Apparition of Splendor

Apparition of Splendor

Marianne Moore Performing Democracy through Celebrity, 1952–1970

Elizabeth Gregory

University of Delaware Press
Newark

A British Cataloging-in-Publication record for this book is available from the British Library.

University of Delaware Press

The paper used in this publication meets the requirements of the American National Standard for Information Sciences—Permanence of Paper for Printed Library Materials, ANSI Z39.48-1992.

udpress.udel.edu

ISBN 978-1-64453-196-9 (hardcover)
ISBN 978-1-64453-197-6 (pb)
ISBN 978-1-64453-198-3 (ebook)

Library of Congress Cataloging-in-Publication Data is available for this title.

Distributed worldwide by Rutgers University Press

Manufactured in the United States of America

Contents

Figures

Acknowledgments

Thanks to everyone who helped me along the many-branched scholarly path this project has taken. Two years out of college in fall 1980, I was working in the Gotham Book Mart (which unbeknownst to me then had been a favorite haunt of Moore's) when John Lennon was killed. That spurred my journey from New York City to the University of Kentucky in Lexington to learn with the inspiring Guy Davenport, who introduced me to Moore's poetry. That immersion then led to further work with John Hollander, Margaret Homans, and others at Yale, and my book on poetic quotation. Patricia Willis, the curator of Moore's papers at the Rosenbach Museum and Library in Philadelphia from 1974 to 1987, welcomed me into the community of Moore-ists from the start, as she did many others. That ever-expanding community constitutes a collective resource of multifaceted knowledge, evolving ideas, and shared enthusiasm—for a brilliant poet whose work compels us to keep reading and reflecting, individually and in dialogue.

After one essay on Moore's late work in the 1990s, I returned to this project in 2003 and since then have benefited from many compelling conversations with Moore scholars, though my argument disputes long-reigning ideas about her work. Particular thanks to Stacy Carson Hubbard, Cristanne Miller, and Alison Rieke for responding to chapters in recent stages, and to Ned Allen, April Alliston, Aurore Clavier, Bonnie Costello, Zachary Finch, Fiona Green, Benjamin Kahan, Linda

Kinnahan, Linda Leavell, Ellen Levy, Tania Modleski, Kirby Olson, Jahan Ramazani, Karin Roffman, Robin G. Schulze, Emily Setina, Rebecca Traister, John Emil Vincent, Nikolaus Wasmoen, Heather Cass White, Melissa Zeiger, all the attendees at the 21st-Century Moore Conference, and the anonymous reviewers of all stages of this project, for their engaged discourse and encouragement. Participants and audience members at panels and discussion groups I was part of at the Modernist Studies Association, the Modern Language Association (especially the Age Studies Group), and the American Literature Association conferences and at the Louisville Conference on Literature and Culture made valuable contributions. Special thanks to Chester Page, Edward Moran, and the wide-reaching group of advocates for a Marianne Moore Memorial in a New York park. Thanks also to the Moore Society listserv community (www.mooresociety.org—please join us!) and the members of the Moore Digital Archive group—for all their insights and generosities.

Closer to home, at the University of Houston my English colleagues Hosam Aboul-Ela, Margot Backus, Jason Berger, Lauren Brozovich, Sreya Chatterjee, Sally Connolly, Chitra Divakaruni, Sarah Ehlers, Karen Fang, Maria Gonzalez, Lawrence Hogue, Carl Lindahl, Auritro Majumder, David Mazella, Kevin Prufer, Martha Serpas, Kavita Singh, Michael Snediker, Lorraine Stock, Roberto Tejada, Cedric Tolliver, Lynn Voskuil, Lois Zamora, and others have provided thoughtful critique and support, and my chairs past and present—Terrell Dixon, Harmon Boertien, Wyman Herendeen, John McNamara, j kastely, and Ann Christensen—have been stellar. My colleagues and co-workers in WGSS and the IRWGS—Dina Alsowayel, Amanda Baumle, Guillermo de los Reyes, Emelie Griffin, Erika Henderson, Kim Howard, Meera Jagannathan, Chinhui Juhn, Claire Kang, Aishwarya Lakshmi, Ayanna Mccloud, Audrey Miller, Sonny Nordmarken, Zelma Oyarvide Tuthill, Andrew Pegoda, Joy Priest, Rachel Afi Quinn, Christiane Spitzmueller, Liam Stone, Jess Waggoner, and many others over the years—along with the amazing networks of faculty affiliates and the Friends of Women's Studies, have built a wonderful community of support for students and for innovative scholarship.

Much gratitude to the University of Houston's Houstoun Endowment in English, College of Liberal Arts and Social Sciences, and Division of Research for generous grants that have allowed me to spend necessary time in the archives and have covered fees.

At the Rosenbach, special thanks to Librarian Elizabeth Fuller, who has shared much wisdom and good cheer, and to the helpful Registrar, Jobi Zink. In nearby Rittenhouse Square, enormous gratitude to my lifelong friends Liz Mednick and Barbara Edelstein, who have kindly provided shelter, inspiring food, and great conversation in Philadelphia, my hometown, for, lo, a long time. At the University of Delaware Press, great thanks to my editor, Julia Oestreich, and to Laura Engel, project manager Tim Roberts, copy editor Jenn Backer, and indexer Enid Zafran, for their insights and for treating this book so well.

Big love to my sister Mindy Gregory Sieber and retroactively to our beloved and excellent parents, Jack and Jackie Gregory, for their wit, kindness, and support of my passions; and to Mark, Geneva, Hannah, Glen, Mike and Perry, Jeanne, Paul, Mark and Alexis, Rachel and Mike, Matthew, Connie and Isaac, Rajal, Maggie and Anya, Mary, JD and Gloria, les français, Victoria and Cathy, Nora and Robert, Alberto and Karen, Joel and Paul, Lydia and Steve, Carl and Moreno, Adriana, Pat and Soren, Melanie, and all my extended family and friends, especially the dear departed Polly Koch, who have sustained and emboldened me.

On the home front, Patrick, Anna, and Sophie Peters have accepted Moore as an invisible but persistent member of the family—a source of humor and eyerolling ("who do you think wrote a poem about that?!"). Thanks for everything.

Apparition of Splendor

Introduction: Democracy, Celebrity, Poetry

To have misapprehended the matter, is to have confessed that one has not looked far enough.

—"England" (*New Collected Poems* [*NCP*], 50)

"Best Living Poet"—so *Newsweek* titled its review of Marianne Moore's *Collected Poems* in December 1951. That summarized the overwhelmingly positive official judgment on Moore's book, which went on to win the 1952 Pulitzer and Bollingen Prizes and the National Book Award, a flourish of victories that made the rather esoteric poet an instant celebrity. But the article qualified the headline: "[Moore] is *probably* the best living American poet, certainly one of the two or three best, and one of the few, in T. S. Eliot's opinion, who has made a durable contribution to the poetry of the English language. Only now beginning to be known outside high-brow circles, . . . her poems have always been readily comprehensible, line by line, though their meaning as a whole is sometimes hard to come by. And they have grown steadily simpler."[1] While in 1925 Richard Aldington admired the complexity of Moore's sui generis prosody and called her the "most high-brow poet in the world,"[2] by 1951 her poetry and that status had changed. *Newsweek* zeroed in on shifts both in Moore's later work and in its reception and linked those to tensions between elite and popular culture. The magazine went on to identify a problem that has plagued Moore studies since, when it noted that unlike her earlier poems, "Miss Moore's newer poems are so clear that . . . ominous mutterings about 'sentimentality' are now beginning to be heard." Nonetheless, the new clarity and the openness to sentiment (which began in her 1940s war poetry)—along with a new cheerfully eccentric celebrity persona, publication in large-circulation periodicals,

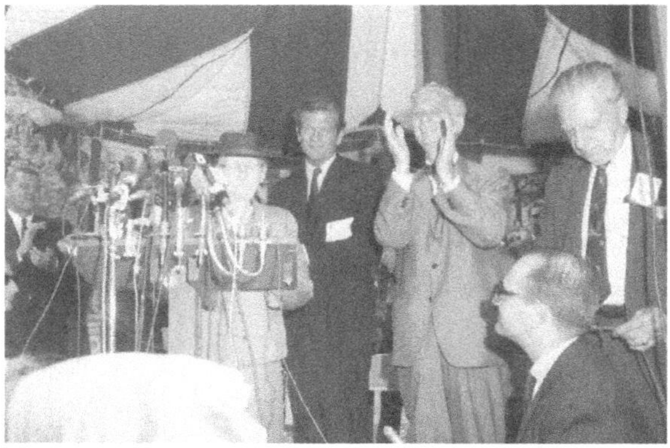

Figure 1. Marianne Moore reading, with Mayor John V. Lindsay and Parks Commissioner August Heckscher. Poets in the Park, Bryant Park. Copyright Academy of Poets, 1968. Reprinted by kind permission, www.poets.org.

a new focus on popular subject matter, and frequent public appearances onstage and in the media—brought Moore a much wider audience in her late phase than she'd had previously.

Since her death, however, without the current topicality or the entertaining persona to connect it to the broader public, Moore's later work has lost its populist base of advocates, and scholars and admirers of her high modernist work of the 1920s and 1930s have defined her posthumous reception. Moore's late success as a celebrity poet and performer have come to be read as markers not of literary value but of triviality. Following *Newsweek*'s lead, her career has been split into two distinct halves, with very different reputations: early Moore—difficult, emotionless, highbrow, great; later Moore—accessible, sentimental, middlebrow, mediocre.[3] That judgment has occasioned an active critical neglect of the extensive body of work that Moore produced in the last two decades of her life.

This volume offers a critical reappraisal and close readings of both the later work and the performance mode within which Moore framed it that challenge this split assessment. While recently critics have begun to engage with individual poems of this period, some quite perceptively,[4] this is the first book in decades to take these later poems seriously as a group, and the first to explore *why* the brilliant, highly skilled Moore would take this down-market route into accessibility. Rather than condemning the later poems for what they *don't*, I explore here what they *do*, which we could now call a variety of code-switching. As biographer Linda Leavell persuasively argues, Moore developed her early elliptical style in part to armor her work against the judgmental intrusiveness of her mother, Mary Warner Moore, with whom she lived in close quarters.[5] In this volume, I demonstrate that, after her mother's death in 1947, Moore employed similar skills in camouflage, or repackaging. In the postwar context of new, democratizing mass media and a heightened celebrity culture that crossed classes and tastes, Moore presented thought-provoking material in new and entertaining ways in order to engage and amuse audiences of all brow levels. Her readers might reflect on this material or not, to the extent they preferred, but all would confront difference in some form in engaging with Moore and her poetry and learn something about democracy and diversity from that encounter.

This 1956 poem speaks straight to the shift:

Values in Use

I attended school and I liked the place—
grass and little locust-leaf shadows like lace.

Writing was discussed. They said, "We create
values in the process of living, daren't await

their historic progress." Be abstract
and you'll wish you'd been specific; it's a fact.

What was I studying? Values in use,
"judged on their own ground." Am I still abstruse?

Walking along, a student said offhand,
"'Relevant' and 'plausible' were words I understand."

A pleasing statement, anonymous friend.
Certainly the means must not defeat the end. *(NCP, 212)*

Note: *The first two quoted phrases are taken from a rousing address that Philip Rahv gave on July 27, 1956[6] in Alston Burr Hall, Cambridge.—M. M. (*Partisan Review*, 1956)[7]

In this clear, rhymed poem, Moore explicitly rejects the artful abstruseness of high modernism for the relevant plausibility of concrete statement that can be easily engaged with by many, reflecting her long-held democratic values in a poem that speaks directly to the audience of intellectual social democrats of the *Partisan Review*, where it first appeared (along with work by her friends Robert Lowell and James Baldwin).

This poem's argument echoes Moore's endorsement of writing "in plain American which cats and dogs can read" in her early poem "England" (1920), though that poem read more complexly overall. Recognizing that even the politically sophisticated *Partisan Review* audience might have difficulty with oblique poems, she offers them an easy way in through straightforward couplets, and she puns in their idiom on the Marxist term "use value" to make an economic case for accessible poetry as another kind of value generator. Her initial readers would have recognized Philip Rahv in the note—a *Partisan Review* founder, he was also a former American Communist Party member, expelled in 1937 for anti-Stalinism (Moore's notes are always part of her poetry, and I include them in quotations throughout). Many would also have heard an allusion to his well-known "Paleface and Redskin" essay (1939) and its call for a synthesis of highbrow and lowbrow (of Henry James with Walt Whitman) in American literature going forward. Few of her more recent readers, however, have recognized this hint that Moore in her later years was engaged in her own critique of high/low cultural relations, or (as she phrased it in a 1959 poem) her own "Combat Cultural."

In arguing against the split view of Moore's career, I make the case that her post-1951 work extends the anti-hierarchical ethics that animated her work from the start, in daring and innovative ways. Putting her egalitarian principles into action in her later work, Moore utilized her new celebrity to cross the tracks from the elite precincts of obliquity where she had earlier flourished, reach a wider swath of the American public, and engage them in a 3-D consideration of a broad range of aesthetic and social concerns while also entertaining them. As the following chapters will show, her later work shares much with her early work—in its deep democratic emphasis, its critiques of gender, race, and class bias, its playful originality, its habitual ekphrases, and its signification through a poem's structure as well as its statement—offering a multidimensional examination of the workings of the culture of its moment. But it does so in new ways, to speak to postwar political and cultural realities and to link poetic means to democratic ends.

To accomplish this, Moore depended upon the interpretive skills and interest in poetry shared by the large and diverse American audience of the period. As Mike Chasar documents, up through the 1950s, readers were surrounded by poems of diverse brow levels—printed in anthologies, newspapers, and scrapbooks, and recited on the radio, in classrooms, and at civic events—and they engaged with them for comfort, inspiration, humor, and reflection.[8] In moving her poetry out of the highbrow little magazine world into more popular and middlebrow venues, Moore met a big audience of skilled and willing poetry consumers where they lived. While the poems still looked and in many respects still were "modernist," she appealed to her new readers by focusing overtly on current events, on the dynamics of celebrity and performance, and on issues in which they all had a stake as citizens of a democracy. She made the poems easy to absorb by presenting them as part of a comedic performance, in which she cross-dressed as George Washington in tricorne hat and cape—a splendid apparition, quite unlike any other.[9]

Underlying its humor, this quondam suffragist's appearance as a female in presidential drag just thirty years after the passage of the Nineteenth Amendment continued the subversive questions about female authority active in her poems across her career. She developed an inclusive community of fans fresh from the hardships and ethical ordeals of World War II, who enjoyed her performances' funny but thoughtful critiques of the various forms of social clampdown rampant in the postwar period. Like Lucille Ball, another celebrity comic of that era, Moore spoke to issues of gender and race through the guise of zaniness, to adopt Sianne Ngai's term.[10]

Celebrity and democracy developed in tandem in the modern West, as both Leo Braudy and P. David Marshall have discussed.[11] Fame, as Braudy notes, long a factor in human relations, transformed in the late eighteenth century to the variety we recognize today, through the effects of democratic revolutions, new media, and widespread literacy.[12] To replace deposed monarchs, the period called forth a new hierarchy—of celebrity, a democratized renown open to all in concept and circulating among many, though often briefly. For those for whom the dream of celebrity goes unrealized, the opportunity remains to achieve a sense of importance, or wholeness, through the sympathetic dynamics of fandom.

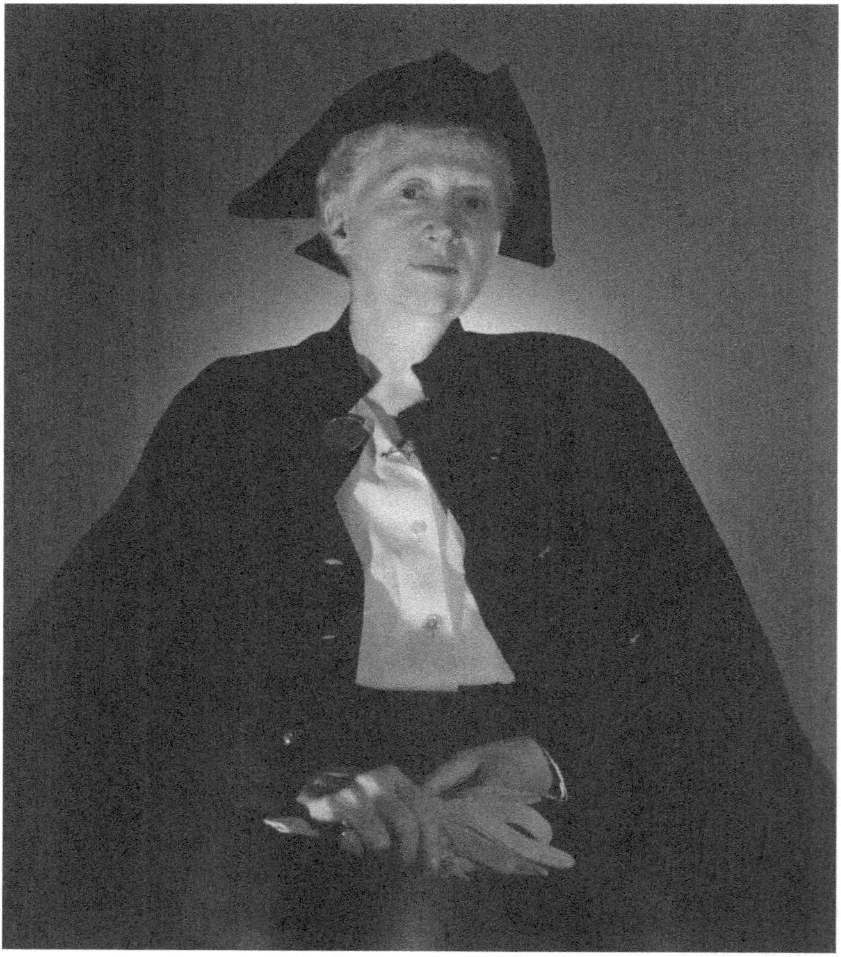

Figure 2. Marianne Moore in tricorne and cape with gloves, photographed by George Platt Lynes, 1953. Reprinted by permission.

As Marshall has outlined, celebrities, who are paradoxically both idealized yet personally idiosyncratic in ways that allow viewers to connect to them as individuals, function to "contain the power of the mass in democracies" while also articulating the possibility of individual agency and change. Though they may be limited in their ability to critique the system that boosts them, they may also activate the instability of social categories and serve as change agents, because they emerge hegemonically "from a legitimation process connected to the people."[13] In Moore's celebrity persona, the idiosyncratic side is emphasized, embodying departures from the norm.

Moore joined in the system of celebrity when she became one, but in a subversive manner that encouraged critique of the failures of our purported democracy, as part of an affirmation of democracy's inherent commitment to ongoing critique and change. She also featured in her late poems the value and ordinary heroism of non-celebrities, a topic she had already engaged with in 1932 in "The Hero," a poem that directly relates to her 1950s cosplay. Set at Mount Vernon, where a frock-coated African American tour guide shows the graves of Martha and George Washington to sightseers, the poem claims the stalwart guide as its hero instead of the president. The guide's "sense of human dignity," maintained in spite of America's history of slavery and mistreatment ("going where one does not wish / to go; suffering and not / saying so; standing and listening where something / is hiding," ll. 13–16, *NCP*, 97), is celebrated and presented as parallel to that demonstrated in the stories of Joseph, Moses, and *The Pilgrim's Progress*. The guide is heroic for his transcendence of injustice regardless of and even because of his lack of recognition.

Unlike heroes of old, modern celebrities spring from the democratic mass (all of whose citizens are valuable in principle) and serve as particularly talented or lucky representatives of all. But the predominance of celebrities of privileged identity groups underscores the degree to which citizens are treated unequally; "The Hero" works to feature and undermine that pattern. In concert with her poems, Moore's late-phase performance as Washington (both democrat and slaveholder), triangulated through "The Hero," complicates pleasure in fame and sports and the other successes she explores by reminding her audience of the ongoing struggle for a more perfect democratic union and by challenging contemporary patriots to follow her nonconformist example, step up, and innovate.

Moore was of course not alone in crossing the boundaries between high and popular literature: as Marsha Bryant has demonstrated, women poets from diverse moments—including H. D., Stevie Smith, Gwendolyn Brooks, Sylvia Plath, and Carol Ann Duffy—have tapped popular forms and venues in order "to write from the cultural center as insiders."[14] Bryant documents that popular culture has provided women poets with important points of access to audiences, though they often critiqued the mainstream even as they invoked it. Moore's transition into popular celebrity in the 1950s also parallels that of Gertrude Stein in the 1930s (with *The Autobiography of Alice B. Toklas* [1933] and *Everybody's Autobiography* [1937]), as explored by Loren Glass and others.[15] The late-phase celebrity of both Moore and Stein differs from that of their male modernist peers, who were celebrated latterly as figures of elite authority. Though modernist difficulty and impersonality were erected as barriers specifically to fence most women writers out,[16] the obscurity and unsentimentality of Stein and Moore in their early phases, combined with their (variously) masculinized physical presentations, set them apart initially from the feminized world of mass culture and won them admission to the modernist canon. In later life, however, both wrote more accessibly and achieved a new celebrity that combined the cachet of their modernist fame (for work that few non-elites read) with the humorous charm of their later work (read by both elites and non-elites). As older women with established reputations, they may have felt secure enough to cast off the difficulty and lack of apparent sentiment required of them early on as means of admission to a "masculine" literary elite, unwelcome enough in the canonical world that embraced them halfheartedly to seek a way out, or overwhelmingly drawn to the various benefits of the popular as they perceived them—or some combination thereof.

The blurriness of the line between popular and high culture experienced by most readers, as opposed to the clear divide assumed by many critics, shaped Moore's material from the start. But her late work even more regularly charts the high/low navigations of the perambulating mind, not unlike the work of her in other respects rather different contemporary Frank O'Hara, who described his method simply: "What is happening to me . . . goes into my poems."[17] Though her late-phase work was not well received by some critics in her day, the *TLS* reviewer of her 1956 *Like a Bulwark* saw Moore's shift in mode as a thoughtful and effective move:

> Here . . . one sees the bird of rare wisdom as well as of rare plumage, whose unique and difficult habitat has for too long frightened away all but the most fearless collectors. Perhaps, at nearly seventy, Miss Moore has not merely had an inkling of this (she must have had that a long time ago, and shrugged her regret) but has decided to do

> something about it. On the evidence of one or two of the poems in this book one has a distinct impression that she is going out towards the world at the same time as the world is coming towards her. . . Taken all together the poems in Miss Moore's book are evidence of a liveliness and freshness of mind scarcely paralleled in a poet of her years.[18]

The later work challenges in new ways received assumptions about what has value and about *whose* voices could be heard as authoritative, challenges in play in Moore's work all along.

While her late work and performances drew on her audience's familiarity with poetry based on cultural patterns past, they also interacted with the younger poets of the postwar avant-garde—including W. H. Auden, Elizabeth Bishop, Frank O'Hara, John Ashbery, Gwendolyn Brooks, Allen Ginsberg, Sylvia Plath, and Robert Lowell. Her modernist poetry had helped shape this cohort's work and her late work also learned from and developed in dialogue with theirs. Like hers, their work blurred high/low and gender lines, questioning many received ideas about "identity." While she didn't always endorse their work, Moore's performances of poetry in character (with rehearsed "impromptu" remarks offered in between poems to break up the tension the highbrow context might create for some listeners) overlapped with the performances of the Beat and the Fluxus poets who also sought to connect with audiences in new ways.

Of course, performance was not a new interest for Moore. All along, her poems' extravagant designs flung across pages and their intensely innovative prosody constituted radical performances—both visual and aural. As Bruce Henderson has noted, quite a few early poems explore the dynamics and ethics of performance by others (from as early as "That Harp You Play So Well" [1915] about King David). But this became a consistent topic in the late poems, simultaneous with Moore's emergence as an active performer herself.[19] At least sixteen of the fifty-two late-phase poems describe action on a stage or a playing field, while many others involve ekphrases, which, though they needn't involve performers per se, do open up a theatrical space wherein the poet tries (and inevitably to some extent fails) to render an image in words, before the audience of her readers.

Moore wrote in dialogue with younger contemporaries on a number of other levels as well. Al Filreis points to connections between Moore's

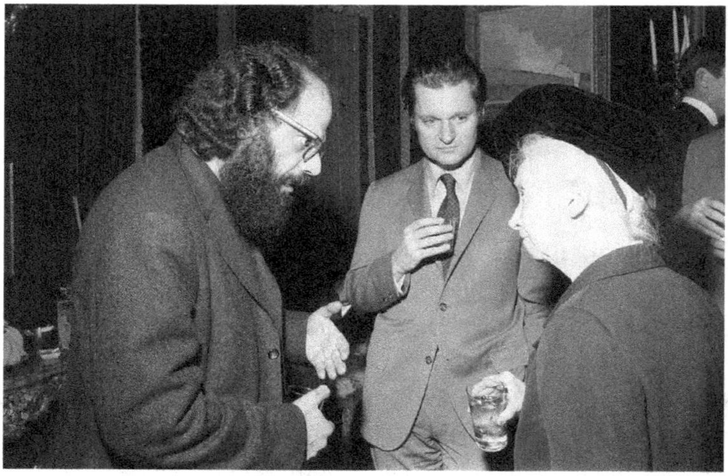

Figure 3. Marianne Moore, Allen Ginsberg, and John Ashbery, photographed by Jill Krementz in 1967 in New York City; all rights reserved. Reprinted by kind permission.

work and that of William Burroughs (whose "cut ups" hark directly back to Moore's methods of quotation), and he notes a coalescing in 1960 of a leftist recognition of commonality with the political and civic rhetoric of the 1920s and "a disorganized but nonetheless effective collaboration of historically distinct avant-gardes," including the modernists on the one hand and on the other "the 'New American' poets, the beats, Black Mountain affiliates, New York School, latter-day Dadaists and surrealists, post-Duchampian conceptual poets," and so on.[20] Leftist poet Muriel Rukeyser, reviewing Moore's *O to Be a Dragon* in 1959, argued that "[Moore] has been a major influence on many people engaged in writing today," and lauded Moore's continued assertion of "living connections . . . qualities for which she has always stood [and which] are here made new."[21] Langston Hughes suggested Moore's anti-racist focus when, at the Poetry Society dinner at which Moore received the Gold Medal in 1967, he "exuberantly" claimed to "consider her the most famous Negro woman poet in America today."[22] In 1964, Robert Lowell sang the praises of Moore's *Arctic Ox* collection to Elizabeth Bishop, noting that "rather to my surprise [I] think it's as good as anything she's ever written—a kind of wild lyrical abandon, and four or five of her most serious poems, and almost everything good."[23] Common interests and methods connected Moore to these and other writers and to artists in diverse realms: poet John Ashbery and collagist Ray Johnson in particular recognized a kindred spirit in Moore.

Upon her mother's death in 1947, Moore mourned but then flourished anew, free to put herself forward and engage with New York in her new celebrity role, full throttle. She provides an unusual case study for the evolution of a long-lived poet, who is both the honored poetic ancestor and also in some respects the peer of her younger contemporaries, as they all respond to their shared scene. Moore's work engaged actively with the community she performed for up until her last days—her last published poem is among her most lively and inventively performative on the page.

Overview

The chapters of this book explore the various means of Moore's democratic outreach through celebrity to a cross-brow audience of Americans, in order to engage them in a poetic community built around entertainment, collaborative interpretation, aesthetic pleasure, and social reflection. She framed her poems within a droll performance, and Chapter 1 begins with a discussion of the development of her stylish cross-dressing persona and of her public appearances, and the attendant media coverage, which I map against Sianne Ngai's analysis of the aesthetic category of the zany in postwar late capitalism. The chapter offers close readings of several of Moore's poems of the early 1950s as narrations of her emergence as what she called in one of them an "Apparition of Splendor"—a poetic and performative character who blends shyness with bold self-flaunting to generative effect.

The chapter also tracks Moore's movement into a new and wider range of publication venues with work framed to engage the interests of each audience. While the first two poems she published after her 1951 collection appeared in literary journals that she'd appeared in previously and employed a recognizably "Moore-ish" style, by 1954 she was publishing in *Vogue* and in Abbott Pharmaceutical's in-house journal. The *Vogue* poem, "Rosemary," for example, directly addresses fashion fans through a story about a horticultural wardrobe change, which invites them to consider both the bonds among kinds of love—religious, erotic, and friendly—and the connections between gender and capitalism that run *Vogue*.

Chapter 2 explores the series of poems about contemporary sports figures, teams, and contests that Moore began in 1953. Of interest to millions, sports offered a point of entry into Moore's work for readers across all brow and class divisions. Once readers were drawn in, though parts of the work might seem odd, her funny poetic persona provided enough reassurance to keep them engaged, creating an emphatically democratic poetry-reading collective of fans. The first of these poems (also her first *New Yorker* poem) celebrates a winning racehorse, the four-year-old Tom Fool, in a context of jest and anti-elitism that operates in humorous tension with her own status as an elite poet. The second and third (about baseball and race, and focused on the 1956 Dodgers and the 1961 Yankees, respectively) explore who is judged worthy of celebration in our ostensible democracy and why. The fourth—about a polo pony, a dancer, several artists, and a contortionist—extends that consideration through a self-conscious enactment of the celebratory ode as a historical form of social-status analysis. In all these poems, Moore proffers a populist model of circulating celebration, featuring herself as a fan rather than a star and stressing the reader's role as poetic collaborator in the construction of any poem's meaning, which evolves across each encounter.

Immediately after Moore's first sports poem appeared to an enthusiastic reception in 1953, she set about utilizing the same connective method to gather readers around other widely shared interests, across new and old media. Chapter 3 explores poems built around a variety of occasions—including cultural events, TV specials, and religious holidays and stories—as well as occasional poems written to be read for the first time at the events they celebrated. Moore often turned the attention of the communities of readers she gathered toward reflection upon the workings of the American community. For example, her 1956 poem on NBC's Colorcast of *The Magic Flute* featuring Leontyne Price subtly explores issues of race relations and human values, while her 1959 poem on CBS's devotion of an entire broadcast of the *Ed Sullivan Show* to the Moiseyev Dancers from the Soviet Union questions both Cold War and high/low divisions. "In the Public Garden" (1958) and "In Lieu of the Lyre" (1965), both formal occasional poems first performed in or near Boston, actively include their audiences and their settings, publicly analyzing the means by which poems are collaboratively produced by writers and audiences.

Though in her early days she'd disdained love poetry as a ghetto for female poets, Moore changed her mind latterly, and Chapter 4 explores the results. Not only had she gradually become more open to expressions of sentiment in her poems of the 1940s, but in the 1950s and 1960s she recognized love, perhaps the most familiar of poetic topics, as another attractive site in which her public could comfortably engage with her performance, though her "spinster" status and her approach upended all norms. Her poems "For February 14th" (1959) and "Saint Valentine," (1960) both expand on the framework of the holiday poems discussed in Chapter 3, exploring the dynamics of personal connection, or love, from a defamiliarized perspective that opens up alternatives to the standard heterosexual romance plot and seeks to engage readers in an "interested" relationship. "Love in America?" (1966) explores the political dimensions of love as the glue that holds democratic societies together, which Moore radically endorses in all its forms, "whatever the deed." Though less explicit, Moore's 1963 poem "To a Giraffe" operates as a love poem in itself, testing the basic modernist assumption that the personal is fatal to good poetry through a teasing treatment of Moore's personal and professional affection for her friend and fellow "impersonal" poet, T. S. Eliot. The poem reflects on the relation of modernism to its reactionary successor confessionalism (which mixes aspects of celebrity gossip with a claim to reveal poets' authentic selves) and on Moore's postwar transition toward expression of personal sentiment and connection.

Chapter 5 takes up another facet of that transition, examining many poems of the later phase in which Moore reflects on mortality and legacy—issues to which her audience could also connect and about which Moore had long been thinking. Bookended by "Granite and Steel" (1966), a poem engaging democratic ethics and the genealogy of Brooklyn poets to which Moore affirms her bond, and "Sun" (1916), which engages with Death and Emily Dickinson, many of the poems of the backwardly chronological volume *Tell Me, Tell Me* (*TMTM*) reflect on time, on Moore's poetic origins, and on her hopes for the posthumous celebrity of poetic immortality. Post-1966, Moore's poem on "The Camperdown Elm" in Brooklyn's Prospect Park moved her at age seventy-nine into new territories of direct activism, connecting her work to the history of poetic advocacy for the environment and for public parks as civic centers that bring together citizens of all ranks. Her last poems reflect remarkably on death, embracing the end with gusto and skill. The Epilogue explores connections between Moore's celebrity performance work and that of two of her late-phase contemporaries, visual artists Andy Warhol and Ray Johnson.

Marianne Moore was an enormously popular poet in her last two decades, for very good reason. Her literary skills were unparalleled—encompassing, as this book will demonstrate, a multidimensional range of effects unlike those of any other writer (Elizabeth Bishop attributed to Moore "a unique, involuntary sense of rhythm, therefore of meter, quite unlike anyone else's" and "the rarity of true originality").[24] Though she was an Eisenhower Republican and older than most counterculture figures at the time, her pro-democracy commitments, her gender-fluid presentation, and her wry intelligence, along with her continuously innovative literary skills, offered her audience liberating alternatives to the rigidly enforced conformism of the 1950s and 1960s. Moore's deeply considered and heartfelt engagement with her audience led to a similar return of affection from her many fans. Ironically, her late work's popular outreach and success, in its difference from her early work, blocked scholarly understanding of and interest in those poems for decades after her death. But, happily, that is changing. This book offers a way into many of the more than fifty poems Moore published post-1951, which have too long gone unread, and into the brilliant late phase of a vital poetic career, too long unacknowledged. The richness revealed in this first survey in decades of Moore's remarkable late period work only hints at a wealth of insight yet to be elucidated by critics who approach her later poems without bias, alert to their dialogues and their context.[25]

For an overview of Moore's early work and career that can contextualize the analysis of the later work offered in the chapters that follow, please consult the Appendix. That section also provides a new analysis of Moore's early use of "literal images," which she continued to employ in her late phase, and a new argument about the increasing democratization of her work over decades, from the 1920s through the 1930s and 1940s—a pattern the later work also builds upon. The Appendix also addresses the status of Moore's shifting texts and explains my methods of engagement with her archive of notebooks, drafts, poems, appointment books, and correspondence.

1

"Apparition of Splendor": Poet as Performance

> Like the fools who say all sorts of things
> They do not mean
> I mean all sorts of things I do not say
> —Poetry Notebook (c. 1951–1952)
>
> Impassioned Ocelot
> I am not jesting; No.
> But sometimes I do.
> —Poetry Notebook (c. 1963–1964)

In the 1950s, Marianne Moore responded to her expanded renown by ditching the highly literary tone that she had previously exhibited and had even enforced as editor of *The Dial* in the 1920s. Building on the increased accessibility she had produced in her work of the war years, she evolved an entertaining new postwar poetics, as well as a charismatic new reading style and a matching iconic persona—becoming both a celebrity poet and a public performance artist. Calmly extraordinary, Moore frequently dressed, as she described it, as "Washington crossing the Delaware"[1]—in a tricorne hat and a cape with a silver-dollar clasp.[2] This transvestite cosplay worked as a three-dimensional metaphor, inviting her audience into a consideration of democracy whenever she entered a room or appeared in a photo. The Washington costume merged his great age with Moore's elder status to create a splendid revolutionary apparition who playfully invited (and still invites) viewers to explore their own standing as members of the community of Americans, as people categorized by gender, race, sexuality, and age, and as spenders of dollars (site of our daily encounters with Washington's portrait).[3] Moore was recognizable all over town in her trademark outfit (John Ashbery, for example, reported running into her in the subway and managing to utter a few words of awed admiration).[4]

Moore debuted the new persona in 1950 (without the costume) at a major public reading at the Museum of Modern Art, where she shared the bill with W. H. Auden. Long a student of performance by others (at circuses, lectures, ballets, plays, concerts, ballgames, etc.), Moore demonstrated herself to be a charismatic comedienne that night, mixing what Leavell describes as "easy erudition and disarming humility."[5] In a letter to her brother, Moore gleefully reported a friend's analysis of her success: "You got much more applause than Mr. Auden—they even shouted after you finished and there was *something in it for everyone*—all the way through—whereas you would have to know a great deal to appreciate all Mr. Auden was saying [emphasis added]." She closed by noting, "This was my best performance so far."[6] Offering something for everyone characterized Moore's purpose in her poetry and performances thereafter.

She took the next step into performance art at the National Book Award ceremony in January 1952, where she received her prize wearing a new tricorne hat that she'd had made especially for the occasion and that quickly became a regular part of her wardrobe.[7] Moore had long sported capes in private wear, and a year later photographer Esther Bubley asked her to wear the cape she arrived in for a *Life* magazine photo shoot in May 1953 and she wore one again along with the tricorne for a shoot with Bubley for *Look* magazine in 1962.[8]

Photographer George Platt Lynes took his renowned portrait of Moore in this gear (Figure 2) in November 1953. Moore enjoyed her celebrity and the dramatic effect of her costume: next to an entry in her 1956 appointment calendar about a party she attended, she records a friend's comment: "'An entrance!' tricorne and cape."

On the textual front, Moore's poems were just one aspect of her presence in the public eye. They were augmented by her many prose publications and talks (essay collections, book reviews, op-eds, lectures, and readings), by reviews of her books of all genres, and by the many media stories documenting her multitude of celebrity appearances. In this phase Moore often wrote poems about events and ideas she encountered in the mass media—and she was then reported upon in those same media, a complete celebrity circuit. Her reputation also expanded through association with the figures she wrote about: for instance, in the middle of the racing season of 1953 she published her first *New Yorker* poem, about Tom Fool, a hot horse who went on to win a triple crown.[9] This poem initiated Moore's late-phase reputation as a sports fan with a humorous

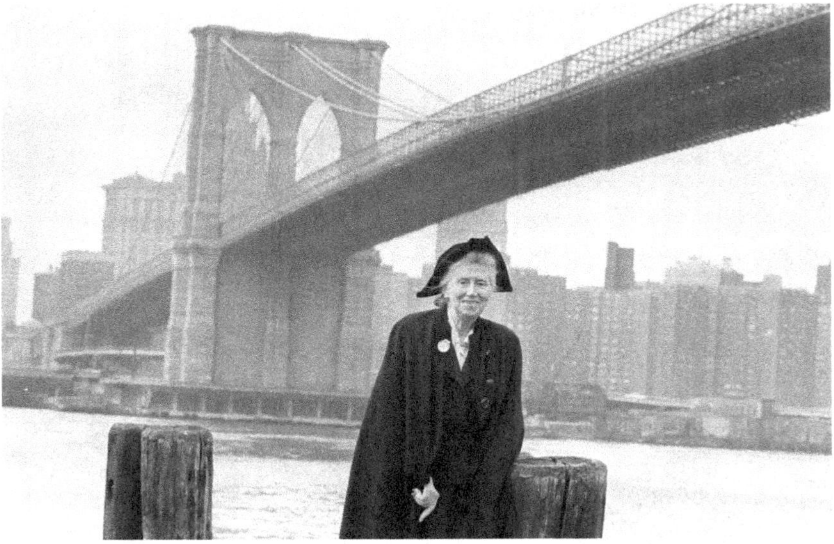

Figure 4. Marianne Moore in cape and tricorne under the Brooklyn Bridge, November 3, 1962, photographed by Esther Bubley. Reprinted by kind permission.

bent, and the horse's growing celebrity ratcheted up her own. A quick scan of some of her extra-poetic activities over the 1950s and 1960s can suggest her pervasive public presence: Her translation of La Fontaine's *Fables* appeared in 1954, to a multitude of mostly friendly reviews in both popular and scholarly journals. The year following, *Predilections*, a collection of her essays, garnered another flood of press and public notice. In 1956, she published a poem hailing the Brooklyn Dodgers on the front page of the *New York Herald Tribune* for game one of the World Series, and though her team lost in the seventh game, her reputation flourished. The *New Yorker* profiled her in 1957,[10] and shortly thereafter her correspondence with the Ford Motor Company on possible names for what became the Edsel struck *New Yorker* editors as so amusing that they published it as a comic essay. In 1958 they offered her a first-refusal contract for her poems. In 1959 she appeared on *The Tonight Show* starring Jack Paar, predicting the winner of the upcoming World Series (she correctly picked the now L.A. Dodgers over the White Sox). In what was likely a first for an American poet, *Sports Illustrated* featured her in an

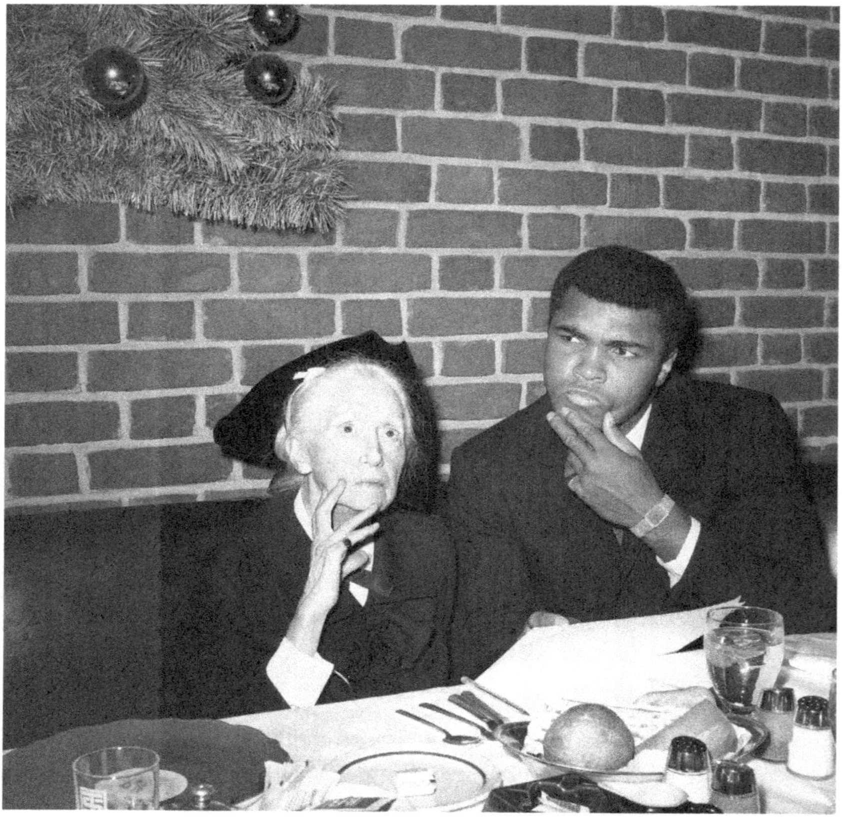

Figure 5. Moore and Ali pose contemplatively while writing a poem together at Toots Shor's, December 21, 1966. AP/Photo by John Lindsay. Reprinted by permission.

article in 1960, exploring her early connections to the legendary sports figures of the Carlisle Indian School. That year, *Vogue* also featured her essay "The Plums of Curiosity," about "really looking at what you see." In 1961, her *Marianne Moore Reader* appeared. Then, in 1963, she wrote the liner notes to Cassius Clay's spoken-word album *I Am the Greatest*,[11] linking her to another sports hero (Clay became Muhammad Ali in 1964), and George Plimpton recounted taking her and Robert Lowell to that year's World Series in a *Harper's* article.

In addition to sports-linked and literary events, her packed schedule included high-profile social gatherings, like Truman Capote's 1966

Black and White Ball (where everyone else wore costumes too). Moore was ubiquitous, across media and in all parts of town: in 1967 she promoted her *Complete Poems* (*CP*) on the *Today Show*, helped New York mayor John Lindsay host Russian poet Andrei Voznesensky at Gracie Mansion, published an op-ed in the *New York Times* to raise funds for a sick tree in Prospect Park, and appeared on Senior Citizens Month subway posters that declared that "Marianne Moore, Pulitzer Prize Poet, is one of New York State's most creative, productive and admired citizens." In 1968 she threw out the first ball of the Yankees season (Figure 6), an event documented on page one of the *New York Times* as well as in the *New York Post*. She appeared again on *The Tonight Show* during the extraordinary week in 1968 in which guest host Harry Belafonte invited a select group of twenty-five civil rights proponents, both black and white, including entertainers as well as politicians, to talk with him and the American people. Martin Luther King, Robert Kennedy, Aretha Franklin, Lena Horne, and other notables were guests as well. Belafonte, a fan of Moore's work, wept in response to Sidney Poitier's reading of "In Distrust of Merits" on the broadcast.[12] This sampling of Moore's charismatic late-life extra-poetic adventures provides a sense of her dynamic pop cultural role.

Though a series of small strokes curtailed her activity in 1969, she still had the energy to segue from playing with the language of ads and the populist dynamics of TV in her poems to making a paid personal appearance in an actual television advertisement, as part of the tongue-in-cheek "When You Got It—Flaunt It" campaign for Braniff Airlines, which paired "mismatched" but "uniquely successful" celebrities—one highbrow, one lowbrow (Figure 7). (Moore's inclusion parallels her celebrity with that of Salvador Dali and Andy Warhol, two of her fellow highbrow showboats in this campaign.) Also an academic celebrity, she received her sixteenth honorary degree, from Harvard, in June 1969. While the active schedule she kept during her last twenty years was physically demanding, she clearly enjoyed it, and her evident pleasure fed her audience's engagement.

Popular renown of the kind Moore developed late in life built on the rather different high-culture fame that she and her fellow modernists had previously experienced, in varying degrees, which involved a niche highbrow readership and some name recognition among middlebrow audiences. Her fame began to expand in the 1940s when she took on

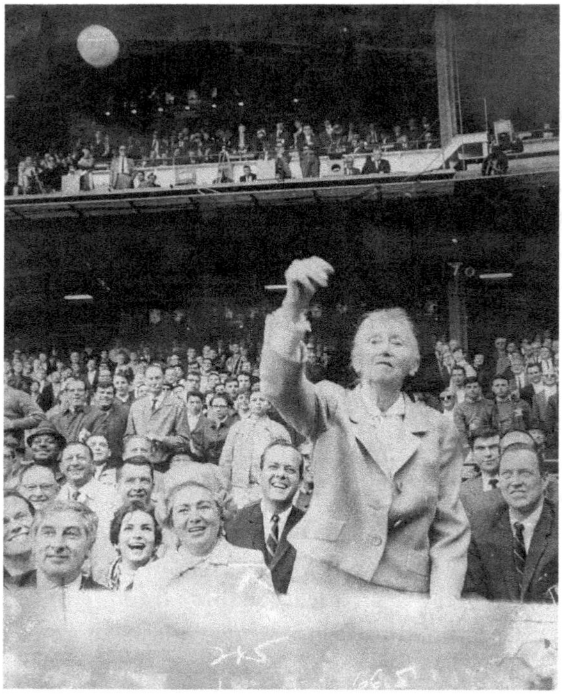

Figure 6. Moore tossing out the first ball for Yankees' opening day, April 10, 1968, photographed by Vic DeLucia, New York Post via Getty Images. Reprinted by permission.

the role of public war poet, and it continued expanding after 1952, when her profile and her sales were raised by her *Collected Poems*' multiple prizes, and by the coverage they brought her in the expanded postwar media market.[13] Her male modernist peers increased their eminence in the postwar environment by continuing to write for the most part in the styles they were known for early on,[14] becoming increasingly recognized as elite figures, whom middlebrow as well as highbrow audiences could recognize as geniuses and perhaps read in college classes (Eliot in particular became widely known after he won the Nobel Prize in 1948 and through his lectures and cocktail-set morality plays).[15] But Moore altered her work as well as her presentation to reach out directly to wider audiences with a new variety of poetry that they might actually read

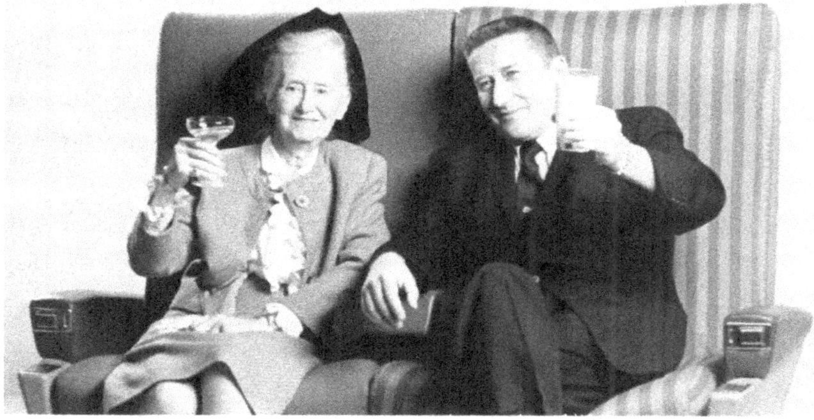

Figure 7. Marianne Moore and Mickey Spillane in advertisement for Braniff Airlines. Reprinted by kind permission. See also http://www.georgelois.com/braniff-moore-spillane-tv-spot.html.

without it being assigned and amusing performances they'd enjoy. Like her male modernist peers, Moore sold many books in her late phase, but for different reasons. Where their mass-mediated authority drew on and consistently affirmed their highbrow status, Moore's involved referencing her highbrow past but differentiating herself and her work from that past in the present.

She took the opportunity that her postwar celebrity provided to forward an ethical, democratic agenda that sought to recognize the contributions of Americans of diverse classes and identities (as well as would-be Americans in refugee camps). Her success grew through her captivating combination of self-flaunting and self-abnegation—playing upon and undercutting her highbrow authority with wry self-critical comments, such as noting at readings that she'd understand if people left when she started to read from her early, and presumably drier, poems.[16] As we'll see in the chapters that follow, within many of the later poems she presented herself as her admirers' surrogate, not as a star but as a fellow fan—of many kinds of entertainment. Such humility aligned with her long-held belief in the importance of forgoing pride, which proved essential not just to moral power but also to charming her audience. Yet she also *was* a star, and in making herself widely known and loved she

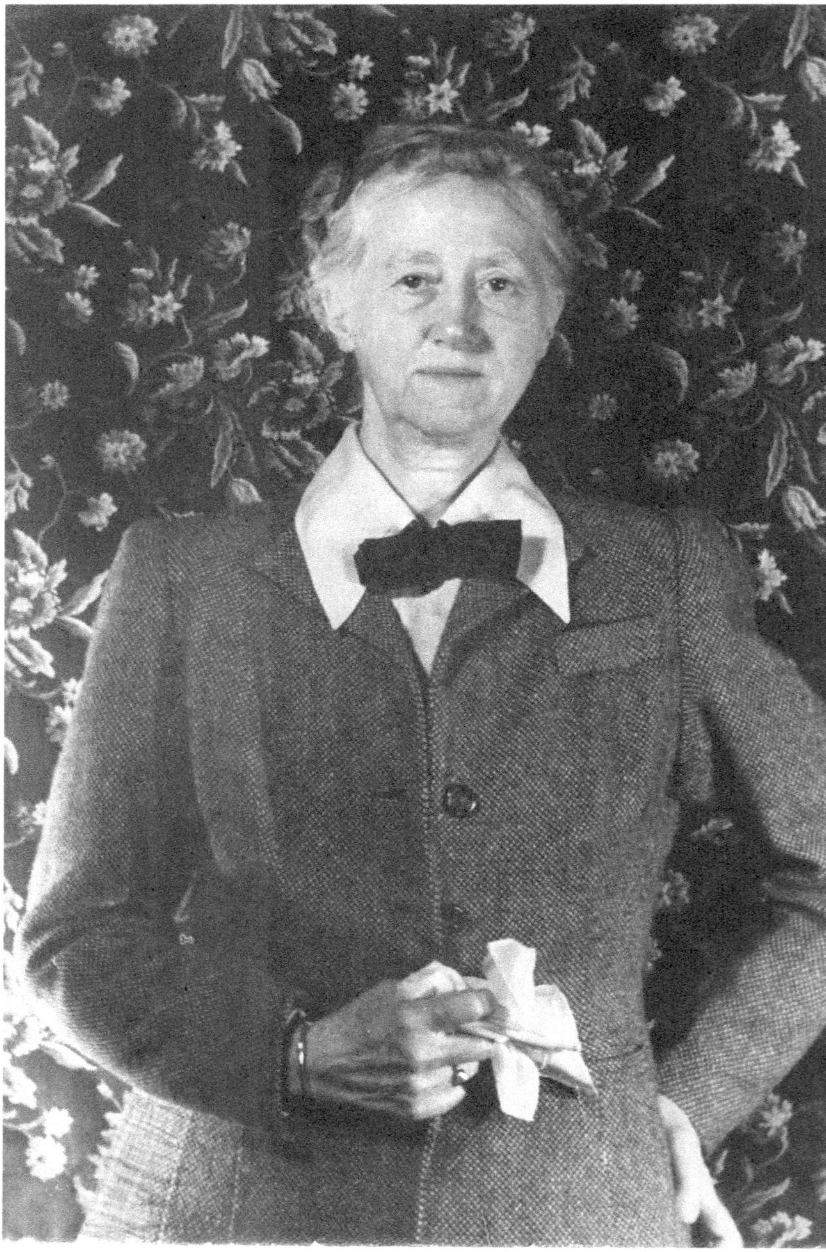

Figure 8. Moore in *Harper's Bazaar*, August 1950, photographed by Marion Morehouse, The Rosenbach, Philadelphia, Moore XII:23:02f | 2006.7453. Reprinted by kind permission.

pushed the limits of who could be celebrated in the mainstream, claiming value for regularly excluded groups of many kinds—gender-defiant old women among them.

Moore's Washington costume has been commonly viewed as patriotic whimsy, not as a philosophic exploration of what democracy means.[17] Nor, with the exception of Kathryn Kent,[18] have critics considered it cross-dressing, since she wore her hair in a feminine braided wreath[19] and sometimes wore feminine clothing beneath the cloak. But sometimes her clothing had a distinctly masculine look.

Her Washington impersonation continues this pattern of pushing the sartorial gender line. Moore, who since childhood had been called by masculine pronouns and nicknames at home, had long preferred clothing with a masculine cast, often wearing oversized men's oxford-cloth shirts and bow ties along with skirts (see Figure 8).[20] While these outfits were not full cross-dress, they actively destabilized the gender line, part of a queer performativity challenging received ideas of and boundaries to identity. The humor associated with her founding-father garb afforded cover for that more direct foray into transvestitism, which enabled her to express in old age the non-binary self-view she'd held all along.[21] At home in New York City she was far from alone in performing challenges to modern sumptuary laws—the whole of Manhattan island was a social theater district. But her challenge to gender norms differed from many, in that, as a lifelong celibate, she did not align her unusual garb with a "forbidden" sexuality and she spoke the language and lived the life of Christian propriety. As a result, she attracted a mainstream audience more readily than obvious sexual transgressors could. Her intimate relationships included those with both her family and her circle of close, supportive friends, who sometimes appeared in fond mentions in her work. Her mixture of apparent acquiescence to social norms and revolt against them added an element of subversiveness that increased her magnetism, and her celebrity gave her an opportunity available to few others to perform gender nonconformity and female authority on a big stage.

The sense of technological and cultural novelty prevalent in the 1950s also marked Moore as a kind of living historical artifact of the prewar modernist period, which produced a patriotic, respectful response from her postwar audience. Normally Moore would have been pushed off the national stage by all the filters that, then as now, make elderly women mostly invisible in American civic life. But her comedic presentation

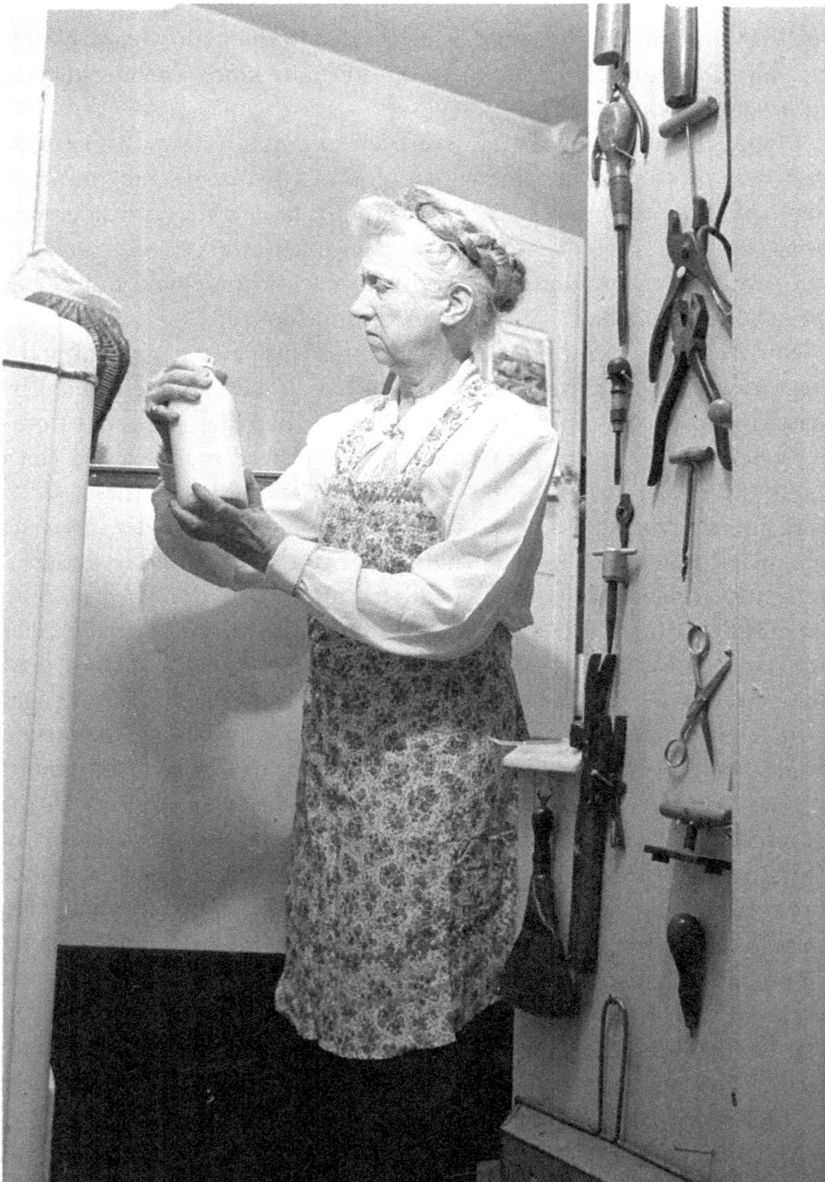

Figure 9. Marianne Moore "suspiciously studies date on a milk bottle," with her house repair tools at right. *Life Magazine*, 1953. Photographer: Esther Bubley. Reprinted by kind permission.

helped offset the anxieties about aging and death that elderly people may produce in a youth-focused culture. As a postmenopausal celibate and childless woman, she met none of the standard qualifications for public celebrity of the day, having escaped the mainstream pressure on women to bear children that was at its height in the 1950s (Figure 9 encapsulates Moore's lack of fit in the housewife mode).[22] Her unsettling refusal to labor on that re-production line was balanced by her humor, her apparent innocence, and her role as a relic of the sainted literary past of the *Dial*.[23] In her cape and tricorne Moore invoked the paradoxical status of Washington, her childfree precursor, known nonetheless as the Father of his country.

Although the costume helped Moore find a place on the public stage by transforming her from a normally excluded figure into an amusing character, the only partially disguised elderly, unmarried, female presence behind the costume created a teasing sense of hide-and-seek—of risk and excitement, as well as connection—that lingers to this day. Her George Washington persona also parallels Moore's long habit of obscured self-display within her poems (an ongoing "reveal-and-veil," as she puts it in "Arthur Mitchell," with an underlying erotic energy), which operated in constant tension with the apparently impersonal dynamic of her work. Whereas early in her career, the multifaceted idiosyncrasy of her prosody was her principal medium of self-display, her later performance persona physicalized that display and her later poems often addressed it as an explicit topic. Moore's shy pleasure in putting herself forward is a consistent factor in these poems; through both the pleasure and the fleeting display Moore forges connections with her audience, while challenging the societal expectation that proscribed identities will be consistently erased or concealed. From the bits peeking out, readers sense there's something hidden in the poems—something that may include elements of grief as well as of excitement, and they have to commit to doing some work to find it. The sense that Moore has invested a lot in making the poems, even the more accessible ones, invites investment from readers, which in itself may create special bonds to these poems.

Both in the poems and onstage, the persona also provided protection—a form of the self-defense Moore had long sought and written of in her many poems about armored animals, shielding her from some of the hazards of direct public vulnerability. Moore suffered from a fierce stage fright, and Leavell has documented the difficulty it took for her to produce even this camouflaged performance. As for many celebrities, being *on* was wearing for Moore, and she sometimes took weeks to recover from major appearances. She often arrived late at gatherings on purpose to avoid having to perform for extended periods.[24] But perform she did, partying regularly with poets, actors, dancers, politicians, and members of the society and arts crowds—most of them decades younger. Moore's carefully annotated appointment books, which provide fascinating documentation of her writing process and daily activities, are also a who's who of 1950s and 1960s New York arts culture.

In the 1940s, Moore had operated as a literary Rosie the Riveter, taking on patriotic literary tasks while many male poets were away (the move to which Randall Jarrell responded negatively).[25] Likewise, in her post-1951 phase, Moore behaved in a manner linked to the postwar fate of her fellow Rosies. Sianne Ngai's work on zaniness can assist understanding of Moore's transition. Ngai characterizes postwar zaniness as the performance of "the experience of an agent confronted with—and endangered by—too many things coming at her at once," which she describes as a response to the changing organization of work, specifically gendered work, in the "hyper-commodified, information-saturated, performance-driven conditions of late capitalism" following the war.[26] Lucille Ball's *I Love Lucy* character (June 15, 1951–April 1, 1960) provides Ngai's chief example. Lucy, as most will recall since the show is still in reruns, repeatedly takes jobs in which she proves herself (and by extension women in general) "incompetent." Ngai argues that the wide range of tasks that Lucy attempts to take on (in addition to her family-building work) represents the market's demand that workers be flexible in an environment of job and gender instability, particularly around requirements that in a service economy workers now bring affective skills into the workplace. In directly related ways, Moore's poetry, her performances of her late-phase public persona, and the interaction between the two seemed increasingly zany after the publication of her *Collected Poems* and the onset of her high magnitude celebrity, reflecting the larger cultural dynamics facing American women in the 1950s. Gender, itself a labor system, assigns certain tasks to certain "kinds" of people, male and female—and further refines the assignment by intersecting gender with race and other factors. For women during this period (like today) the allotted tasks typically included emotional work as well as reproductive and productive labor, which were compensated at lower pay grades than was work by men. Poetic labor was similarly regulated by gender, and the expression of poetic emotion was gender-marked. Moore's work disputed this regulation from its start—both topically and structurally, and her disputation continued in new form in the later work as well. Although she had rejected the realm of overt sentiment standardly associated with the feminine in her early efforts to establish an authoritative voice in her poetry, her later work repurposed the platform her earlier work had built. The combination of her celebrity persona, her documented history of accomplishment and contribution, and the altered cultural context now allowed her to speak directly about sentiment and about democracy and rights struggles (long linked to sentiment).[27]

As the close readings that follow will demonstrate, Moore's performance in the 1950s and 1960s parallels Ball's zany characterization in several ways. Both women enjoyed successful careers before the war, Moore as an influential poet and Ball as "the queen of the B's" (with an occasional A movie thrown in), and both remade themselves drastically in the postwar context, in which many women workers were sent home after successfully staffing the nation's jobs for the duration. The character "Lucy" affirmed the logic behind the gender division of labor that the 1950s male establishment (complexly represented by Ricky, a Cuban, in a role that also challenged race hierarchies) pushed upon American women (from "We can do it!" to "We totally can't do it anymore"). But that overt message was also undercut by the audience's awareness that Ball was the most highly paid woman in the same showbiz at which Lucy Ricardo proves endlessly inept. Ball proved herself supremely capable of performing this incompetence, undermining the argument and marking the tension that still characterizes our attitudes toward women's work.[28] In the 1950s, Moore began performing a similar kind of paradoxical "incompetence" for her audiences. Whether or not they liked Moore's new work, both highbrow and middlebrow fans could recognize that she was not writing in the approved highbrow way (for example, see the *Newsweek* review cited in the Introduction), though her awards made clear that she could and had.

In itself, Moore's George Washington outfit looked zany, both in the root sense of the word meaning *imitation*[29] and in the modern sense of *erratic*, *silly*, or *daft*—but it represented a choice, not a failure. As we will see, a certain zaniness characterizes the poems as well, and that too has its own logic, born of an effort to balance direct statement with an obscurity that harbors the possibility of many and subversive readings. Ngai notes that much of "serious" postwar writing is zany, and she points to the work of Ishmael Reed, Kathy Acker, John Ashbery, and Donald Barthelme, most of it post-1970.[30] By adding Moore to this list, I underscore her contemporaneity with the younger writers of the 1950s and 1960s, though her prewar work was already on this path. Clifford Mak describes the comic dynamic in Moore's early work, particularly her amusingly clumsy animals, as partaking of a "slapstick grace," which draws on her early love of Chaplin and "incorporate[s] failure itself (without erasing its constitutive precarity) into an authoritative kind of surplus style."[31] That dynamic evolves in the later work into her own performance of hilarity, in both her texts and her onstage delivery. Moore summarized aspects of her comedic technique in letters to family members at various points, noting that "I am something of a strolling player & interpolate trivialities that perhaps are out of keeping" and that "It all depends on knowing the text thoroughly and seeming to talk impromptu."[32] It makes sense that a celebrity comedian like Chaplin would serve Moore as an example in her own celebrity turn and that Lucy, herself a former film star, would provide a contemporary parallel, since film generated the contemporary notion of celebrity, as an interface between an individual star and a mass audience. But while Moore (like Lucy) plays with received comedic techniques, postwar concerns and the expanded 1950s celebrity culture inflect them anew.

Post-1951, Moore sought out a wide audience, many of whom felt uncomfortable with elite poetry and its perceived rejection of ordinary readers; to reach them she crossed the high-cultural border into something odd but accessible. She made this move in a humorous framework that blurred gender lines and brow lines simultaneously and in the process explored the operation of those lines. Her work made these transgressions less threatening by inviting her audience in on the joke—and readers and fans came in droves, welcomed into the big tent Moore pitched. But since her death, critics have too often mistaken the performance of "incompetence" (at being fully *high*brow) for reality, missing the ways in which her method, like Lucy's, engaged and challenged the context in which her work was received.

Reveal/Conceal

Moore's late-phase poetry began with "Apparition of Splendor" and "Then the Ermine:" (both 1952), a pair of linked poems that coyly introduce a poetic character—a shifting and stylish "apparition" who seems linked to the emerging public persona. The new figure steps onto the poems' stage as a prelude to the major cultural performance to follow. Emphatically not static, the figure transforms multiply into a variety of animals and plants within and across the two poems, as various manifestations are revealed and concealed. The hide-and-seek dynamic suggests big emotional reservoirs of both shyness and desire to come forward and connect ("dignity with intimacy" as the second poem has it) that are in themselves appealing. Above her notes for "Then the Ermine:" Moore wrote: "I am in an affectionate frame of mind this year," reiterating the connective sentiment.[33] That mood continued for two decades. Though there are instances of similar "reveal and conceal" dynamics in Moore's early poems, they appear more overtly in the late work. In her revolutionary hat, Moore was not obviously a political or social activist, but she and her public persona regularly modeled rebellion and self-confidence-in-nonconformity through her unusual fashion choices, on the subway platform and across all the available media platforms of her day. The equally nonconformist poetry affirms the same, reassuring those in the audience who feel pressured to conceal socially proscribed qualities.

Though the two 1952 poems transition toward the more accessible phase of her work, they are stylistically similar to Moore's earlier, more oblique work.[34] As the title "Apparition of Splendor" adumbrates, that poem demonstrates absorption with dramatic display, but it starts off as a series of refusals to display any one character or object clearly. Instead we are presented with dramatic creatures that are *like* other dramatic and sometimes elusive creatures, starting with yet "another armored animal" (*NCP*, 141), as in so many of Moore's prior poems.

Apparition of Splendor

Partaking of the miraculous
    since never known literally,
Dürer's rhinoceros
    might have startled us equally
    if black-and-white-spined elaborately.

Like another porcupine, or fern,
    the mouth in an arching egret
was too black to discern
    till exposed as a silhouette;
    but the double-embattled thistle of jet—

disadvantageous supposedly—
    has never shot a quill. Was it
some joyous fantasy,
    plain eider-eared exhibit
    of spines rooted in the sooty moss,

or "train supported by porcupines—
    a fairy's eleven yards long"? . . .
as when the lightning shines
    on thistlefine spears, among
    prongs in lanes above lanes of a shorter prong,

"with the forest for nurse," also dark
    at the base—where needle-debris
springs and shows no footmark;
    the setting for a symmetry
    you must not touch unless you are a fairy.

Maine should be pleased that its animal
    is not a waverer, and rather
than fight, lets the primed quill fall.
    Shallow oppressor, intruder,
    insister, you have found a resister. (*NCP*, 196)

Notes: Lines 16–17: "*train . . . long*" Oliver Goldsmith in one of his essays refers to "a blue fairy with a train eleven yards long, supported by porcupines." Line 21: "*with . . . nurse.*" "All over spines, with the forest for nurse." "The Hedgehog, the Fox, and the Flies," Book Twelve, Fable XIII, *The Fables of La Fontaine* [Translated by Moore] (New York: The Viking Press, 1954). (*NCP*, 322)

The poem begins with a direct reference to Dürer's famously inaccurate drawing ("never known literally") of a rhinoceros (Figure 10), which is followed by more inexact descriptions, of wavering animals. Through the first five stanzas we are refused a stable apparition, as Dürer's imaginary rhino turns into a porcupine, a fern, an egret, and then back into a porcupine, in company with fairies (who appear in a lightning flash).

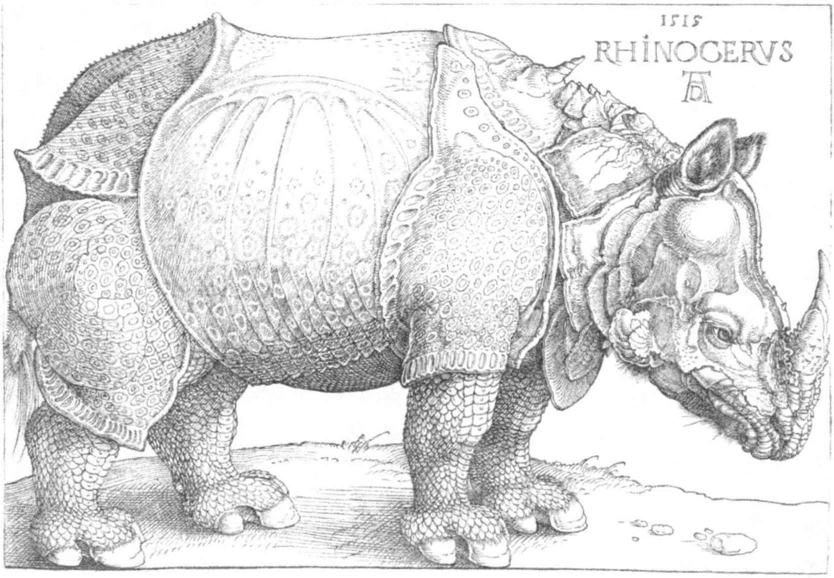

Figure 10. Albrecht Dürer, "Rhinoceros," woodcut, 1515, public domain.

The splendid apparition of the title could allude to the wild morph of creatures itself, which suggests a wide range of natural splendor. Like the forest floor, the springy symmetry of the poem's stanza shapes and rhymes (ABABB) bounces readers around and resists our attempts to stop the flow of characters and to make sense of the poem's story.

But in the final stanza, an "animal" does step into a clearing in this forest of meaning—"not a waverer" but a "resister." The poem closes with an affirmation ("Maine should be pleased") of a porcupine, or quill hog, which, though not Maine's official animal, is an inhabitant of the state. Although porcupines may not shoot their quills (as legend sometimes has it), the sharps do detach when touched, damaging predators, so while this closing image is not aggressive, neither is it quite pacific. This animal also shares qualities with Moore—herself a Maine resident in summer and, as a writer, armed with a primed quill of her own—and Moore's diversely armored animals always figure her and her work in some measure.[35] The poem demonstrates its skill at resisting our efforts to grasp it; like a porcupine or the rose in Moore's 1917 poem "Roses Only," it's prickly. Through its closing contrast (insister vs. resister), readers suddenly find themselves in the poem, cast as the "[s]hallow oppressor, intruder, / insister," who is trying to shape a recognizable narrative out of the resistant poem. But the dialogue between the resister and the insister here is fruitful—together, at the end, they produce the poem, in which the poet/resister/porcupine is revealed at the close.

After its active obfuscation to that point, the poem's closing revelation of the quill hog, a splendid resister, employs the same structural hide-and-seek dynamic that John Emil Vincent has identified as a pattern in Moore's very late work.[36] In his analysis of three poems from Moore's last years—"Love in America?" (1966), "Tippoo's Tiger" (1967), and "The Magician's Retreat" (1970), Vincent argues that what Harriet Monroe disapprovingly described as "the coruscating succession of ideas" in a Moore poem actually represents "an erotic hide-and-seek in which Moore conceals and divulges her presence by turns across the body of a poem . . . the final outcome breathlessly anticipated" by readers.[37] The pattern of "closural appearance," or apparition, that Vincent describes tends to involve a Moore-ish figure, her textual accomplishments, or an animal or character proxy. He distinguishes that from the pattern in the earlier work, where, he feels, the texts dissolve the narrative at the close, and the artist and her art disappear (e.g., "People's Surroundings," which closes with a long, actively confusing parataxis). Although I would argue that Moore's disguised self-flaunting at the close of poems appears in her work at least as early as the image of Daniel Webster at the end of "Marriage" (1923), and that self-figuration occurs in many ways throughout Moore's oeuvre (cf. "Roses Only"), this habit does thicken in the later phase in parallel to Moore's increasing openness to life in the public eye, and "Apparition of Splendor" heralds her transition into celebrity.

Both poems in the pair continue Moore's long-standing pattern of self-figuring through stylish animal surrogates (who do also represent the animals). Her poems on animals and plants extend her long-standing interest in clothing and style beyond the human, into the realm where surface markings and physical features serve both as identifiers and as camouflage. Her descriptions of zebras ("supreme in / their abnormality") and of the tiger ("that Gilgamesh among / the hairy carnivora"), both in "My Apish Cousins" (1917); of elephant skin in "Melancthon" (aka "Black Earth," 1918); of the lizard in "The Plumet Basilisk" (1932); of the eponymous anteater in "The Pangolin" (1936); and of the ostrich in "He 'Digesteth Harde Yron'" (1941) all explore the significations of animal "style." A biology enthusiast since college, Moore recognized connections across organisms, and her college poem "Tunica Pallio Proprior"[38] (1909) brings that home, declaring, "My coat is nearer than my cloak; / Inside / My coat is an integument of pride,"[39] using a term for plant rind or animal skin to suggest the integral nature of her self-confident outfits. Alison Rieke calls such moves "reverse anthropomorphism," wherein Moore, rather than representing humans via animals, "reinvents herself as an animal in human skin."[40] Her evolutionarily correct affirmation of such continuity constitutes a form of boundary crossing not unlike her post-1951 crossing of the high/low cultural line.

The pattern of animal morph established in "Apparition of Splendor" continues in "Then the Ermine:," which operates as a sequel, extending the action into a new setting. Moore's Poetry Notebook suggests that she began this poem about the inevitability and beauty of change (among other things) just after the publication of her *Collected*.[41] Full of compressed logic and oblique references, "Then the Ermine:" may seem hard to follow and even contradictory (although this then becomes part of its argument for change of various kinds and for "skill in obscurity"). Like "Apparition of Splendor," this poem too insists on being hard to locate, beginning with the title, which opens in medias res with the setup to what is apparently the second speech in a series ("then" implies a preceding "first"), this one attributed to "the Ermine," with the colon serving as a dialogue marker. The eccentric inclusion of punctuation in the title makes the Ermine speak its own motto, as though in a play.[42] This is followed by the Ermine's punfully hard to decipher phrase "rather dead than spotted" (*spotted* means at once "sinful," "seen," and "marked with spots").[43] As in many Moore poems, the title also functions as the first line, a technique familiar to her readers that nonetheless continues to surprise.

THEN THE ERMINE:

"rather dead than spotted"; and believe it
    despite reason to think not,
I saw a bat by daylight;
hard to credit

but I knew that I was right. It charmed me—
    wavering like a jack-in-
the-green, weaving about me
insecurely.

Instead of hammer-handed bravado
 adopting force for fashion,
momentum with a motto:
Mutare sperno

vel timere—I don't change, am not craven;
 although on what ground could I
say that I am hard to frighten?
Nothing's certain.

Fail, and Lavater's physiography
 has another admirer
of skill in obscurity—
now a novelty.

So let the *palissandre* settee express
 change, "ebony violet,"
Master Corbo in full dress,
and shepherdess,

at once; exhilarating hoarse crow-note
 and dignity with intimacy.
Foiled explosiveness is yet
a kind of prophet,

a perfecter, and so a concealer—
 with the power of implosion;
like violets by Dürer;
even darker. *(NCP*, 197)

Notes: Line 2: "*rather . . . spotted*" Clitophon; "his device was the Ermion, with a speach that signified, Rather dead than spotted." Sidney's *Arcadia*, Book I, Chapter 17, paragraph 4. Cambridge Classics, Volume I, 1912, edited by Albert Feuillerat.
Line 12: *motto*. Motto of Henry, Duke of Beaufort: *Mutare vel timere sperno*.
Line 18: *Lavater*: John Kaspar Lavater (1741–1801), a student of physiography. His system includes morphological, anthropological, anatomical, histrionical, and graphical studies. Kurt Seligmann, *The Mirror of Magic* (New York: Pantheon Books, 1948, page 332). (*NCP*, 322)

Moore borrows the title and the pun in "spotted" from Philip Sidney's wild *Arcadia*, perhaps the zenith of zaniness in English literature, with its multiple cross-dressers and hugely confusing romance narrative (a pastoral about shepherds and shepherdesses, paired with a literary conflagration of jousts in the name of honor, mistaken identities, rapes, and courtly intrigue), which Moore knew from her freshman readings at Bryn Mawr. By invoking Sidney, Moore sets herself as heir to the sixteenth-century zany tradition, though she evolves it to speak to the twentieth-century context of gendered work. After the motto, the speaker seems to shift, so that we are no longer hearing the discourse of the Ermine; instead we hear from a person who has things in common with ermines.

The poem's shifting series of reflections on certainty and change are emblematized in its borrowing from the Duke of Beaufort's motto (ll. 12–13), which is documented in a note as "*Mutare vel timere sperno*" (I spurn change or fear), but which is changed in the poem to "*Mutare sperno / vel timere*," which means the same thing but alters the phrasing. The comparison with the note undermines the speaker's claim to spurn change (and fits Moore's rhyme scheme)[44]—a joke that is continued in the rest of the stanza, especially in its closing assertion that "Nothing's certain." As in her 1930s poetry, Moore here destabilizes both the mottos she has introduced—the Duke's and the Ermine's—and opens them to multiple meanings. In stating her double intention to both not change and change, Moore marks her new work as continuous with the pre-1951 material, but importantly different too.

This poem beginning "Then" creates a sequence in which the Ermine follows on the heels of the Porcupine in "Apparition of Splendor." Here, too, the initial animal immediately turns into another, this time a bat—who appears in an unusual context (by daylight). "Hard to credit," but true: as with the porcupine and its quills, the bat does not behave as expected. Whereas the porcupine in "Apparition of Splendor" was lauded for not wavering, in this poem the bat's insecure wavering gives it "charm," both sweet and magical. "Marianne Morph," Vincent's appellation for the poet,[45] well describes the shifting imagery in both of these poems, as it does her oeuvre overall. These morphing images second the morphing meanings introduced by the puns that flash multiple referents in and out of readers' minds and tempt them to toss off the chains of grammar and propriety and enter the associative wilderness within. The poem moves from assertions of mutability in stanzas 3 and 4, into affirmatively obscure references to dark magic, to failure as a prelude to new skill (specifically, like Moore's, "skill in obscurity") or even a skill in itself, and to multifaceted colors, like the "ebony violet" of a settee Moore admired in her friend Katherine Anne Porter's apartment, which she links to the blue-black colors of crows' feathers.

Like the prior poem, "Then the Ermine:" also includes characters that evoke Moore, again presented within a framework of concealment. "Master Corbo in full dress," a crow character (from the French *corbeau*) carried over from Moore's translation of La Fontaine's *Fables*, suggests Moore in her cape—especially as it is marked as both male *and* female, "Master . . . / and shepherdess // at once."[46] The reference to "jack-in-the-green," a Druid green-man figure from May Day rites (which were celebrated quadrennially at Bryn Mawr), also suggests Moore (whom H. D. remembered wearing a medieval green brocade dress at the celebration).[47] So does the Ermine, whose motto, "rather dead than spotted," Ellen Levy reads as ventriloquizing Moore's views on her "special chastity [that] holds passion in reserve."[48] Of course, ermines are themselves rather unstable animals: their white coats with the black spot at tail's end exist only in cold weather; in other seasons, their pelt changes (to brown) and their name changes too. *Ermines* are called *weasels* in summer; and Weasel was one of Moore's childhood nicknames.[49]

Across the final three stanzas the male/female "Master Corbo/shepherdess" expresses an "exhilarating hoarse crow-note / and dignity with intimacy," which reframes the whole poem as a dignified intimate communication, a libidinized expression without explicit statement. In contrast to the reveal of the porcupine at the close of "Apparition of Splendor" (oblique but emphatic), the closing images of "Then the Ermine:" focus on concealing (and in so doing, paradoxically, they also reveal—that something is being concealed):

> Foiled explosiveness is yet
> a kind of prophet,
>
> a perfecter, and so a concealer—
>   with the power of implosion;
> like violets by Dürer;
> even darker. (*NCP*, 197)

Both poems close with a simultaneous conceal and reveal (condensing the action that unfolds across the poems), but "Apparition of Splendor" puts more weight on the reveal while "Then the Ermine:" stresses the conceal.[50] Levy reads the closing six lines of "Then the Ermine:" as an expression of and commentary on Moore's own "foiled sexuality," which pursues pleasure in art by others, like Dürer. But Moore's own writing—her own art—is also an erotic engine here, giving pleasure not only to Moore in creating it but to its audience as well, with whom it shares its "affectionate mood" through the coy hide-and-seek and self-featuring. The foiling of explosive pleasure anticipates a different but also powerful, perfected, feminine pleasure of implosion, resonating within. The poem thus becomes a vehicle of "dignified yet intimate" internal connection of poet with readers—triangulated through various objects of delight invoked in the poems. In both poems, Dürer provides such an object—the miraculous rhino at the start of "Apparition of Splendor" and the almost-black violet revealed at the close of "Then the Ermine:" (Figure 11)—further linking the poems, with this pair of masculine and feminine images, the second one reminiscent of the lesbian tradition of the erotic garden that Lisa Moore traces.[51]

The two invocations of Dürer place these among Moore's many ekphrastic poems, beginning from as early as her college publications "To a Screen-Maker" (1909) and "A Talisman" (1912) and continuing through to her final poems. As Bonnie Costello has noted, "Almost every poem Moore wrote involved a picture or art object at some stage of composition," some more "submerged," in Elizabeth Loiseaux's phrase, than the direct references here.[52] Moore's sustained efforts to suggest specific visual images through words, inevitably unsuccessful in some degree, echo the shy self-flaunting of her many reveal-and-veils. They align Moore with the pattern that Brian Glavey calls "queer ekphrasis" and traces in the work of twentieth-century writers Gertrude Stein, Djuna Barnes, Richard Bruce Nugent, Frank O'Hara, and John Ashbery. He names this group "the wall-flower avant-garde," pushed by "conflicting desires to critique, to shy away from, but still to remain at the scene of the dance."[53] While in poetry "pictures promise the presence that might satisfy desire," they never quite come through, remaining elusive and alluring, and opening up a productive space for exploring sexuality within the aesthetic, particularly alternative sexualities which one might feel shy about and wish to represent indirectly.[54] Drawing on Lisa Moore's analysis of the "sister arts" as figuring alternativity and relationality per se, Glavey argues that the parallel embedded in ekphrasis (of poetry and visual art) creates "an unpredictable spectrum of relationality, multiplying ways of desiring."[55]

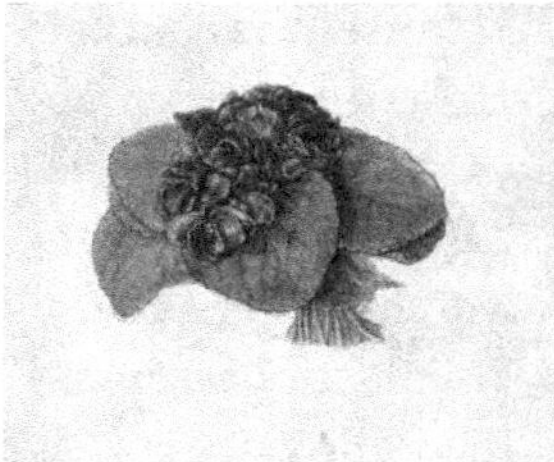

Figure 11. Albrecht Dürer, "Violet Bouquet," watercolor, ca. 1502, Albertina, Vienna, public domain.

Simultaneously, ekphrasis symbolizes an implicit self-revelation; the slippage between poem and painting figures a similar slippage between poem and poet. Stein's remark that "all literature is me to me; that isn't as bad as it sounds,"[56] is largely characteristic of Moore as well. Likewise the slippage in Moore's poems between the imaginary (gardens) and the real (toads) is directly instantiated by her late-phase performances—in which she appears before her public as "Marianne Moore," poet/character, inhabiting both sides of the literary line at once. In doing so she literalizes the gesture at three-dimensionality embedded in all ekphrases and underscores the structural play with 2-D form active in so much of her work.

Among Moore's contemporaries, Donald Hall saw "Then the Ermine:" as among the last of Moore's poems "in which oblique style harbors depth of emotion."[57] But such depth is expressed throughout her later oeuvre, in both overt and oblique ways. However you parse her history, Moore's self-flaunting performance in all aspects of the poetry invokes the many-layeredness of human connection: at once erotic, humorous, spiritual, and intellectual. With their playful "reveal and conceal" dynamics, "Apparition of Splendor" and "Then the Ermine:" anticipate Moore's stepping out into the more accessible poems that follow. But they stand on the brink, doing so in still-obscure terms that require readers to actively engage in efforts to decipher/construct the text and find the hidden and revealed figures. The later work's greater accessibility never erases a core obliquity, an irresolvability that spurs forward movement and persists in spite of Moore's "burning desire to be explicit," as she puts it in 1966. *Mutare sperno / vel timere.*

Shifting Venues, New Audiences

The process of getting published often involves matching a poet's literary style to that of the target venue. In tandem with the evolution of her poetry and persona, Moore shifted the range of the journals in which her work appeared from literary magazines aimed at a small readership to those favored by wider audiences. Though her two 1952 poems were published in *The Nation* and *Poetry*, both journals with established literary reputations with which she had long been associated, those were her last appearances there. After that she branched out, and between 1953 and 1958 venues in which her new poetry appeared included the *New Yorker*, *Vogue*, *Times Literary Supplement*, Abbott Laboratories' *What's New*, *Art News*, *BBC Listener*, *Shenandoah*, *Ladies' Home Journal*, *Partisan Review*, *New York Herald Tribune*, *Sequoia*, *Virginia Quarterly Review*, *Atlantic Monthly*, and *Boston Globe*—a broad spectrum. In late 1958 the *New Yorker* offered her a first-refusal contract, which meant that most of her new work from then on (a total of 20 poems between 1959 and 1970, and 23 poems overall) appeared therein.[58] But there were some exceptions to Moore's contract (as well as a few refusals when the *New Yorker* found the work too "puzzling"),[59] in which case Moore found alternate venues. In that period, she also published new work in *Harper's Bazaar*, *City Center Ballet Program*, Steuben Glass's *Poetry in Crystal*, a Stinehour Press broadsheet, *Harvard Advocate*, *Saturday Evening Post*, *New York Post*, *Tambourine*, *New York Times Magazine*, and a Phoenix Book Shop pamphlet. While some of these venues were academic, most were middlebrow or popular and brought Moore a wide variety of readers. In order to meet their diverse needs, she had to be inventive and flexible.

Since its start in 1925, the *New Yorker* had combined humor with seriousness as part of what Faye Hammill describes as a sophisticated middlebrow culture, aimed at thoughtful Americans who aspired to elite cultural status but weren't willing to be deeply critical of the social status quo or to work very hard at interpretation.[60] Addressing readers alert to a wide cultural spectrum, the magazine published in-depth news-linked reflections and aesthetically sophisticated literature alongside limericks, comic stories, and multiple wry cartoons. Though the proportion has reduced over time, in the 1950s the magazine still ran many humorous poems—by Ogden Nash, Phyllis McGinley, and others[61]—and while the aesthetic standards overall were relatively demanding, poetry editor Howard Moss didn't want readers (including both experienced literati and wannabes) to have to work too hard; submissions were regularly sent back to authors for alterations to fit the magazine's view of their audience's needs. Though Moore felt comfortable with such demands, Elizabeth Bishop complained in 1949 that Moss often enforced a limiting code of "clarity" and middle-class politeness: "I think the convention of situating everything clearly and immediately can get to be boring, make the reader lazy."[62] The magazine's role as purveyor of urbanity to the nation gave it a dubious cast in the eyes of many literati.[63] But Moore took a more generous view, seeing the magazine as a means not just to reach but to engage a wide audience.

As *Dial* editor in the 1920s, Moore required that work accepted for publication fit her audience's expectations in regard to the style or level of work they would find in that journal, and she recognized the need to do the same with her own submissions. Her late poems were often written in response to a request from a magazine, with its audience in mind. Such invitations were part of the poetic culture of the day, which often involved poems written to order for special issues or collections (though that's less the case today, it still occurs). Moore's celebrity and accessibility combined to mean that she received many such requests in her latter days. She didn't accept them all, but those she did served as prompts, which she would evolve to fit her own interests. Sometimes the development process involved negotiation on how best to meet the needs of both editor and poet. The diverse topics she engaged with in skipping among literary magazines, fashion rags, science journals, newspapers, and so forth bespeak the big range of Moore's interests, allowing her to channel diverse aspects of herself and to connect with audiences in their comfort zones.

For instance, in 1954 Moore was invited to contribute to the Christmas issue of the Abbott pharmaceutical company's bimonthly magazine, circulated to 165,000 doctors (poets Carl Sandburg, Edna St. Vincent Millay, and Archibald MacLeish, among others, had contributed previously). The topic was to be seasonal, though not necessarily about Christmas, and could be concerned with doctors or medicine, or not. Moore replied that "I have never been able to write about Christmas; but have an ardent interest in products bearing on medicine and science . . . Christmas is a thought that glows in the mind and there should be a way of exteriorizing it, but as I say, I had best turn my mind to medicine!" The editor welcomed the poem she submitted,[64] titled "The Staff of Aesculapius" (a son of Apollo, Aesculapius was the Greco-Roman god of medicine). His staff with a single snake winding around serves here as a symbol of both medicine and science. While the poem closes with an image of renewal that may also suggest the Christmas season, Moore devoted most of the six stanzas (all of which snake around their centers, adding up to an abstract "literal image" on the page) to directly addressing the concerns of the journal's medical audience, through emphasis on rigorous research and details about virology, lung resection, and other cancer-curing techniques.

THE STAFF OF AESCULAPIUS

A symbol from the first, of mastery,
experiments such as Hippocrates made
and substituted for vague
speculation, stayed
the ravages of a plague.

A "going on"; yes, *anastasis* is the word
for research a virus has defied,
and for the virologist
with variables still untried—
too impassioned to desist.

Suppose that research has hit on the right one
and a killed vaccine is effective
say temporarily—
for even a year—although a live
one could give lifelong immunity,

knowledge has been gained for another attack.
Selective injury to cancer
cells without injury to
normal ones—another
gain—looks like prophecy come true. (*NCP*, 201, ll. 1–20)

Notes: Line 11: *Suppose . . . one. Time*, March 29, 1954, article on the Salk vaccine. Lines 17–20: *Selective . . . true*. Sloan-Kettering Institute for Cancer Research, *Progress Report VII*, June 1954; pp. 20–21. (*NCP*, 326)

Stanza 2 describes a hardworking contemporary virologist trying all the possible experimental variables in his search for a cure, and the poem goes on to explore his methods.

Science had always informed Moore's writing, both in terms of her interest in biology and animal behavior, which she'd been engrossed by since college, and in terms of her own methods—precise observation being her watchword and syllabic meter being itself structured around a genetic metaphor. ("I never 'plan' a stanza," she told Donald Hall.

"Words cluster like chromosomes, determining the procedure," and stanzas then replicate on the same pattern, though with some variation, as in life.)[65] As David Anderson points out, Moore values the parallel in the evolution of knowledge through experiment and disciplined perception that science and poetry both depend upon,[66] and the development of her methods across her career documented in this volume offers an instance of precisely that kind of evolving experiment.

Stanza 5 describes a successful cancer surgery, leading to the celebratory close:

> Now, after lung resection, the surgeon fills space.
> To sponge implanted, cells following
> fluid, adhere and what
> was inert becomes living—
> that was framework. Is it not
>
> like the master-physician's Sumerian rod?—
> staff and effigy of the animal
> which by shedding its skin
> is a sign of renewal—
> the symbol of medicine. (*NCP*, 201, ll. 21–30)

> *Note*: Lines 22–25: *To . . . framework.* Abbott Laboratories, "Plastic Sponge Implants in Surgery," *What's New*, Number 186, Christmas 1954.[67] (*NCP*, 326)

Just as the sponge serves as a framework for healthy cells to grow upon, Moore builds a celebration of medicine and the scientific process in selfless service to the community onto a framework of syllabics, indentation, and rhyme (ABCBC) and brings the poem to life, first for her audience of doctors and then for the wider audience reading her books, who are reminded of these passionate scientific laborers on our behalf.

Though this kind of writing to order (a form of occasional poetry, discussed at more length in Chapter 3) may raise questions about whether the poet sacrifices her aesthetic to the context, Moore's praxis, less acquiescently, consistently combines her own ideas and formal preferences with the venue's context, on purpose to include her venue's audience in her wider discussion of the operations of community—a dialogue among individuals, all valued and all contributing their own insights in their own distinctive styles.

In *Vogue*: Fashion Miracle

> one's style is not lost in such simplicity
> —"People's Surroundings" (*NCP*, 56)

That same year Moore's work took an especially fashionable turn, in a poem written for *Vogue*. The magazine provided a new and bigger audience, of readers who shared Moore's strong sense of style. From hats to hair and on down, her sartorial choices had always signified, both as part of her interest in gender blurring and, somewhat differently, as expression of her personal aesthetic.[68] Unlike those who choose their clothes to blend in, Moore aimed "to have to wear, what keeps life from becoming a parcel of uniformities."[69] In letters home from Bryn Mawr, she detailed and analyzed her own outfits and those of others. Later she displayed similar focus in correspondence with her friend Hildegarde Watson, often about clothes Hildegarde was giving her. Discerning a difference between modish fashion (which "can make you ridiculous") and style ("which is yours to control"),[70] throughout her life Moore wore outfits that supported her active sense of her self-presentation as reflective of her idiosyncratic personality. Though hats were the crowning signifier in Moore's late career, she dressed snappily on all levels, on her own terms.

Moore's habits of highly conscious dressing, early and late, rhyme with her careful curating of her portrait photographs, for which she posed regularly. Poets, like actors, need publicity shots, and Moore's sharp style sense prepared her for her postwar celebrity turn. Stacy Hubbard has examined the staging of the early 1920s image in Figure 12, taken by Sarony Studios (which was known for theatrical work, including portraits of the young aesthete Oscar Wilde). She notes that Moore's hand placement echoes Mannerist portraits of the late Renaissance (see Figure 13), in ways that draw attention to the artfulness of the pose and the artist's role as maker, and thereby "invit[e] speculation about what it means to look and to represent" and themselves constitute "poetry by other means."[71]

Through the gender-blurring outfit and the positioning of the hands, head, and gaze, Moore's photo invokes Bronzino's *Portrait of a Young Man*—though Moore avoids the full "teapot pose" often also adopted by nineteenth-century gay aesthetes.[72] Details, like the echo of the young man's cap in the shape of Moore's wreathed braid and their shared penchant for pinky rings, further the parallel. Moore repeats similarly

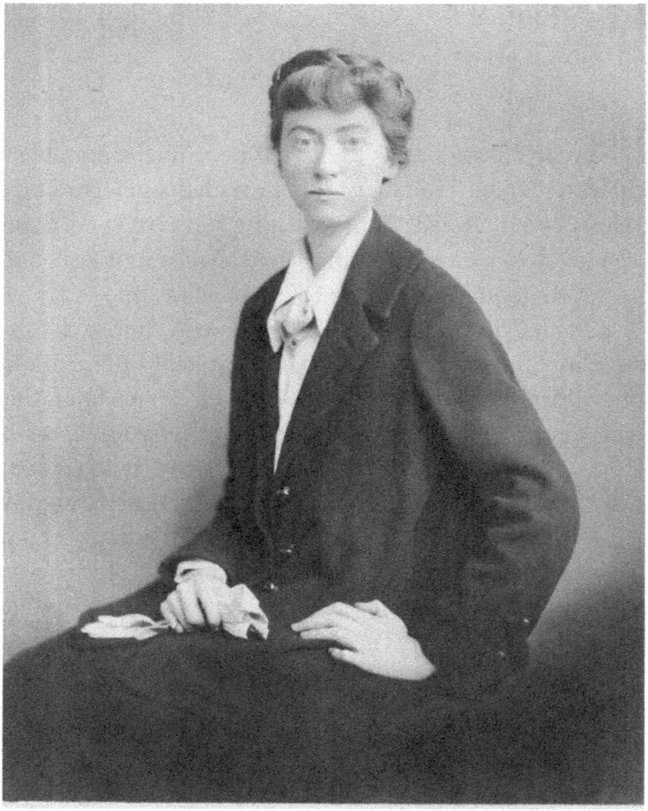

Figure 12. Marianne Moore, 1924, photographed by Sarony Studios. Reprinted by kind permission.

marked hand gestures in several later portraits, including the 1950 Marion Morehouse image (see Figure 8).[73] Moore's passion for visual signification through dress and pose mirrors her poetry's deep engagement with visual art.[74] Her revisions of poems' layouts over decades keep them in motion and create the fashion effect of ongoing refittings.

Allene Talmey, the literary editor at *Vogue*, invited Moore to submit "a Xmas piece" just days after she completed "The Staff of Aesculapius" for *What's New*.[75] Moore must have quickly recognized that such invitations would be both frequent and flexible in her new incarnation as a celebrity poet, and were indeed an opportunity to be seized rather than avoided. So this time she did not protest, writing to Talmey, "I do not

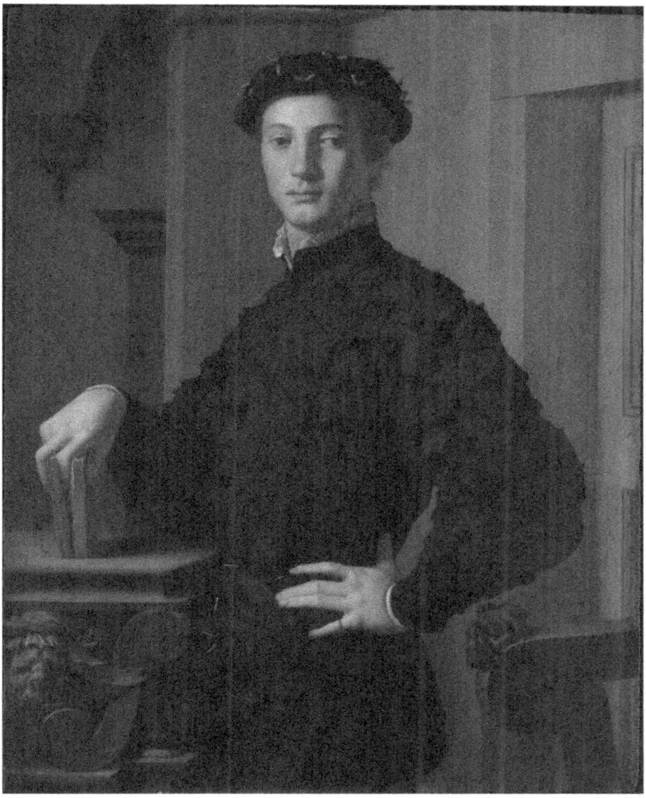

Figure 13. Bronzino, *Portrait of a Young Man*, c. 1530, Metropolitan Museum, New York, public domain.

know what to think of writers who undertake to 'serve' a magazine and find themselves unable to subordinate their material to the needs of the magazine."[76] "Rosemary," the resultant poem (originally titled "A Kind of Christmas Tree"), takes the seasonal assignment more seriously than did "Aesculapius" while again aligning directly with the magazine's basic realms of interest: in *Vogue*'s case, fashion and eros. Though the poem, which appeared in the December 1954 issue, explicitly states its intention to "speak plainly" for this less literary audience, and arguably does so relative to some Moore poems, it still requires readers to lean in a bit as it recounts the myths associated with the rosemary herb that link it to Venus and to the Blessed Virgin Mary. Like many of Moore's later poems, it engages with sentimental material directly: starting out with Beauty and Love (both of immediate interest to *Vogue* readers) it turns quickly to Christmas, and then caters even more specifically to *Vogue*'s audience by focusing on fashion.

ROSEMARY

Beauty and Beauty's son and rosemary—
Venus and Love, her son, to speak plainly—
born of the sea supposedly,
at Christmas each, in company,
braids a garland of festivity.
    Not always rosemary—

since the flight to Egypt, blooming differently.
With lancelike leaf, green but silver underneath,
its flowers—white originally—
turned blue. The herb of memory,
imitating the blue robe of Mary,
    is not too legendary

to flower both as symbol and as pungency.
Springing from stones beside the sea,
the height of Christ when thirty-three—
not higher—it feeds on dew and to the bee
"hath a dumb language"; is in reality
    a kind of Christmas-tree. (*NCP*, 203)

Note: Marianne Moore is one of America's great poets. These are her own footnotes for this Christmas poem: The rosemary of Europe, unlike ours, grows four to eight feet high, and according to the British scholar, Eleanour Sinclair Rohde, "never grows higher than the height of Christ when He was a man on earth." . . . A Spanish legend explains that the flowers of rosemary turned from white to blue, when the Virgin threw her cloak over a rosemary bush while she rested on the Flight into Egypt. (*Vogue*, 101)[77]

As in "The Staff of Aesculapius," Moore builds an unexpected narrative here around a familiar symbol. The trio of gods introduced in line 1 were relatives in Greek mythology, Rosemary being the least renowned. As Brewer's *Dictionary of Phrase and Fable* (which Moore consulted) describes it: "Rosemary is Ros-marinus (sea-dew), *and is said to be 'useful in love-making.' The reason is this:* Both Venus, *the love-goddess*, and Rosemary or sea-dew, were offspring of the sea; and as Love is Beauty's son, Rosemary is his nearest relative [emphasis added]."[78] The presence of Venus and Love/Eros is reiterated in the first two lines, to clarify "plainly" who is being discussed, though their connection to Rosemary (Eros's aunt) is not made explicit in the poem. The poem's start suits the sexy focus of *Vogue*'s stories and ads, and in a draft Moore linked Rosemary more clearly to that focus, by echoing Juliet's nurse's comment that "Rosemary and Romeo begin with the same letter." But in the final poem, that detail is repressed and the reference to Venus is left to do the work of marking the erotic connection here.

The poem segues in line 4 to the holiday theme (for *Vogue*'s hallowed gift-buying season) with Christmas revelers braiding garlands, and we learn that Rosemary, though born a minor Greek goddess, soon (effectively) converted to Christianity. Moore links *Vogue* readers' presumed interest in beauty and fashion as a spur to erotic love[79] with the religious love associated with Christmas by recounting two legendary "fashion" changes undertaken by the rosemary plant itself, which enact the conversion. First, the plant, when touched by Mary's blue cloak during the Flight into Egypt, signified its change of faith by turning its flowers from white to blue in coordinated solidarity. Later, the poem holds, the herb (in its upright European variety) altered its growth pattern: from that point forward, never growing beyond the height of Christ.[80] The changes enact both miracle and fashion statement, together. To mark that marvel, revelers thereafter weave Rosemary into holiday garlands, which seems, given the narrative, to effectively braid both her aspects—religion and erotic love. *Vogue*'s commercial context adds the additional thread of capitalism to this poem's garland, raising questions about the values of the gifts for sale in the magazine relative to love and spirit.

The miraculous transformations also suggest Moore's aesthetic transformation, from her high modernist mode to its mixed-brow, *Vogue*-worthy cousin: a poetic fashion change. "Rosemary" thus offers a variant on an idea Moore had introduced decades earlier in "The Past Is the Present": what matters in most poetry is not form (including brow level) but the ecstasy that occasions it.[81] Embedded in *Vogue*, "Rosemary" likewise activates its context to suggest that love too may take various forms, all of which also share a basis in a common ecstatic energy. Both in its title and in its exploration of the nature of beauty and attraction via gardening lore, "Rosemary"' echoes the early poem "Roses Only" (see Appendix); both affirm the erotic body while refusing it status as sole source of feminine value—both affirm mind and spirit as well. The expansion of the plant name in the second poem to include "Mary" adds a reference to the Blessed Virgin, while also continuing Moore's pattern of poetic self-figuring. In drafts, Moore cites Brewer on the etymology of Rosemary as "*ros-marinus*, sea-dew."[82] It's a short trip through "Ros-marine" to "Rose-Marianne,"[83] a vogue-ish blend of poet and plant, sporting another prideful integument, of personal style.

The Christmas story of the holy family underlying "Rosemary" may be the most recognized Bible tale, known by shoppers of all faiths. By reshaping it into a fashion narrative, Moore follows in a long history of telling Bible stories through media that reach out to people where they are—including sermons, carols, and stained-glass windows. But once they're snagged by the popular hook of what may seem to be the familiar Christmas narrative, and the also widely familiar story of Venus and Eros, Moore carries her readers off in new directions. These relate initially to her audience's established interest in fashion, which she shares, but they quickly lead readers toward new methods of engaging with poetry, activating them as interpreters of the poem's braided layers. Attentive readers find they've stumbled into a more complex text than expected, where they're asked to negotiate conjunct realms of sexuality, religion, and authority through the (ancient) body of the Ros-mari[an]ne. Moore's poem deemphasizes the capitalist aspect of Christmas by featuring not gifts (the focus of the many ads in the pages surrounding the poem in *Vogue*) but the miracle of the fashion change, and the religious miracle celebrated by believers that it heralds. Though the poem can't radically undermine capitalism in *Vogue*, its bastion (and Moore, who appreciated the usefulness of money, wouldn't have wanted to), it can and does invite critique of excess and of objectification.

In reaching out to non-elite audiences through venues like *Vogue* (and later the *Saturday Evening Post* and the *New York Herald Tribune*), Moore fulfills avant la lettre Daniel Tiffany's wish for an avant-garde outreach to wider audiences. "In order to broaden its accessibility and political influence," he asks, "should avant-garde poetry be exploring models of expression—from melodrama to mottoes to kitsch—that might broaden its scope and bring it more directly in contact with larger numbers of people?" He wonders "to what degree can the historical polarity between vanguard experimentation and popular taste, between difficulty and accessibility, be overcome?"[84] Were avant-garde poets to do as he describes, they would be following directly in the steps of Moore, who variously conducted just such explorations, particularly in her late phase. Play with diction was her calling card from the start (recall the "plain American which cats and dogs can read"), but many fans of her early work discount the diction and material of the 1950s and 1960s precisely for representing a "decline" into sentiment (as in the *Newsweek* quote above) or kitsch.[85]

Tiffany goes on to insist that "the poetic avant-garde must invent a fugitive language to circulate as widely as possible," while noting that "the historical record of attempts to overcome the tension between popular taste and vanguard experiment is—with the arguable exceptions of Brecht, Godard, Warhol, and a few others—largely one of failure. Preoccupation with the conflict between vanguard experimentation and popular taste undermines the basic political objective of revolutionary aesthetics, which is to dissolve the autonomy of the poetic artifact—to integrate art and life."[86] The exclusion of Moore from this and other discussions of chic kitsch suggests that while poetry and art by elite men may include kitsch and still get respect, kitsch-engaged poetry by women tends to be sneered at as abject, presumably because kitsch is already gendered feminine, which is part of the dynamic of its abjection. Too often, women's realm is still understood as that of the thoughtless body to which poems like Moore's "Roses Only" reject exclusive assignment. Delighting in the complementarity of petals and thorns, body and mind, Moore demonstrates the pleasures and importance of both. While the embrace of kitsch or non-elite realms by male poets and artists, gay or straight, may signal a claim to femininity, that's implicitly ironized by their sex and reads as subversive, but for women it has read as just a reversion to type. And such has been the case for Moore. (For more exploration of Moore's links to contemporary cross-brow artists Warhol and Ray Johnson, see the Epilogue.)

In looking anew at her later poetry and at her apparition as a splendidly avant-garde performer in her last two decades, we can now recognize the wide range of improvisations enacted and skills involved in Moore's utilization of her late-life celebrity to make the case for democracy to a cross-brow audience. Her later poems move among many concerns—performance, style, participatory democracy, sexuality restrained and expressed, post–World War II workforce patterns, celebrity dynamics, human/animal relations, war and pacificism, ethics, evolving age and gender experience, active dialogue with multiple moments in literary history, with diverse prior texts, and with personal friends—and, of course, *more.* As such they mirror the many layers of lived experience—often chaotic, rarely hierarchical. Moore's poems' engagements with multiple topics and audiences in themselves feed her case for democracy, representing the diversity of knowledge and experience, and reinforcing her argument for valuing the world's complexity and its wide variety of people. Not that she herself realizes that complexity fully—Moore too had biases, of which her unfriendly response to Sylvia Plath's work and Plath's position as a poet with children may be taken as representative, since it offers a clear example of failure to include, based perhaps in a combination of very different experience and some rivalry.[87] Likewise, Moore's anti-racism, though active and committed, was nonetheless of its moment. But the tumult in her poems in itself gestures toward an ideal polity, in which the panoply of voices may both speak and be heard, each performing in its own style.

2

Sports Poetry: Populism, Race, and the Ethics of Celebration

> the bat, . . .
> the base-
> ball fan, the statistician— . . .
> all these phenomena are important.
>
> —"Poetry" (*NCP*, 27)

As honors rolled in for Moore's *Collected Poems* in 1952, her tiny appointment calendars overflowed with celebratory engagements,[1] and multiple news stories and features made her prize-winning status common knowledge. Many Americans who were entirely unfamiliar with her poetry suddenly found her new celebrity incarnation interesting,[2] and Moore obligingly began producing playful, more accessible poems for this expanded fan base. Several focused on sports and athletics—blurring the lines among highbrow, middlebrow, and popular cultures to widen the potential audience, and drawing parallels between the playing of sport and the playful poetry itself. Focused on the nature of fandom and on sports stars, whose fame was based on the authentic exercise of hard-earned skills rather than on beauty as with many Hollywood celebrities, Moore's sports poems also furthered her exploration of who deserved celebration and of the roles of race, gender, and identity politics in both sports and American democracy more broadly.

Sports, Race, and Democracy

Moore was no newcomer to sports in 1952: a lifelong tennis player herself, from 1911 to 1914 she also had an inside view of both the global machinery of sports and of the dynamics of race in America when as a recent college graduate she taught commercial subjects to Olympian Jim Thorpe and the other legendary athletes of the U.S. Indian Industrial School in her hometown, Carlisle, Pennsylvania (the entire backfield of the champion national collegiate football team were in her class at one point). As Siobhan Phillips surmises, she may refer to these athletes in the first version of her poem "The Student" (1932) when she speaks of "football men," who possess a genius combining the wisdoms of calculus, physics, strategy, and physical skill.[3] Moore observes that "There is a vitality in the world of sport. / If it is not the tree of knowledge, it's the tree of life." Phillips sees reference to the Carlisle School also in Moore's comment in this poem that "Education augments our natural forces and / prompts us to extend the machinery of advantage / to those who are without it" (*NCP*, 96). Lesley Wheeler and Chris Gavaler also see echoes of Moore's Carlisle School experience of sports and race in "To an Intra-Mural Rat," "Like a Bulrush," and "You Are Like the Realistic Product of an Idealistic Search for Gold at the Foot of the Rainbow."[4] Though she didn't overtly document more about her experience at the Carlisle School in poems, those were momentous years for several reasons and had enormous effect on her, not least on her productivity (she published fifty-one poems during the period 1910–17[5] and, Wheeler and Gavaler calculate, wrote another forty-plus).[6]

Eight years before Moore's birth and three years after the Battle of Little Bighorn, the Carlisle School was the first of the residential schools founded by the Bureau of Indian Affairs in 1879, to assimilate Native Americans into the Anglo world—cutting them off from their cultures and families, at substantial risk to their health and happiness, and training them for future employment. The admissions office favored athletes and the Carlisle team was extraordinary, shattering records. Among these athletes, and all athletes of his day, Jim Thorpe was preeminent: winning two gold medals in the 1912 Olympics (for decathlon and pentathlon), later playing for the New York Giants *baseball* team, then leading the Canton Bulldogs *football* team to three championships, and serving as the founding president of the NFL. Moore reported to Robert Cantwell in 1960 that "we were just proud of them. The whole town was." In his *Sports Illustrated* essay on Moore, Cantwell opines that "when the school was started, [Native Americans] were despised, feared, hated, exploited, fought—and while the achievement of Thorpe and his teammates could not end that altogether they certainly worked a transformation in the attitude of the nation as a whole toward the red men."[7]

In their essay on Moore's years at the Carlisle School, Wheeler and Gavaler portray the multilayered political, ethical, and aesthetic world that she inhabited, and they emphasize that she recognized race as a shifting performance there, not a static category. Many of the students were mixed race, and the whole structure of the institution was based on ideas of "strategic imposture and racial chameleons." Moore's eventful tenure overlapped with that of Thorpe, her student, and also included the period in which a student petition against the administration's "cruel neglect and abuse" (including beatings and inadequate food) led to a national hearing and the school's eventual closing. Because the petition was generated from students in her classes on, among other things, how to negotiate a contract and avoid being swindled, the superintendent accused Moore of spurring it, though she was not a signatory. She replied, "You mustn't hold me responsible for my pupils' stubbornness. I crush out disrespect and rancor whenever I see it, and I give the students as thorough a training in political honor as I can."[8] As Wheeler and Gavaler note, given Moore's ironic tendencies, her "understanding of disrespect, rancor and honor, of course, may have been very different from [the superintendent's]."[9] She speaks fondly of Thorpe in the *Sports Illustrated* profile and her archive preserves a postcard Thorpe and fellow student Ivy Miller sent to Moore while on their honeymoon in Japan. At the Carlisle School and elsewhere Moore did not avoid all participation in the racist dynamics of the world around her, but she was part of the resistance and went on to take a pro-integrationist stand in major poems, as well as through many of her private and public actions and associations.

The elephant speaker in her 1918 poem "Melancthon" (later "Black Earth") discusses its thick black skin ("Black / but beautiful, my back / is full of the history of power. Of power? What / is powerful and what is not?" [*NCP*, 41]), which led Ezra Pound to ask Moore in an early letter whether she were indeed "a jet black Ethiopian Othello-hued."[10] Edith Sitwell noticed the same poem in her positive review of Moore's *Poems* (1921), attributing to it "a strangeness like that of negroid art" (a not-uncommon figure for modernist outsidership, as Michael North has shown).[11] Unlike Pound and Sitwell, Moore spoke actively against race prejudice of all kinds in many of her poems,[12] noting, for instance, in "Virginia Britannia" (1935) that

> . . . Like strangler figs choking
> a banyan, not an explorer, no imperialist,
> not one of us, in taking what we
> pleased—in colonizing as the
> saying is—has been a synonym for mercy. (*CP*, 110, ll. 110–14)[13]

In "Labours of Hercules" (1921), citing a sermon, she endorsed her Greenwich Village pastor's view that, in spite of the unceasing flows of racist rhetoric and eugenicist polemics against immigration,

> . . . one keeps on knowing
> "that the Negro is not brutal,
> that the Jew is not greedy,
> that the Oriental is not immoral,
> that the German is not a Hun." (*NCP*, 54, ll. 31–34)
>
> *Note:* "the Negro is not brutal": The Reverend J. W. Darr (*NCP*, 299)

As we've seen, her poem "The Hero" (1932) awards that title to the black guide leading a tourist to Washington's grave at Mount Vernon, a place that resonates with the history of slavery as much as or more than it does of freedom. Years later, Moore's Washington impersonation signaled not just cheerful patriotism but an ironic reminder of the essentially flawed version of democracy that he and the other founding fathers brought forth upon this continent, with its many omissions from equality—including people of color and women.

David Kadlec connects Moore's anti-racism to her anti-eugenicist views, built through studies of biology and of Jamesian pragmatism at Bryn Mawr and of the work of John Dewey and Charles Darwin, among others, in the 1910s and 1920s. He understands those to have directly affected her prosody, so that she "derived from modern genetics an aesthetic based on semiotic contingency that enabled her uniquely to confront the essentialist logic of modern eugenics, or the science of racial engineering."[14] But Moore's discussions of race, being of their moment, also involved elements that can make contemporary readers uneasy. For instance, she did sometimes express stereotyped ideas, as when she writes in "Nine Nectarines" that "A Chinese 'understands / the spirit of the wilderness'" (*CP*, 30),[15] as if such understanding were a stable, race-based characteristic. As Cristanne Miller has argued, "Moore works within the [racial] stereotypes of her nation and era at the same time that she attempts to work out of them."[16] Her play with the pun on Moor in her own last name may seem appropriative, at the same time that it signals a pride in claiming connection through a shared marginalization. Moore activated that pun as early as 1916, in "Sun!," where the poem seems to refer to itself as "a device of Moorish gorgeousness," and she deployed it in poems at intervals throughout her life. Her frequent though fleeting representations of performers of color—including Chinese, African American, and Hispanic artists and athletes—also combine elements of appropriation with a sympathetic connection that leads her to seek to not objectify or "to cage" those she describes, as she puts it in "Arthur Mitchell" (1962). These representations also suggest some identification, and like many of her tropes and habits (including her armored animals, her cross-dressing, her celibacy, her insistently peculiar prosody, and her ekphrases) likewise suggest her discomfort with, and model escape from, many of the norms and social hierarchies of her day.

Moore's connection to the race struggle in the United States, like her Republicanism, had roots in her family's defining experience at the battle of Gettysburg (see Appendix), which resonated through their generations.[17] Asked at one point what was the most significant event "in her lifetime," she said, "Lincoln's assassination,"[18] in spite of its having occurred twenty-two years before her birth. In Brooklyn she worshipped at an integrated church and, as noted earlier, Langston Hughes (who also sought to connect poetry with the people and appreciated Moore's related efforts), after describing Moore as "a wonderful and lovely lady," quipped that "I consider her the most famous Negro woman poet in America today" (1967), marking Moore, as Benjamin Kahan notes, as "a fellow traveler in demolishing racial difference."[19] Though she speaks from a situation of relative privilege that complicates her identifications, Moore continued her lifelong advocacy for racial equity in her late sports poems.

Tom Fool: Circulating Celebrity at the Races

In "Tom Fool at Jamaica" (1953) Moore chose as subject a non-human athlete whose situation turned out to mirror her own, though she couldn't know that when she first noticed him in 1952. The horse's "foolish" name paired with his April Fool's Day start date at Jamaica Race Course attracted Moore, who was fond of jest: "out on April first, a day of some significance / in the ambiguous sense" (*NCP*, 178, ll. 11–12).[20] Soon thereafter she became a "winner" in the poetry games (bringing home the Pulitzer in May 1952 for her 1951 *Collected Poems*), and the three-year-old thoroughbred Tom Fool was predicted to do the same in the racing world that season.[21] Responding to her own exciting year, the newly celebritized Moore began writing about Tom Fool in her poetry notebook in July 1952, as his star was also climbing. In the poem, she presents herself as a fan (the horse is the luminary) and utilizes her growing fame to proffer a populist model of circulating celebration for hard-won accomplishment by characters of whatever class or rank, rather than the static up/down dynamic of admiration for idealized celebrities by the lowly masses.

Moore details her writing process in the three pages of notes to this less-than-two-page poem (the notes—her longest set—were added in the 1956 book version), reporting that she'd first been drawn to the horse by a March 1952 *New York Times* sports article that described him as having "that mark of a champion, the extra / spurt when needed" (*NCP*, 198).[22] When she then saw his photo on April first, she "felt I must pay him a slight tribute" (*NCP*, 325), and her appointment book tracks her submission of a version titled "Letter Perfect Is Not Perfect" to Fleur Cowles's deluxe *Flair* magazine on August 3, 1952.[23] But while the stallion had a strong start in the 1952 season, a fever sidelined him for the big races, and the poem went unpublished (though perhaps for other reasons).[24] After he recovered, Moore and her housekeeper Gladys Berry took the trip to see Tom Fool run at Jamaica Park in Queens that October (where he came in second). By May 1953, he was back on course, prognosticators foresaw great things, and the *New Yorker* accepted the poem, with the title change and minor edits.

Given Moore's highbrow status, her choice to associate herself with Tom Fool's popular context both affirmed her humility and allowed a further teasing out of the operations of rank in American culture. That Moore viewed this as a moral and philosophical move, and as connected directly to her own past, is suggested by her starting the poem with the story of the prophet Jonah (also an animal tale). In 1909, in letters home from a visit to Manhattan, Moore had described her stay there as a Jonah-esque "sojourn in the whale"[25]—both a trying exercise in humility and a blessing. She embraced that paradox permanently in 1918 when she and her mother moved to the city—and her early poem "Is Your Town Nineveh?" (1916) directly engaged the Jonah story.[26] Almost forty years later "Tom Fool at Jamaica" begins like a sermon, also with a lesson on Jonah:

> Look at Jonah embarking from Joppa, deterred by
> the whale; hard going for a statesman whom nothing could detain,
> although one who would not rather die than repent.
> Be infallible at your peril, for your system will fail,
> and select as a model the schoolboy in Spain
> who at the age of six, portrayed a mule and jockey
> who had pulled up for a snail. *(NCP*, 198, ll. 1–7)

Jonah, a sacred snob, avoided Nineveh because he knew YHWH would find value in the sinners there and forgive them, a kind of democratic view that Jonah's sense of superiority could not condone. Moore reminds herself here not to stand apart from others as he did, feeling better than, but to go among them and learn humility ("be infallible at your peril"). Jonah's eventual decision to travel to Nineveh to warn the people to repent could be understood here to stand in, jokingly, for Moore's transition toward the popular and her goal to democratize culture, in this poem and in her later work generally. In both her poetry and her performances, the forgoing of pride in her high literary status, her public acknowledgment of flaws, and her assertions of common interests endeared her to audiences across the brow spectrum.[27]

Moore plays a humorous high/low game in "Tom Fool," inviting the sports-loving public to read work by a highbrow poet that mixes erudite and street-level styles around variously popular material. By commenting on unfolding events, and thus joining the wider cultural occasion around Tom Fool's growing success, the poem crosses into the realms of both sports journalism and a sportive brow game exploring the connection of celebrity to democracy, which Moore herself is playing. The first stanzas cite or allude to several sources in addition to Jonah, who as a prophet is an old-style celebrity with whose story most readers would have been familiar. These sources include a drawing by an unknown six-year-old Spanish student and two literary quotes—one attributed within the poem to Victor Hugo (the still famous nineteenth-century author of the popular *Hunchback of Notre Dame*), about how the true value of things may not always be obvious, and a quotation in French from a funny poem by the now little-known eighteenth-century poet Mme. de

Boufflers. Her tongue-in-cheek 29-line poem is cited in full in Moore's notes, vaunting at length the value of succinct expression. Moore offers this poem as a precursor/contributor to her own joke here, in this long poem made longer by the extended notes, which combine texts of diverse brow levels and, in terms of length, represent an uprising by the poem's subordinate elements. This comedic apparatus parallels other significations through a poem's structure, in poems like "Silence," "To a Snail," and others.

The borrowings from literary Europeans are followed by extensively annotated quotes from nonliterary Americans—Tom Fool's jockey Ted Atkinson and Belmont racetrack announcer Fred Capossela (ll. 10–11, 13–14, 19–20), both of whom many readers would have recognized. The poem goes on to cite from the *I Ching* on the interaction of control and chance in all things—including races and poems:

> . . . "Chance
>
> is a regrettable impurity"; like Tom Fool's
> left white hind foot—an unconformity; though judging by
> results, a kind of cottontail to give him confidence.
>
> (*NCP*, 198, ll. 14–17)

> *Note:* Lines 14–15: "*Chance . . . impurity.*" The *I Ching* or *Book of Changes*, translated by Richard Wilhelm and Cary Baynes, Bollingen Series XIX (New York: Pantheon Books, 1950). (*NCP*, 325)

Moore reframes impurity here as "unconformity" and as a distinct positive. This endorsement, made at the height of McCarthy's power, reminds readers of Moore's own nonconformism and speaks up for that of many others, including Julio Gomez, the Spanish schoolboy cited in the poem, whose drawing and signature are reproduced in the notes, and who is associated there with the anti-fascist struggle against Franco:[28] "Line 6: *mule and jockey.* A mule and jockey by 'Giulio [*sic*] Gomez 6 años' from a collection of drawings by Spanish school children. Solicited on behalf of a fund-raising committee for Republican Spain, sold by Lord and Taylor; given to me by Miss Louise Crane" (*NCP*, 323).

The poem goes on to almost predict Tom Fool's continued success, in a protean series of human and animal images:

> Tom Fool is "a handy horse," with a chiseled foot. You've the beat
> of a dancer to a measure or harmonious rush

of a porpoise at the prow where the racers all win easily—
like centaurs' legs in tune, as when kettledrums compete;
nose rigid and suede nostrils spread, a light left hand on the rein, till
well—this is a rhapsody. (*NCP*, 198, ll. 23–28)

This pointed morphing through species (horse, dancer, porpoise, centaur), as in "Apparition of Splendor," suggests networks of connection among all creatures—refusing stable divisions or ranks, and bespeaking what Dancy Mason calls Moore's form of *posthumanist thought*, which "escapes reductive categorizations of self and other, human and animal."[29] Atkinson's reflections in the notes on Tom Fool's superior intelligence (contra his name) feed the poem's affirmation of the links among the human race and animals of all kinds, including the implied pun on the horse race.

With the competition now reenvisaged as a dance set to the beat of Tom Fool's own internal kettledrum rhythm and accompanied by harmonies, its result is left to the reader's imagination ("till / well—"), and the poet points back to her text, naming it a *rhapsody*—an improvised form of poetry or music of free-flowing structure and extravagant moods. The musical reference leads her to associate to another musician, the brilliant jazz pianist Fats Waller (described in the *New York Times* article to which Moore's note refers us, as a "protean jazz figure" and as a "hoarse" and playful singer, whose eyes in a photo remind Moore of a giraffe's). Waller's trademark tagline "One never knows, do one?"[30] plays along the same high/low line that Moore walks here. Moore then associates to two more black musicians—drummer Ozzie Smith and pianist and composer Eubie Blake (whose Broadway musical *Shuffle Along* [the first with an all-black cast] Moore had seen in 1921)—who "ennoble the atmosphere," further expand the range of the poem's popular material, and carry the poem into yet another kind of race territory, adding a case for race equity in a democracy to the case for brow equity already in play. Moore describes all three men as champions, like Tom Fool, and then moves on to another set of protean animals—Lipizzaner horses, Ted Atkinson on a horse called Tiger Skin "cat-loping along," and a monkey riding a greyhound. "But Tom Fool . . ." the poem concludes, suggesting that he is the greatest champion (and/or the most protean) of the group (*NCP*, 199).

Adding a race-equity argument as an addendum to an argument about animals is jarring, and setting the three black musicians in the same stanza with the morphing animals may seem by association to assert the very kind of racist hierarchy that the poem to that point seems to contest. A danger of populist poetry may be that the poet risks falling victim to cliché—to phrases and systems of thought that are easily recognized by a wide audience but that may also be objectionable for reasons beyond their ordinariness. The closing stanza may have the effect of defusing the effort to not only engage but also challenge middlebrow readers that the poem had offered to that point. But Moore views animals as superior not inferior to people and offers animal comparisons not as insults but as praise. While the juxtaposition may still be offensive, Moore affirms the posthuman interspecies bond here. The monkey on the greyhound image comes from a story current at the time about capuchin monkeys fastened to dogs as part of a horse-race parody and refers back to the poem's race-track core. Clearly Moore was not infallible; the associations rhymed with and could have played to racist humor of the day regardless of her intentions, and the ending undercuts the poem's humor for readers today. But the work that follows "Tom Fool," also on the populist path, reaffirms her anti-racist challenge to readers.

Baseball Poems: Fandom and Race Politics

Three years after "Tom Fool," Moore again took up sports in "Hometown Piece for Messrs. Alston and Reese," a paean to the 1956 Brooklyn Dodgers. There followed two more sports poems, "Baseball and Writing" in 1961, and an ode to a polo pony named "Blue Bug" in 1962. These three, along with a linked poem on New York City ballet dancer Arthur Mitchell, continue Moore's reflection on performance and her relationship with her public, but expand that to examination of 1950s race struggles and the ethics of who is celebrated.

Sports stars have a special kind of celebrity, not glamorous or deeply personalized but based on stellar physical skill and having the "heart" to sustain high-level performance under duress. They play games seriously, and Moore is drawn to celebrate the discipline and effort involved. Sports as topic, and baseball in particular, expands the number of likely readers of a poem to fans of all classes and brow levels, all drawn to the familiar American game about which they often feel passionately. The game provides economically disadvantaged players with opportunity for class advancement, making it emblematically "American" in that respect too. In "Hometown Piece for Messrs. Alston and Reese," Moore offers lower-brow readers a way into a more complex poetic ground, while also offering her higher-brow readers access to a democratic cultural experience—effectively convening two teams on this poem's field.

Like "Tom Fool," "Hometown Piece" concerns an ongoing competitive season—the 1956 Dodgers' race to capture a second World Series title—so the poem participates in and helps build the city's excitement. As a renowned Brooklynite with a developing pedigree as a public sports fan, Moore had authority in this realm. To their borough's delight, the Dodgers had won the 1955 subway series against their hometown rivals, the Yankees; Moore's poem celebrates that victory and teases them to do it again, invoking their star players by name.[31] "Hometown Piece" continues Moore's ongoing experiment with mixed-brow play:[32] The title starts the game off by assigning the fancy title "Messrs." (for Messieurs) to people generally referred to as Smokey and Pee Wee (Manager Walter Alston and shortstop/team captain Pee Wee Reese). The epigraph asks that the poem be sung, to the tune of the folksong "Hush, Little Baby," a lullaby with a hard message of ongoing disappointment and hope (a dynamic familiar to many, including the poor and, of course, baseball fans), which Moore invokes by citing the first two lines from a variant she heard in a Travelogue.[33] The poem adopts the song's couplet rhyme scheme and adapts its quadruple meter (four beats to each measure) into poetic tetrameter,[34] a pattern usually antithetical to Moore but familiar to all audiences from childhood. Moore creates a comic tetrameter, with lines combining iambs, anapests, dactyls, trochees, single beat feet, and extra unaccented syllables where needed, creating a slapstick effect of rhythmic excess, while continuing her long-standing method of frequent enjambments—an "elite" literary mode that requires readerly attention when it breaks a line in the middle of a phrase, causing the reader to stumble. The combination undermines expectation by disconnecting some line breaks from the sense of the text, while insisting through the rhyme and the tune that those breaks be emphasized. The text below suggests a way to read it to the beat:

HOMETOWN PIECE FOR MESSRS. ALSTON AND REESE

To the tune:
"Li'l baby, don't say a word: Mama goin' to buy you a mocking-bird.
Bird don't sing: Mama goin' to sell it and buy a brass ring."

"Millén | nium," yés; | "pandemón | iúm"!
Roy Campanél | la leaps hígh.| Dód | gerdóm

crówned, | had Johnny Pód | res ón | the móund.
Búz | zie Bavá | si and the Préss | gave gróund . . . (*NCP*, 213, ll. 1–4)

If readers try singing this quick recap of the 1955 Dodgers win to the tune they know, the multiple patterns of rhythm and sense around the line breaks create a comic counterpoint ("Dódgerdóm / crówned had Johnny Pódres"), giving them at least two brow experiences at once. This contrapuntal experience thickens further in stanzas 6 and 7 when the Sym-Phoney fan band in the stands is described singing still another song (the pop standard "All of Me"), the tune of which readers now have in their heads layered above the mockingbird song and the additional rhythmic challenges:

And would the Dód | ger Bánd |in 8, row 1′| reláx
If they sáw | the colléc | tor of ín | come táx?

Réady | with a túne | if thát | should occúr:
"Why Not Take Áll | of Mé |—Áll of Me, | Sír?") (*NCP*, 213, ll. 11–14)

Add in the breaking news context of this poem published on day one of the World Series, and you have a simultaneously highbrow, folksy, journalistic, pop poem, blending many levels of culture within a retelling of America's game and echoing the "plain American" high/low argument in "England."

Moore wrote the first draft of "Hometown Piece" very quickly, having been urged to do so by friends at the conference on Little Magazines at Harvard in the second week of August (the same conference that generated "Values in Use"). It responded to an article in the *New York Times* about the Sym-Phoney,[35] a band of Dodgers fans who brought their instruments to every home game and played musical accompaniment to the action.[36] This band of fans provided the idea of setting the action to music as well as the poem's fan-focus,[37] but once the poem was set in motion, it evolved. Moore was invited to write and submit the poem in less than a week to the *Hudson Review* for consideration for publication months later,[38] timing that would have prevented the poem from continuing in the "Tom Fool" vein of building up an ongoing contest. Fortunately for Moore, the first draft was rejected as "not [her] best," which left her free to work further on it for the *New Yorker*.[39] But in

September editor Howard Moss also turned it down, regretfully, because that magazine's weekly print schedule would delay publication and "if [in the interim] the Dodgers lost to the Braves, for instance, the poem would no longer be useable, for our purposes"—as culturally engaged poetry.[40] She then sent it to *Life* and *Sports Illustrated*, who also said no (likely for the same reason).

Fortunately again, the Dodgers survived, the poem continued in play, and the *New York Herald Tribune* could give it full journalistic status. "Hometown Piece" slid into home plate on page one just in time for the World Series' opening game, feeding the thrill and proving one of the poem's points: that fans are as much part of the team as the official lineup (some called for the poem to be enshrined in Ebbets Field). An early version of the poem (called "Brooklyn on the Mound") closed thus: "Cóme on | Dódgers. | You've wón; | we're yours. What's fáme! / We're satisfíed | Recíp | rocáte: | say, 'Fans, you're gáme.'"[41] In the final version, the poem still features fans, though without using that word—in the "Hometown" crew of the title, the Sym-Phoney band in the middle, and the "Dodgerdom" watching and urging the team on in the last stanza:

> Yóu've | got plén | ty: Jackie Rób | insón
> and Cám | py and big Néwk, | and Dód |gerdom agáin
> watching év | erything you dó. | You won last yéar. | Come ón.
> (*NCP*, 214, ll. 49–51)

This rhythm is pointedly hard to assign, especially in the last line, which breaks the couplet pattern—but the reader gets to experiment. Here again Moore's celebration of sports emphasizes its participatory, democratic element.

Along with its playfulness, this poem also seriously explores the race struggles that were an essential part of the Dodgers' story. Team owner Branch Rickey (along with manager Smokey Alston and business manager Buzzie Bavasi—both mentioned in the poem) had integrated the Dodgers minor league team by signing Roy Campanella (Campy) and Don Newcombe (big Newk) in 1946. In 1947 Rickey hired Jackie Robinson as the first black major league player. Tensions were high and Robinson faced challenges on the road and in the dugout, but team captain Pee Wee Reese was his advocate; Reese famously silenced hecklers by putting his arm around Robinson at a game in Cincinnati in 1947. By 1956, attitudes had advanced and the Dodgers had four black players in the

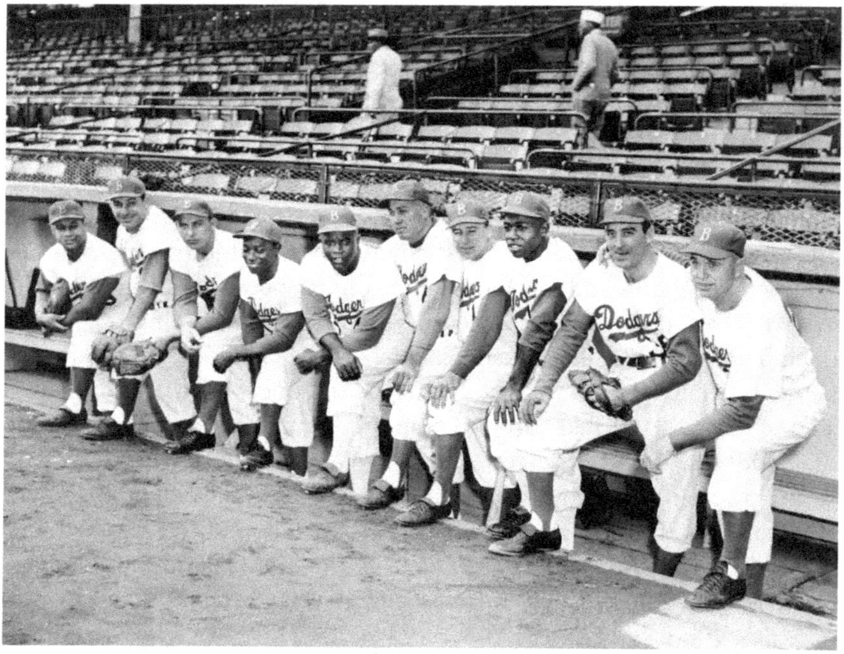

Figure 14. The Brooklyn Dodgers' starting lineup of 1956 is ready to take on the New York Yankees in the World Series at Ebbets Field: Roy Campanella, Carl Furillo, Gil Hodges, Sandy Amoros, Jackie Robinson, Duke Snider, Pee-Wee Reese, Jim Gilliam, Sal Maglie, and Manager Walter Alston (l. to r.), photographed by Walter Kelleher/*New York Daily News.* Reprinted by permission.

starting lineup for game one, and five black players (a majority) started game two, when Don Newcombe pitched.

All five appear in Moore's poem—beginning in line 2 with Roy Campanella, the first player mentioned. The three players named in the final stanza are also all African American ("Jackie Robinson / and Campy and big Newk"). The two other black players, Jim Gilliam and Sandy Amoros (whose amazing 1955 series catch is recalled in ll. 6–9), are featured in the middle, and Willie Mays, a black player with the Giants, another local team, makes an appearance as someone who "should be a Dodger" (l. 25). Contemporary readers would recognize the integration process as a big part of the "everything you do" that Dodgerdom and America were watching and that the poem celebrated. The Dodgers' 1955 World Series victory and their follow-up presence in the 1956 series together make the case that integration is not only equitable and moral but beneficial to team success. The poem's contrapuntal structure is itself both a literal form of integration, and a metaphor for it.

In "Hometown Piece" Moore celebrates the Dodgers' breaking of a race barrier, as well as the skills of both their black and white players. Although the poem celebrates the whole Dodgers team, by featuring its black players the poem challenges the way identity markers have historically limited the options for who may be celebrated. In choosing "Hush, Little Baby" (the folk precursor to the R&B "Mockingbird Song"), Moore sets the game to a tune that blends Scots-Irish with African roots, like much American folk music. The mockingbird has an ambiguous status in Moore's work,[42] as in the song, which teaches that things can be expected to disappoint you but you should keep on shopping for what works, paralleling what Moore admired about Tom Fool: the will to keep trying. This trait she shared with the horse and the Dodgers: though elderly women and sports may not seem a match, the performance lesson Moore espouses is seconded in her own sustained innovative effort over decades.

In setting the poem to a folk lullaby, Moore also connects her poem to the ballad tradition. In so doing she creates a striking example of the historical byplay that Daniel Tiffany traces across the two centuries of the history of what he calls kitsch but which others may call, more generally, non-elite poetry. Moore's poem condenses that history: readers can access the poem as a sports celebration of fondly presented athletes, set in a humorous rhyming frame, requiring no reflection for the consumer to absorb, and linked patriotically to President Eisenhower and to George Washington (aka Moore) through its packaging on the front page of the *Herald Tribune* ("Eisenhower Will Throw First Ball" reads a headline beside Moore's photo above the poem).[43] Though the poem's imagery and meter are available to readers as familiar, prepackaged units of received ideas (meeting Tiffany's definition of kitsch), it also undermines those received ideas with its enjambed modernist line breaks and its race and gender politics.

In this poem, received ideas about race also turn out to be varieties of kitsch in its negative sense—part of a falsified, whitewashed "tradition," the terms of which the poem (like the team) undermines with its newfangled, modernist sonic dissonances. But Moore's poem also critiques any cultural mode that claims to rank itself above the patriotic sentimental work of equality (also a received American idea, so therefore "kitschy" in a positive sense, here represented by the people's sport and standard meter), or above folklore, also ranked as lowbrow but honored here. In manipulating the high/low lines in this poem, Moore plays the field of innovative poetics.

The Dodgers lost the 1956 World Series against the Yankees in the seventh game, 0–9, and then further broke Brooklyn's heart by moving to L.A. in 1958. Like all Brooklynites, Moore had to process her grief, but by 1961 she was ready to publish a poem about her new team, the Yankees. "Baseball and Writing," published in December 1961 in the *New Yorker*, describes a September Yankees vs. Detroit Tigers game for the American League pennant. Moore doesn't focus on the contest (by the time the poem appeared in December her team had already won that year's World Series) but on the temperament of the players, beginning with Elston Howard, the first black man to play for the Yankees (debuting in a very late 1955) and the only person of color in the 1961 starting lineup. He'd been denied batting prizes at several points, for reasons thought by some to do with the same racism that had kept the Yankees lily white for so much longer than other teams and that continued to keep Howard in the shadows in spite of his strengths.[44]

> It's a pitcher's battle all the way—a duel—
> a catcher's, as, with cruel
> puma paw, Elston Howard lumbers lightly
> back to plate. (His spring
> de-winged a bat swing.)
> They have that killer instinct;
> yet Elston—whose catching
> arm has hurt them all with the bat—
> when questioned, says, unenviously,
> "I'm very satisfied. We won."
> Shorn of the batting crown, says, "We";
> robbed by a technicality. (*NCP*, 236, ll. 13–24)

Howard took that robbery in stride and went on to win other titles in later years, including the first American League MVP prize given to an African American and two Gold Glove Awards. The team's other black player, Panamanian Hector Lopez, appears in the last stanza, as does the team's second Hispanic player, Luis Arroyo, and earlier Manny Montejo—a young Detroit pitcher who once grazed the legendary Mickey Mantle with a pitch—is praised (as a "premature prodigy" who will "be tough" [l. 60]), as is the rest of the team's starting lineup, with added focus on Mantle.

Moore begins the poem by distinguishing her level of interest from what it had been for the Dodgers. She may be a Yankees supporter now, but she is no longer a fan-atic. She then makes explicit the title's parallel between poetry and the game:

> Fanaticism? No. Writing is exciting
> and baseball is like writing.
>   You can never tell with either
>   how it will go
>   or what you will do; (*NCP*, 236, ll. 1–5)

Moore does affirm her excitement, but while this poem takes on topics related to those of "Hometown Piece," it is nowhere near as lively or unexpected as its precursor. The poem has a recognizably Moore-ish stanza form and a fairly steady syllabic meter. She replays recent team highlights and lauds the collaborative spirit of the crew: "Who in that galaxy / of nine won the pennant? Each. It was he" (ll. 47–48). Moore is portrayed as in the stands with her readers, hoping to catch a home run ball ("meant to be caught by you or me" [l. 36]), though she actually didn't go to games, preferring to watch at home on her black-and-white TV. We hear that the price of fame (especially Mantle's) is harassment by "ruffians"—"(Drat it! / Celebrity costs privacy!)" (ll. 69–70)—and the poem closes with a pun on the star status of the players, whom she compares to the galaxy above ("Studded with stars in belt and crown, / the Stadium is an adastrium. / O flashing Orion, / your stars are muscled like the lion" [ll. 81–84]). Moore joins in the process of celebrating these stars, again stressing the link in sports between celebrity and skill, and connecting that also to group effort, as opposed to stardom of a less effortful or solely individual type. Though highly individualistic herself, Moore endeavored consistently to connect to readers in both their roles as individuals and as members of a democratic community, out of which stars might emerge but in which all members had value.

In baseball as in writing, you never know what will happen, but the most surprising thing in this poem—unstated but known to all at the time—is the poet's own situation (like that of many of her fellow

Brooklynites): finding herself cheering for the opposition team five years later! Though Moore demonstrates a fondness for and knowledge of the Yankees in "Baseball and Writing," the lowering of the poetic energy level in itself makes its own commentary on the star-fan relationship, providing evidence that fanaticism doesn't transfer and marking Moore as a true Dodgers fan through the low amplitude of even her concerted effort to get excited about the Yanks. Two years later, in 1963, Moore kept a notebook tracking the action of the World Series battle between the Yankees and the L.A. Dodgers, which the Dodgers swept in four games.[45] From that moment of divided loyalty for thousands of former Dodgers fans, no poem emerged—after all, what would there have been to celebrate, no matter who won?

Blue Bug: Odes, Eyes, and Ethics

Though Moore may have tired of baseball poetry, she continued to be drawn to questions of celebrity and identity, specifically who is celebrated and why. Two months after publishing "Baseball and Writing," she returned energetically to these issues in a tour de force poem about, among other things, a polo pony named Blue Bug.

Blue Bug

(After looking at a picture of Dr. Raworth Williams' polo pony,
photographed, with seven other ponies, by Thomas McAvoy,
"Sports Illustrated")

In this camera shot,
from that fine print in which you hide
(eight-pony portrait from the side),
you seem to recognize
a recognizing eye,
limber Bug.
Only partly said, perhaps, it has been implied
that you seem to be the one to ride.

I don't know how you got your name
and don't like to inquire.
Nothing more punitive than the pest
who says, "I'm trespassing," and
does it just the same.

I've guessed, I think.
I like a face that seems a nest,

a "mere container for the eye"—
triangle-cornered—and
pitchfork-pronged ears stiffly parallel:
bug brother to an Arthur
Mitchell dragonfly,
speeding to left,
speeding to right; reversible,

like "turns in an ancient Chinese
melody, a thirteen
twisted silk-string three-finger solo."
There they are, Yellow River-
scroll accuracies
of your version
of something similar—polo.

Restating it:
pelo, I turn,
on *polos*, a pivot.

If a little elaborate,
Redon (Odilon) brought it to mind,
his thought of the eye,
of revolving—combined somehow with pastime—
pastime that is work,
muscular docility,
also mentality,

as in the acrobat Li Siau Than,
gibbonlike but limberer,
defying gravity,
nether side arched up,
cup on head not upset—
China's very most ingenious man. (*New Yorker*; *NCP*, 231–32)

While this many-layered poem, initially published in the *New Yorker*, offers readers a wide range of engaging figures, the poem's form is just as essential to its argument as any of the characters invoked. Moore reflects here upon the promulgation of celebrity through the celebratory ode, a form with roots reaching back at least to the Greek poet Pindar (fifth century BCE) and which Moore here revives, though that has not been obvious to readers, who get absorbed by the poem's other narratives.[46]

The explanatory epigraph tells us that the poem's stimulus was a photo of a pony called Blue Bug in *Sports Illustrated*, a magazine in which Moore herself had recently appeared and which she could expect a wide range of readers to know.[47] This creates a casual waiting-room mood, but the epigraph also alludes to the grand traditions of overt allusion and ekphrasis, in which poems refer directly to prior texts or art objects (like Chapman's Homer or Grecian urns). Although a sports-magazine photo is not usually considered great art, polo is an expensive sport requiring horses (the "sport of kings"), so from the start, the poem inhabits several brow realms at once. Also significantly, the epigraph describes our access to this pony as highly mediated: Readers (us)/Moore (poet)/Moore (reader of *Sports Illustrated*)/McAvoy (photographer)/Williams (owner, who is pictured in *Sports Illustrated* looking at the ponies)/and then Blue Bug.

The first few lines expand the image being described from the photograph alone to the whole page on which the photograph appears, portraying the pony hiding in the "fine print" of the surrounding story:

In this camera shot,
from that fine print in which you hide
(eight-pony portrait from the side),
you seem to recognize
a recognizing eye,
limber Bug. (*NCP*, 231)

This reframing of the ekphrasis alters the situation of the pony, emphasizing the viewer's role in delimiting her or his field of regard. Moore's reframe brings the pony toward us from the Dallas farm, through all the layers of remove emphasized in the epigraph and into the *Sports Illustrated* page. There Blue Bug attempts to hide among the words that share that page (unlike most figures on display who are generally refused the option to hide). This effect produces another kind of "literal image," this one located *among* the letters—rather than shaped by them. The poem's reference to the print on the page points to the ways in which our perception of any entity is shaped by habit and to the power that a reader has to alter this. We can view the photograph as separate or as part of the larger page, which in turn comprises only part of our even larger visual field.

DOC WILLIAMS *continued*

"But it's perfectly possible, isn't it," I said, "that you could captain another great team to represent the Dallas Athletic Club and go after the National Open championship again next year? Maybe sign up Bob Skene again? I believe that, along with Cecil Smith, Skene is one of the two 10-goal players in the country?"

The doctor nodded.

"But," I persisted, "I'm not thinking of tournaments and championships. I'm thinking of a man who has been playing polo for 35 years and is still playing two

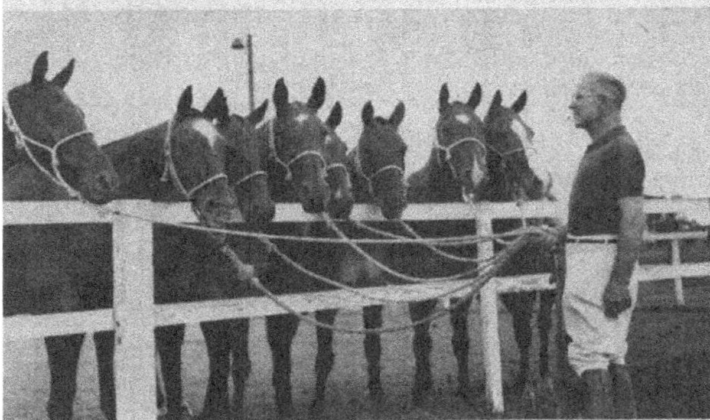

Dr. Williams keeps a string of eight ponies at his polo field on farm near Dallas.

and three times a week, even if only in pickup matches out at your own field. I'd like to find out how a man of 66 can do it—how he can stay in shape to do it. I mean to say, you take a 66-year-old golfer. Show me one who isn't using a cart."

"Golf carts should be outlawed," said the doctor. He reflected a moment and then chuckled. "I remember some years ago in Chicago, a reporter asked me, 'Doctor, how do you get in shape for tournament polo?' I said, 'Hell's bells, young man, I have never been *out* of shape.' Oh, I was a goin' dude then, as we say in Texas. But it was the absolute truth. I was raised on a ranch in West Texas and I swear to you I can't remember when I learned to ride. At the University of Texas, before I went on to medical school at Columbia University in New York, I played quarterback on the football team and first base on the baseball team. When I finished my internship at St. Vincent's Hospital in New York I set up practice here in Dallas and started playing polo as a member of a National Guard team and have been at it ever since."

"And you don't think all this justifies a write-up?"

The doctor shook his head. "I'm speaking of lately—lately."

"All right. How about just last spring when you were awarded the Governor of Texas Polo Award? Cecil Smith got the first one, you got the second. And on the occasion of your award, somebody said that you had the physique of a man of 35. How about all the things you've done to promote polo in Dallas? How about your term as governor of the Southwestern Circuit of the U.S. Polo Association?"

The doctor rubbed his chin.

I said, "I see only one thing that could militate against this write-up."

Dr. Williams' eyes narrowed. "What?" he said.

"Well, to be frank with you, doctor, as I am sure you would be with a patient, the one thing that would give me pause would be to learn that you're easing up in polo and that some of the younger players are easing up on you. Pulling up for you, I believe the phrase is. Avoiding any hard-riding body contact. Making allowances for your age."

The doctor's eyes flashed, and he seemed to blanch under his tan.

"Nobody pulls up for me," he snapped. "And I don't pull up for anybody else. The day they start pulling up for Doc Williams, that's the day I quit—and quit for good."

He nodded his head vigorously and slipped out of his white coat. He started back to the examining rooms. "I'll be with you in a minute," he said. "We'll get on out to the farm and look at some horses."

A little later Dr. Williams, wearing a broad-brimmed Stetson, was behind the wheel of his air-conditioned Cadillac, holding the speedometer needle at an even 70. He was pointed for his 100-acre farm, which is about 12 miles northwest of Dallas.

"We were speaking," he said, "of the Dallas Athletic Club winning the National Open in 1958. You must remember that another Dallas team, the Circle F, captained by Russell Firestone Jr., won the Open the following year and took the National 20-goal championship as well."

"Isn't it true, doctor, that polo is enjoying a modest sort of renaissance throughout the country?"

"Yes, and particularly in Florida and the Middle West. A magazine had quite a write-up this past summer on what Robert Uihlein and his associates have done to popularize the game in Milwaukee."

"I read that write-up," I said. "I was surprised to see that the polo games played at Mr. Uihlein's farm drew crowds as large as 3,000 regularly."

Dr. Williams laughed shortly.

"That's very encouraging, of course," he said, "but I can remember when the East-West and International games

continued

Figure 15. Dr. Williams with eight ponies, photographed by Thomas McAvoy, © 1961. Reprinted by kind permission. Text reprinted from *Sports Illustrated*, November 13, 1961: "Don't Pull Up for Doc," by Gerald Holland, copyright © 1961 by Time, Inc. Reprinted by permission.

Moore thus reminds us of the alterability of our perceptions, and of our power to simply see the world differently if we so choose.

Moore then brings the pony still closer in, when she addresses it, saying: "you seem to recognize / a recognizing eye, / limber Bug." There the pony—"you"—may seem to recognize the eye of Dr. Williams within the photo; or the eye of McAvoy, the photographer; or even the mechanical eye of his camera. Or the pony may be again moving forward into the poem and looking more directly at Moore's eye, or even at us readers—providing *we* are up for recognizing her or him. These shifts in perspective demand our input and make us part of the poem. Similarly, in stanza 2 the speaker comments "I don't know how you got your name / and don't like to inquire"—as if, were Moore less respectful of the pony's privacy, she could ask and get a reply. This chatty form of address differs from standard apostrophe, such as in "The Sun Rising," where John Donne calls upon the unruly sun to say why it rises so early without any expectation that it will respond—a paradigmatic rhetorical question. But in almost asking about the pony's name, the poet gets much closer to actually expecting a reply, even as (or because) she then renounces the question, as a matter of privacy. In so doing she accords the pony status as a respected individual, involved in a process of mutual recognition, a process that allows each member of a dyad to understand something not only about the other but also about themselves and their own value, as worthy of attention. Mutual recognition accomplished would be the opposite of Spectacle, as described by Guy Debord, which dispenses images without allowing for dialogue between the viewer and the entity imaged.[48] The recognition dynamic here engages not just the pony but the reader as well, who has to work hard to make sense of, to re-cognize, what's going on in this unusual poem.

Most readers won't look up the *Sports Illustrated* reference here, but there's interest in the backstory. The article concerns Dr. Raworth Williams, a sixty-six-year-old Dallas urologist and longtime polo player, who three years previously had captained his team to the national championship. The piece is called "Don't Pull Up for Doc" because when the reporter asks whether his opponents go easy because he's older, the doctor insists he'd quit if they did. Along with the pun on Moore's friend and fellow poet "Dr. [W. C.] Williams," part of the attraction for Moore may have lain in this story's parallel with her concern with her own age, expressed in several later poems (see Chapter 5), and with maintaining her fitness in the poetic playing field. Dr. Williams tells stories of his early residency in Greenwich Village, at St. Vincent's Hospital—right by the offices of *The Dial*, Moore's former employer. The doctor reflects on the operation of celebrity, doubting he deserves a "write up."

But back to the pony. The doctor remarks to the reporter: "You see those three ponies looking at us over the fence? They've been to the polo wars, all right. On the right there is Blue Bug, my favorite." The scene described is not the image displayed, however—the photo includes eight ponies not three, along with Williams himself. There is no way to identify which pony in the picture is Blue Bug, or even to aver that Blue Bug appears at all, though these ponies also overlook a fence. So, Moore guesses, much as the reader must deduce and, in some measure, invent the meanings of the poem—within the framework provided.

Readers don't know that Blue Bug is not identifiable in the picture, unless they read the article. But we are given several hints that the poem's information is questionable: We're told in stanza 1 that "Only *partly said, perhaps*, it has been *implied* / that you *seem* to be the one to ride [emphases added]"—a statement with at least four qualifiers. In the second stanza, the poet tries to figure out why Williams named his favorite pony Blue Bug—again based on no information ("I don't know")—and claims not to want to get the facts ("don't like to inquire"). She connects herself to the pony by characterizing herself as a "pest"—another metaphorical insect who "bugs" you. In spite of her disclaimer, she does seek the source of the name, however, and asserts that "I've guessed, I think"—though she doesn't say what she's concluded. Taking the pony on the far left as Moore's surrogate, Leavell understands the references to its face as a "'mere container for the eye'" to signal that its eye, like Moore's, might be blue—or that Moore might imagine it so—and that the darting blue eye is what Moore understands as the source of Blue Bug's name.[49] While that is a plausible reading, Moore pointedly leaves it to us to interpret (or guess) what she's guessed.[50] In the poem, as in the world, the guess often constitutes an effective truth, or what we work with as truth until a more compelling truth appears. The poem foregrounds both that tentativeness and the abyss of unknowability behind efforts at recognition of signals offered—which both makes those efforts all the more important and models the free-play of meaning, with the implicit possibilities of transformation of all kinds inherent there.

Punning again on the insect link, Moore next segues to describing Blue Bug as "bug brother to an Arthur / Mitchell dragonfly." Though Mitchell, the only African American in George Balanchine's New York City Ballet (NYCB) until his departure in 1970 and the founder of the Dance Theatre of Harlem, was a dancer not a sportsman, Moore makes a link around quick motion across space. At the time Moore was writing "Blue Bug," she had also been commissioned by Lincoln Kirstein, the artistic director of the NYCB, to write a poem celebrating Mitchell and his premiere performance as Puck in the company's *Midsummer Night's Dream*, for the souvenir program. That poem opened with a similar dragonfly image:

ARTHUR MITCHELL

Slim dragonfly
too rapid for the eye
  to cage—
contagious gem of virtuosity—
make visible, mentality.
Your jewels of mobility

  reveal
   and veil
    a peacock-tail (*NCP*, 240)

Note: Puck in Lincoln Kirstein's and George Balanchine's New York City Center's Music and Drama Inc. production of *A Midsummer Night's Dream*. (*NCP*, 334)

Because Moore connects Mitchell and polo ponies via a shared ability to pivot sharply, like a dragonfly, we can derive that she views this skill at turning quickly as a possible source of the "Bug" in the pony's name (her "guess"). Since "Arthur Mitchell" was written before the premiere, Moore had to imagine his Puck costume, and in her version it trails long and peacock bright.[51] The second stanza physically imitates the trailing peacock tail it names (another literal image),[52] but the first stanza actively refuses to "cage" or objectify its subject, whose mentality is emphasized. This poem prefigures concerns that Moore explores in greater depth in "Blue Bug," and it reaffirms her enduring fascination with the hide-and-seek dynamic that she here calls a simultaneous "reveal and veil."

Moore admired Mitchell, and in a letter described the poem named for him as "just fanmail" about "the least affected and most graceful 'outright' fellow in the troupe."[53] Her twofold reference to him signals her approval also of Kirstein and Balanchine's project of creating an innovative American ballet, strengthened but not stultified by traditions. "Arthur Mitchell" continues her writing about dance begun with an essay on the Russian ballerina Anna Pavlova (1944), especially her performance in "The Dragonfly," and continued later in Moore's poem "Style" (1956), which describes a flamenco troupe.[54] The evanescent nature of both in-person cultural performances and journalism, ephemeral "texts" that are widely known momentarily and then disappear from the general consciousness, make Moore's late poems full of invocations of such texts also similar to them. While, unlike the performances and the stories, the poems do continue to be accessible after their initial moment, their invocation of events in their first audience's immediate sphere of reference changes quickly into something like the Cornell-box detritus of the "inconsequential past" that Ellen Levy writes of, an inconsequence that is repurposed through inclusion in the poems, as in the boxes, as advocacy for the less powerful. Internet archives transform forgotten events to some extent, by making them at least accessible again, if still not widely recognized.

Initially, Kirstein and Balanchine intended that their company would be fully racially integrated, but they failed utterly in that.[55] Mitchell's solitary blackness in the company and in the poem underscores his fragile status as a black man (also a gay ["outright"] man) in a white industry, along with the fragile cultural standing of ballet. Like Blue Bug and the other athletes and artists in this poem, he also works as an analogue for the fragile status of Moore, elderly, cross-dressing lady poet. In addition to their cultural fragility, all of them share a stalwart strong-mindedness that allows them to utilize their anomaly and their celebrity in pursuit of cultural and political change.[56] In its moment, "Blue Bug" (and all Moore's later work) pirouetted boldly, shaping new meaning out of what was going on around the poet and her readers. In our moment and ever after they bridge the gap between the reader's present and the pure now that was, and offer meaning in that tension, according to the level of attention each reader brings to bear. After linking Mitchell and Blue Bug through their turns, Moore then connects the two athletes to her own poetic exercise, representing the back-and-forth motions of the pony and the dancer in the left and right motions of her lines on the page:

speeding to left,
  speeding to right; reversible, *(NCP*, 231)

The stanzas stay in motion; the poem moves on to accumulate more turns that lead from one thing to another and accrete new meaning, as the reader works to build the connections into an overarching QED.

The next stanza makes a similar pivot, this time to two Chinese art forms also connected to turns. Moore begins with a phrase marked as a quotation (source yet unknown) referencing "'turns in an ancient Chinese / melody'" played apparently on a Tang dynasty 13-string zither; then she connects these to "Yellow River scroll[s]," some of which portray the river bending right and left and which themselves turn, as they are unwound, to reveal a series of scenes in sequence.[57] Moore refers also to the "accuracies" of these paintings, which include minute details of landscape and culture, which she then links to Blue Bug's "version / of something similar—polo," with its similar demands for accuracy of movement. Readers familiar with Tang dynasty paintings and sculptures of polo players (including female players) may see references to those here,[58] along with, given the pun-play of the rest of the poem, allusions to Marco Polo, famed East-West traveler.

All these networked references are further connected by the poem's genre, which is quite insistently an ode. The form—built for celebration—well suits the poem's consideration of celebrity. Originally written to celebrate athletic victories and accompanied by music and dance, odes have evolved over the centuries to treat a variety of subjects. But "Blue Bug" goes back to the genre's origins in equine sports: most of the Olympian odes of Pindar (the preeminent sports writer; 522–443 BCE) honor horse and chariot races. Pindar's "Olympian 1" lauds both Hieron of Syracuse, the owner of the winning horse and Pindar's patron, and the horse himself—the graceful Pherenikos ("Victory Bearer"), the "most famous horse in antiquity" largely because he was celebrated in several long-lived odes.[59] Similarly, Moore's ode begins with a celebration of a victorious polo pony (a minor celebrity featured in *Sports Illustrated*), and then goes on to extol a dancer, musicians, and artists in the stanzas we've tracked so far and, in what follows, another artist and an acrobat.[60] All these athletes and artists of various periods she characterizes as engaged in "pastime[s] that [are] work," which require command of both body and mind ("muscular docility, / also mentality").

Formally, the poem's prosody flaunts its characteristic odic structure. Greek odes are comprised of a variable number of triads, the sections of which are called *Strophe*, *Anti-strophe*, and *Epode*. Movements from one section of a triad to the next mark turns in the poem's argument or themes, and such is the case with "Blue Bug." Historically *Strophe*, Greek for "turn," also indicated turns in the physical direction of the Greek chorus dancing back and forth across the stage, singing as they went.[61] For English odes the section names are translated from the Greek as "*Turn*," "*Counterturn*," and "*Stand*." Each section may be singular and lengthy, as in Wordsworth's "Ode: Intimations of Immortality," or there may be one or several short triadic units.

While the equine-lauding start in "Blue Bug" in itself suggests a Pindaric ode, in stanza 5 the poem declares the connection directly, by drawing attention to that tercet's status as a turn. This self-reflexive stanza both narrates its own unfolding and "literally" embodies a pivot (another literal image), in the slenderness of its lines around which the two longer sections revolve:

> Restating it:
> *pelo*, I turn,
> on *polos*, a pivot. (*NCP*, 231)

This pivot speaks in both ancient Greek and English to restate the poem's argument thus far as: "I turn on a pivot," *pelo* on *polos*. It's a poem both full of turns and about turns, a reinforcing pattern that also offers a guide to the associative logic and interactive relations between "form" and "content" of much of Moore's work. The emphasis on turning in stanza 5 suggests that the prior four stanzas may be considered the Strophe or Turn; stanza 5 the Anti-Strophe or Counterturn; and stanzas 6 and 7 the Epode or Stand.

Accentuating the Pindaric connection by her use of Greek words here, Moore, who studied Greek and experimented with Greek meter at Bryn Mawr,[62] chooses a Greek verb for *turn*—*pelo* (πελῶ), which sounds like "polo" and means *to become, to be in motion, to exist in process*, in a way associated with dance and change (*to turn into*).[63] Turning takes on a primal meaning here associated with the energetic motions of life and progress through time. *Pelo* also associates to words to do with round shapes and turning motions—like balls (Greek root—βαλ, Ps and Bs being linked), which bounce around in our words *balloon*, *ballet*, and *ball* (of the dancing type), all active in this poem.[64] Moore next does something similar with *Polos*—a Greek word related to *Pelo*, meaning a pivot or end of an axis, from which we derive our word *pole*, as in North Pole. This is not the direct root of the name of the game polo, however, which apparently comes from a Tibetan word *pulu*, also meaning "ball."[65] The two meanings overlap, since polo does involve lots of quick, pivoting turns by the ponies. Thus, the stanza *pivots* and *turns* around alternating definitions of those words. And, of course, the "*I*" in "I turn" brings the poet into the linked set of artists under consideration here, in a context in which she shows off her skill at poetic pivoting. "Blue Bug" turns into poetry polo, with Moore as lead athlete or player, and with the reader (included along with Blue Bug in the "you" addressed throughout) arguably serving as teammate, adversary, spectator, or ball—and perhaps a bit of each.

This brief stanza also "talks" about the role of form in the poem—in highlighting form's aspect as the shape and body of all poems as well as invoking the specific odic literary form of this poem through the emphasis on turns. This "statement" is made as much through the image created (the slender pivot formed by the layout of these words) as through the words' denotation. This section actively embodies the poem, stressing its physique and demonstrating Moore's control of her poem's docile (obedient) muscles. This emphasis on the text's double life as image also engages with the earlier reflection on images introduced with the horsing around about the "fine print."

The next stanza pivots again, sharply, to a very different image, which Moore asks readers to recognize and recall. In these lines, the poem's "mind's eye" narrates its own turn to the lithograph titled *To Edgar Poe: The Eye, Like a Strange Balloon, Mounts toward Infinity* by French proto-Surrealist artist Odilon Redon (another submerged ekphrasis), which many of her *New Yorker* readers would have seen recently either in person at MoMA in the exhibition *Redon, Moreau and Bresdin* (December 1961–February 1962) or reproduced in an *Arts Magazine* article about the exhibition by John Simon, which Moore took notes on and to which she refers several times in this poem.[66] Like Moore, those of her readers who subscribed to that journal would have had the image ready to hand.

> If a little elaborate,
> Redon (Odilon) brought it to mind,

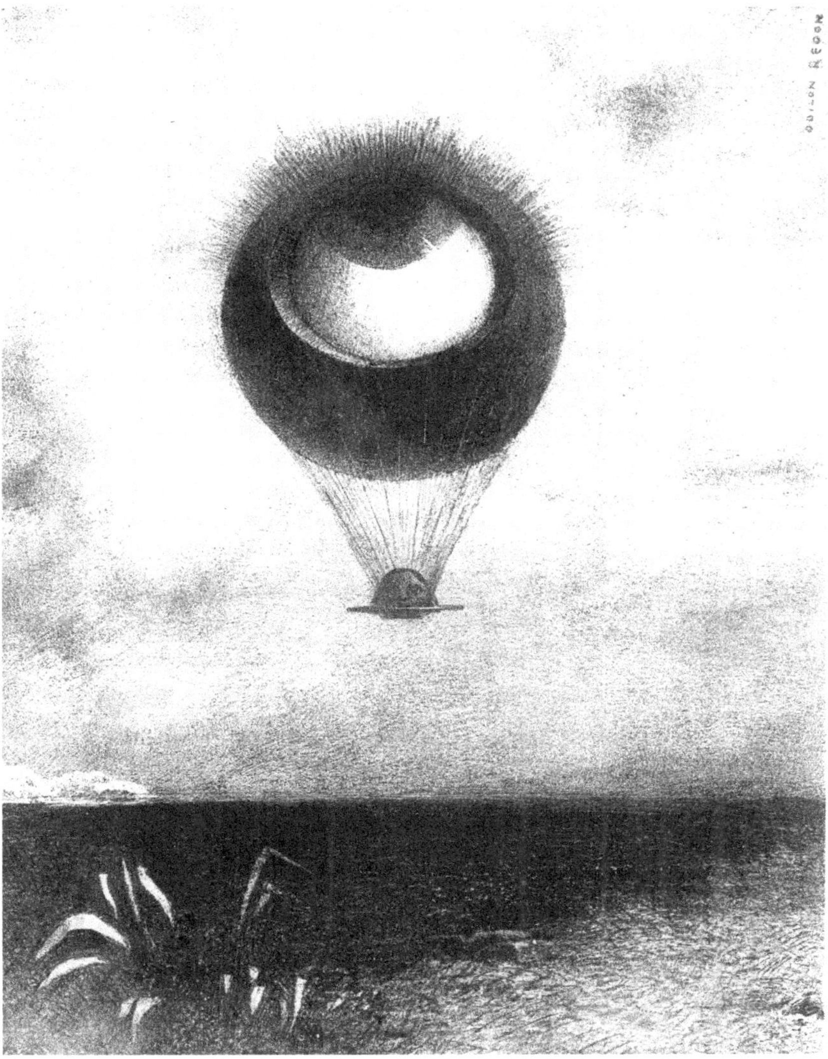

Figure 16. Odilon Redon, *À Edgar Poe: L'oeil, comme un ballon bizarre se dirige vers l'infini* (To Edgar Poe: The Eye, Like a Strange Balloon, Mounts toward Infinity), 1882. Lithograph, 17¼ x 12¼ in. Los Angeles County Museum of Art. Reprinted by permission.

his thought of the eye,
of revolving—combined somehow with pastime—
pastime that is work,
muscular docility,
also mentality, *(NCP*, 232)

"Pastime that is work" makes a neat description of any active poetry reader's task, and one that is especially apt for Moore's readers. The "e-laborate" efforts of the poet condense and multiply the poem's meanings in ways that require an active combined unpacking and contribution by the reader, in order to galvanize the poem's meaning-production engine. This is a very different kind of reading from the passive reception of the one-way spectacles that Debord deplores, and which Moore also critiques here. On its own, Redon's image of an eye looking upward, with a severed head in the basket, could take us in many directions![67] The image summons up connections for Moore between thinking ("mind"/"thought"/"mentality") and vision, which she imagines in motion, "revolving." Her synopsis of Redon's work summarizes her own revolving thought processes fed by what she sees, presented here via the poem's chain of associations—a mental map. The stanza also reminds us that the most satisfying pastimes—including poetry—involve effort, and constitutes each of us as a character in the poem (perhaps represented by the severed head), whose reciprocal contributions (further turns in the ongoing process of meaning-making) are requested by the poem's refusal to fill in the connectors between its points. Including the world outside the poem within it, through the works of art and the progress of time since the Greeks and the Tang dynasty, Moore asks us to Think, in 4-D.

Redon's image presents a spectacle to observe (an odd balloon that invites your eye) and simultaneously suggests the possibility of an exchange of glances (an eye-ball-oon), of recognition, of dialogue between the viewer and the image and perhaps the artist. (John Simon remarks on the active gazes of the many eyes in Redon's work in the review that prompted Moore's reference.) This uncanny exchange challenges standard passive (though predatory) image consumption (in which we obey the homey dictate that you "Eat what you're served"); it operates even more strangely than the already odd exchange of looks between human and horse. The "revolving" spectacle looks back twice: the head gazes directly at us, and the revolving eye, as Moore characterizes it, soon will (though in Redon's image it seeks the infinite new realms above). Moore's account of an active eye brings our own more sedentary spectation to our attention, asking that we put it aside and take a more participatory role in the poem, if we haven't already. The active, world-traveling poem points beyond its borders too, asking that we similarly engage with and ask questions of the wider world.

The poem's call for reciprocity expands on Moore's career-long efforts to counteract the rapacity inherent in description with an ethics of looking, aimed at creating a non-predatory poetry of "imaginary possessions"—entities of all kinds, acknowledged to exist apart from the terms in which the poet defines them.[68] Her insistence on acknowledging the sources of her material, in prior texts from diverse cultural levels and speakers of various identity positions, and her oblique portraits of the people and creatures she treats (the "fleeting glance rather than the fixing gaze")[69] allow her to reveal and critique oppressive power relations while working to limit her reenactment of such. By creating a poem that is itself in motion and in conversation with its readers, like the pony who moves through the many levels of mediation at the start to (almost) talk with her, Moore not only undermines the operations of objectifying spectacle but liberates the spectator from the prison of mechanical consumption as well.

The insistence here that art involves both "muscular docility" and "mentality" points backward to the previous stanza, where the building of the literal pivot into the shapely body of the poem activates its form as a powerful part of its meaning system. In laying out the words as a pivot Moore emphasizes the physical aspect of this and all her texts—claiming for the poem's "body" (or form) the muscularity to go along with the mentality demonstrated through its "argument," often the aspect of Moore's work given exclusive attention. Moore insists here on the interdependence of the two. She connects athleticism with mental effort in Redon's lithograph as well (ballooning is also a sport).

Moore segues into the next stanza with an analogy between Redon's active image and a mixed-race German Chinese acrobat (practitioner of yet another sport) whom she and many of her initial readers saw perform in 1962 on Don Ameche's *International Showtime*, a weekly TV broadcast of European circus acts into American living rooms.[70] Like the balloon, Li defies gravity, contorting his body in surprising ways while balancing a cup on his head, in a more difficult variation on a headstand.

as in the acrobat Li Siau Than,
    gibbonlike but limberer,
  defying gravity,
    nether side arched up,
    cup on head not upset—
  China's very most ingenious man. (*NCP*, 232)

In calling Li "ingenious" Moore employs a term she's used previously, with apparent self-reference (the "criminal ingenuity" of "Marriage"). This acrobat joins the series of players in the world of artful movement of thought, body, and materials that Moore celebrates across the poem. Using his head acrobatically, Li combines muscularity and mentality in his show-stopping feat, lowering himself backward to the ground, with "his nether side arched up," two plates twirling on sticks, and a full cup balanced on his head, without spilling a drop. At the poem's close, Li and Moore become one, as Moore performs her own ingenious display, by ending the poem formally (and punningly) with her own odic Stand—paralleling his acrobatic stand.

The celebrities paraded in the various forms of spectacle we take in daily generally model the favored forms of identity within specific markets, but they may occasionally include exceptions meant to prove rules or serve as tokens. And sometimes, if enough of the audience is supportive, they may challenge rules. In "Blue Bug," Moore invites us to notice and make sense of her featuring of athletes and artists marked by difference of color and nationality from the mainstream media model of her day. The poem's set of named characters includes: Blue Bug, Dr. Raworth Williams, Thomas McAvoy, Arthur Mitchell, Odilon Redon, and Li Siau Than. In addition, ancient Chinese musicians and scroll painters are described without specific names, and allusion is made to Pindar. All but Williams and McAvoy are represented as actively pivoting—but even these two fit the athlete/artist criterion.

While all these characters differ from Moore in gender (except perhaps Blue Bug, whose gender is unspecified), the two humans in the epigraph parallel her and differ from the poems' other characters in being white Americans. As white American men, they inhabit the norm of public power and their approving gazes authorize what follows. The poem joins the long line of Moore poems populated with emphatic and respectful references to individuals from non-dominant cultures. While some of these poems specifically address colonialism or questions of cultural oppression,[71] others, including "Blue Bug," make their case against dominative vision by example. Moore's attention travels the globe as a kind of eye balloon itself here, recognizing beauty and skill far and wide, in the work of African American, Chinese, French, and Greek artists, but refusing to allow her "eye to cage" it (per "Arthur Mitchell") through extended description. In "Blue Bug" Moore presents a band of outsider artists, marked by race, nationality, gender, and/or species, in which she includes herself, to raise questions about the operations of power and celebrity, about who sees and is seen, and how individuals are valued. By featuring them in this ode, as in her earlier sports poems, she explores and challenges the terms of celebration. In embodying only two people, Arthur Mitchell and Li Siau Than, in "Blue Bug" (the other artists are invoked via their work but not described) and doing so through analogy with a pony, Moore distinguishes and objectifies them as people of color—within a context that specifically critiques the process of objectification. Mitchell and Li are portrayed working to escape the limitations of portrait (an objectification that is often part of celebrity—especially of women and people of color), through motion and contortion. The poem also affirms its own shapely body as part of its argument about dialogic looking, insisting on acknowledging the subjectivity of the observed and the embodied-ness of the subject.

Even as they streak by, these adroit artists register as Moore surrogates. Like her and like Blue Bug (whose name adds further differences of both color and species), they work hard to entertain their audiences. In presenting this parallel, Moore links and critiques race bias and gender bias simultaneously, even as in some measure she continues the race objectification by talking about race at all. The framework spectatorship of the white men, McAvoy and Williams, provides the poem's performers with a kind of safety net. At the same time, of course, the need for such sponsorship betrays the fragility of the artists' status—singing for a supper not otherwise guaranteed. This dynamic resembles that surrounding Moore's own regular presence in the *New Yorker* of the 1950s and 1960s, to which she is admitted as a kind of performing pet, though a well-pedigreed one.

Moore identified herself with Mitchell when she submitted her poem named for him to Kirstein, who had commissioned it.[72] She refers to Mitchell in the accompanying note as "a certain young blackamoor with peacock-wings plucked from Puck" and then signs off as:

Your great admirer though slight acqu
A Moor
like the jet black tomcat by the door
on the rear cover of the N. Yorker[73]

The abbreviated "acqu" (for acquaintance) in this quatrain accentuates the internal rhyme with "black" in line 3 and creates her as an "acqu-a-Moor." The term "blackamoor" may technically mean a person of Moorish extraction, but it also refers to a history of Venetian sculptures of black slaves decorated with jewels and posed in attitudes of servitude. Moore connects Mitchell's peacock-costumed Puck to such a figure. This may register as derogatory—but her identification of herself as "a Moor" complicates that.[74] She invokes an image of a black male cat from a *New Yorker* ad (October 28, 1961) for vinyl flooring, to represent herself. The letter's signature rhymes on Moor/door/Yor. Reflecting upon the racist context and stereotypes of its day, Moore's references to Mitchell here and elsewhere affirm a bond and underscore the predatory role of spectacle in the looks-based economy of race categorization, in which one group's wealth depends on the theft of another's liberty and labor. Moore's references engage this biased dynamic, even as they challenge it.

Moore's sense of connection with races and cultures other than Anglo also drew her toward Asia, particularly China.[75] As they did for Pound and Stevens, the perspectives that Chinese art offered American museumgoers magnetized Moore, who claimed in a letter to William Rose Benét that she "was born pro-Chinese."[76] Moore valued the connection to the wider universe that Taoist meditation on abstracted Chinese nature images provided. As Cynthia Stamy emphasizes, respect for China's antiquity also served to triangulate and lessen the power of European culture over the American upstart culture that Moore inhabited.[77] References to Chinese art populate her poems from as early as "Critics and Connoisseurs" (1916) to "In Lieu of the Lyre" (1965), with many art and dragon references between.

"Blue Bug" mentions three Chinese arts, which all employ turns: music of the Tang dynasty, paintings from the Ming or Qing dynasty, and the contemporary acrobat Li Siau Than, "China's very most ingenious man," in the poem's last few lines. The close focuses the poem's gaze on China but may seem to dissipate the poem's overall logic on a tangent about a little-known performer, making no attempt to circle

BLUE BUG

(AFTER LOOKING AT A PICTURE OF DR. RAWORTH WILLIAMS' POLO PONY, PHOTOGRAPHED, WITH SEVEN OTHER PONIES, BY THOMAS MCAVOY, "SPORTS ILLUSTRATED")

In this camera shot,
from that fine print in which you hide
(eight-pony portrait from the side),
you seem to recognize
a recognizing eye,
limber Bug.
Only partly said, perhaps, it has been implied
that you seem to be the one to ride.

I don't know how you got your name
and don't like to inquire.
Nothing more punitive than the pest
who says, "I'm trespassing," and
does it just the same.
I've guessed, I think.
I like a face that seems a nest,

a "mere container for the eye"—
triangle-cornered—and
pitchfork-pronged ears stiffly parallel:
bug brother to an Arthur
Mitchell dragonfly,
speeding to left,
speeding to right; reversible,

like "turns in an ancient Chinese
melody, a thirteen
twisted silk-string three-finger solo."
There they are, Yellow River-
scroll accuracies
of your version
of something similar—polo.

Restating it:
pelo, I turn,
on *polos*, a pivot.

If a little elaborate,
Redon (Odilon) brought it to mind,
his thought of the eye,
of revolving—combined somehow with pastime—
pastime that is work,
muscular docility,
also mentality,

as in the acrobat Li Siau Than,
gibbonlike but limberer,
defying gravity,
nether side arched up,
cup on head not upset—
China's very most ingenious man.

—MARIANNE MOORE

Figure 17. "Blue Bug." *New Yorker*, May 26, 1962, 40. Reprinted by permission.

back to summarize or clarify. The original publication of the poem, however, provides another way to read the close.

All of the poem's seven stanzas have seven lines, except the first (8), the pivotal fifth (3), and the last (6). If, as printed here, we read Moore's name as the missing seventh line in the final stanza, a riddle is both posed and answered. Earlier the questions (put indirectly) were: Who is Blue Bug and how did s/he get that name? Here the question morphs to: Who is Li Siau Than, China's most ingenious man? And the embedded answer is: Marianne. The internal rhyme connects all three (Than/man/Marianne), in a manner similar to the rhymes on Moor in the letter to Kirstein. The poem flaunts its shape best when printed on one page as originally. This kind of invisible visibility—more disguised self-flaunting—repeats the similar presentations of a paradoxical self at the close of other Moore poems.

In identifying herself with Li the inverted acrobat, Moore also refers us back to an early negative review by Marion Strobel included in Harriet Monroe's "Symposium on Marianne Moore" (1922) of Moore's first book, *Poems*. Strobel compares Moore to a gymnast, characterizing her poetry as strained: "Even a gymnast should have grace. If we find ourselves one of an audience in a side-show we prefer to see the well-muscled lady in tights stand on her head smilingly, with a certain nonchalance, rather than grit her teeth, perspire, and make us conscious of her neck muscles. Still, we would rather not see her at all."[78] Discussing this review, Vincent notes the contempt implied in Strobel's portrayal of Moore as a side-show freak and gender outlaw.[79] Decades later in "Blue Bug," I suggest, Moore nonchalantly demonstrates the skills Strobel seeks, for the miniscule audience of those who remember the review and get the joke and, more importantly, for her own satisfaction. By clothing herself in Li's male persona, Moore even fulfills Strobel's wish that female gymnasts (masculinely muscular and generally improper in her view) would disappear as a group. Reading the acrobat of "Blue Bug" as an allusion to this review from an emotionally fraught moment in Moore's literary career underscores the autobiographical aspect to Moore's work that has generally gone unrecognized. This, along with the continuation of the literal imaging from "Roses Only" to "Blue Bug," further underscores the many levels of connection between Moore's later and early work.

The Strobel allusion also exposes another tie between "Blue Bug" and Monroe's "Symposium," which also quoted a short review by Moore's friend Bryher.[80] Like Strobel, Bryher views Moore's work as masculine, but Bryher sees this positively and wishes that Moore would behave in even more overtly masculine ways. At both the start and close of her commentary, Bryher calls Moore "Marco Polo":

> [*Poems*] is the study of a Marco Polo detained at home. It is the fretting of a wish against wish until the self is drawn, not into a world of air and adventure, but into a narrower self, patient, dutiful and precise. . . . The temperament behind the words is not a passive one, however much environment may have forced meditation upon it as a form of "protective coloration." The spirit is robust, that of a man with facts and countries to discover and not that of a woman sewing at tapestries. But something has come between the free spirit and its desire . . . [Miss Moore's] *Poems* are an important addition to American literature, to the entire literature of the modern world. Only, Marco Polo, your sword is ready and your kingdoms wait. May it soon please you to leave the fireside and ride forth.[81]

Bryher and her partner H. D. disapproved of Moore's choice to live under her mother's scrutiny, lamenting what they deemed a waste of life and adventure. But Moore turned down their efforts to draw her into the wider world. Bryher's connection of the China-traveling Polo to Moore's gender nonconformism reinforces the reading of Li as a figure for Moore in this poem about polo—and indeed of the whole context of polo reference as a form of self-figuring. The echoes from decades past in play in this punning poem suggest that Bryher's invitation to Moore to expand her horizons remained important to Moore long after.

As a well-known playful cross-dresser, in ties and masculine jackets as well as in her George Washington costume, Moore's gender is in question throughout her oeuvre, as in the world. Her otherness in the realm of poetry inheres not just in her femininity but also in her gender nonconformism, and both are invoked here through parallels with others excluded from the approved set—by nation and by race. Indeed, Moore seems to characterize herself as a race apart. Just as in her view her poems are not really poems, but work for which there is no better name, she is herself in her own and her family's view not exactly a woman, but someone for whom there is no better name. Except, as in the Moore family correspondence, when that name is "brother," or, as here, "ingenious man," to represent her regendering. Like Li Siau Than, she is a kind of contortionist—finding a way to present herself within the available, ill-fitting gender options. Like Arthur Mitchell, who speeds between historically white and black dance contexts, redefining both, Moore too maneuvers in two worlds, and a third that she invents as she goes.

Reading the poem as self-reflexive reveals another Pindar parallel, since he too closes several odes with reflections on his own status. At the same time that they celebrate victories, Pindar's poems raise profound questions about who deserves celebration, and about how power and riches contribute to that determination. Though the patron is honored in an ode, Nigel James Nicholson demonstrates that the mode itself bespeaks tensions in Pindar's era around changing social roles. The patron's claim to status depended on the understanding (or pretense) that he had earned it either as an athlete (rider or charioteer) or through preparation of the victorious horses in other ways (trainer or breeder), not merely a purchaser of horseflesh or hirer of trainers or jockeys. These odes explore not just who holds power, but why.

Similar questions percolate in Moore's ode: who has power, who does what work—including that of entertainment, performance, and provocation, and how are they recognized and compensated? Class and patronage—of arts and sports—are embedded issues here. Gender and race have long served as work-stratification systems along with class and age—assigning forms of employment as well as physical, cultural, and emotional tasks and setting pay scales. Moore's presentation of the global collection of nondominant figures here celebrated invites reflection upon how our world economy operates, who is valued, who decides value, and how all that might alter. Likewise her framing utilization of her own celebrity to focus reflection and call her readers to action recalls P. David Marshall's description of celebrity's combination of ideals with idiosyncrasy to "both contain the power of the mass in democracies" and represent the possibility of change."[82] Refusing to fade into invisibility as expected of elderly women, Moore (idiosyncratically) models and remarks on the activist side of celebrity while providing her readers with opportunities to affirm their own agency, qua active readers of many kinds of texts, and, by analogy, to affirm their own individual identities as valuable citizens.

In a letter home from college in 1909, Moore recounted a conversation she held with her Greek professor Henry Nevill Sanders, while ice skating. They "talked about Pindar and Aeschylus and Dr. Mahaffey and Oscar Wilde and Kipling and Poe and the value of making your work real, in at least some respects, so the majority can grasp it."[83] Several aspects of this confluence of concerns anticipate those of "Blue Bug" fifty-three years later. Across her late career, in choosing to celebrate athletes and artists, many of them locatable on her average reader's culture map, Moore gives her audience a "real" hook of popular knowledge and pleasure to grab onto, while simultaneously inviting reflection and active participation in the "pastime that is work" of engaged reading. That work also has "real" resonance with the cultural debates of its period, debates that remain current.

Though detained in New York City, Moore did become a kind of modernist Marco Polo, exploring the foreign lands of post-1951 popular culture in her own backyard. Moving from the book review to the sports section, Moore finessed her highbrow fame into a popular role as celebritized commentator on celebrity that gave her an entrée into the lives of her readers around their mutual experience as fans. Like her poems, Moore's example destabilized received ideas about who could and should be celebrated and on what terms. In her sports poems and through her public persona, she modeled the possibility that those currently excluded from recognition need not always be, and that we need not be passive spectators to media messages or to our own lives. Instead we may be democratic agents, both in our reading and viewing practices and in our inclusive interactions with those around us, advancing integration and affirming the full citizenship of Americans of all kinds.

3

Occasional Work: Culture, Spirit, Community

"'Ecstasy affords
the occasion and expediency determines the form.'"

—"The Past Is the Present" (*NCP*, 29)

The epigraph above, from an early poem, suggests that Moore viewed all her work as occasional, in a broad sense.[1] Ecstatic encounters of diverse kinds—with works of art, animals, individuals, situations, objects, phrases, ideas, and even with the process of writing—created occasions worth communicating, and in each case she employed the form she gauged most likely to accomplish that. While complex forms and methods gave her access to an elite audience early on, expediency of communication to a wide audience became a key concern in her late phase, as I've argued, so her forms and methods altered, making the poem into a new kind of performance space for creating the occasion of the encounter of the poet with the reader. Additionally, Moore utilized "occasion" in more specific ways in her later poems: many of them comment on shared cultural occasions like holidays, popular shows, and even moments when great paintings are featured in national magazines. Two poems were written to be delivered by Moore at events referred to in the work, and they became occasional poetry of the formal type. All of these poems build in consideration of community's meaning and mechanisms and themselves catalyze the audience's group performance of community.

As with her sports poetry, Moore's poems about shared cultural occasions drew readers who might not otherwise like poetry, because they directly address those readers' experience, giving them a special expertise, access, and stake in the poem. Such occasions also locate the poems in a particular moment, which later may connect readers looking back. One of this book's early readers vividly recalled a performance treated in a poem from the 1950s, which she'd attended as a child, and found the poem especially compelling therefore. Although later audiences who do not share direct experience of the events will have more work to do to plug into such poems, they can still recognize similar events in their own histories or the gestures of Moore's active efforts to reach out to her audience, which, decades later, now includes them.

The occasional dynamic in Moore's work also extends its political aspect, sometimes through allusion to specific sociopolitical events and consistently through creating a collective experience and a dialogue among readers of different social and political positions. Her citations remind readers (and particularly New Yorkers) of their parallel consumption of media—of a daily newspaper, a weekly magazine, a book, or a show or event on TV—which links the members of a dispersed audience of citizens. This community-building element of Moore's work parallels the "connective reading" that Juliana Spahr recognizes in the work of Gertrude Stein and of later writers like Lyn Hejinian, Bruce Andrews, Harryette Mullen, and Theresa Hak Kyung Cha.[2] Their poems, like Moore's, also seek to overcome barriers to poetry, to "use reading to contribute to, contest and expand how we think of public (and thus cultural) spheres," and to encourage readers' participation in "co-producing" poems, inspiring autonomous interpretations that resist merely reiterating status-quo assumptions.[3] Moore's poems had made this effort to engage readers as collaborators from early days, but it intensified and became more broadly populist in her later work. She attained a wider readership than did the poets Spahr studies because, while her poems were still often oblique, she found a middle ground of topicality, humor, and venue, made glamorous by her celebrity, which attracted and enabled readers of all kinds. While requiring that readers fill in blanks and actively co-produce the work to make sense of the pointedly odd presentation, Moore also provides them with a framework of familiarity and fun so that they aren't put off the effort and do engage, in varying ways and to varying extents.

Highbrow Culture for the Masses

At the same time that Moore's poetry began to engage with popular culture, her busy social circuit also took her to quite a few "highbrow" performances—including operas, ballet, art exhibitions, concerts, lectures, and poetry readings. Many of these performances both in content and context posed their own questions about brow dynamics and the relation between the high and low elements of a purportedly democratic culture; when she refers to these events in her poems, Moore extends these questions.

Opera on TV

Several years before Moore wrote "Arthur Mitchell" (1962) at the behest of Lincoln Kirstein, she had written a poem based on a January 15, 1956, performance of her friend W. H. Auden's translation of Mozart's Masonic opera *The Magic Flute*, for which Kirstein served as special production consultant. That opera, performed in the NBC Studios at Rockefeller Center (in the RCA Building, now called 30 Rock), had been broadcast nationally in an NBC Opera Theatre "Colorcast," promoting color receivers in a time when few people had them. Although Moore did not get even a black-and-white GE portable until the fall of 1956,[4] she saw that performance—at Kirstein's invitation, in color and in person—in the studio.[5] This mixed-brow presentation of opera on a mass medium featured (in the role of Pamina) Leontyne Price, then a young African American diva and already an international celebrity whose first performance on Opera Theatre the previous year had led several southern affiliates to cancel the broadcast.[6] That context spurred Moore's poem "Logic and 'The Magic Flute.'"[7] The racial tension behind the show goes unstated in the poem or its notes but would have been well known to Moore's contemporary readers, reframing the meaning of "Colorcast." Even in black and white (or even more so), the evolving story of democracy's confrontation with its own unfulfilled principles of equal and fair treatment for all citizens, including the highly skilled Price, was conveyed into living rooms across the nation by the broadcast, and Moore's poem documented and continued that story, along with related reflections.

As part of its Cold War efforts to counter international views of the United States as rampantly racist, the Department of State underwrote or assisted racially mixed performances around the globe, promoting a narrative of ongoing racial improvement, as Mary Dudziak and others have shown.[8] Price's 1952 appearances in Virgil Thomson's *Four Saints in Three Acts* in Paris and in the U.S. and in the international tour of Gershwin's *Porgy and Bess* were financially supported by the State Department. Her Met TV performances fed the same narrative of progress (though that message was undercut by the southern cancellations). Price's struggles to have her performances recognized as legitimate or even heard by racist audiences would have been entirely clear to Moore, who had also had to negotiate the terms on which she could meet a sympathetic audience, for different reasons. Moore's letters indicate that she made efforts to take Price to a meal, and that she called ahead to book a table and confirm that the restaurant would be gracious to an African American, though it's not clear whether they were able to find a workable date.[9] Simultaneously, the poem questions the operation of high/low distinctions, since in the United States a TV opera specifically aims to make available to the general public material usually reserved for the elite. Moore's democratically inspired but still complex poem distributed to the middlebrow audience of the *New Yorker* has that line-blurring effort in common with this opera performance.

Auden's translation also contributed to the progress narrative. In contrast with the integrationist aspect of the NBC broadcast, *The Magic Flute*, which recounts a Masonic battle between the forces of darkness and light, itself has a directly racist subplot that revolves around a servant of the high priest Sarastro called Monostatos, who is described in the German libretto as a Moor ("ein Mohr"). In the direct translation, Monostatos explains that, in this opera's ranking of levels of access to enlightenment and love, its hero Tamino achieves the supreme combination of both; its comic relief figure Papageno finds love only; and its villain Monostatos finds neither, intoning, "I must forego love / because a black man is ugly." But since Monostatos nonetheless has a heart, he falls for Pamina (played in this version by Price), singing that "a white skin has seduced me. White is beautiful, I must kiss her." This text is both repugnant and, with Price as Pamina and white singers as both Tamino and Monostatos, nonsensical. When Pamina feels no similar attraction, Monostatos first attempts to attack her but is foiled, and then attempts to blackmail her into love. The original's racial contrast aims to put into flesh the battle of dark vs. light in the rest of the plot. In Auden and Kallman's translation, however, the race plot is suppressed: although Monostatos is described as ugly, no racial difference is mentioned. The new text argues that he is attracted to Pamina because they are opposite in other ways:

And her beauty in relation
To my ugliness is right:

In the order of creation
Only opposites excite
The contrasting appetite.
She is frank and I am scheming,
I am warm and she is cold;
She is young and I am old,
I'm awake and she is dreaming:
So, Monostatos, be bold![10]

The translation reinforces the anti-racist effort of the broadcast.

Moore's poem then extends Auden's project further, playfully translating elements of the story of *The Magic Flute* into a new setting. Her poem reworks the opera's allegorical quest narrative:

LOGIC AND "THE MAGIC FLUTE"

  Up winding stair,
here, where, in what theater lost?
was I seeing a ghost—
a reminder at least
  of a sunbeam or moonbeam
that has not a waist?
  By hasty hop
  or accomplished mishap,
the magic flute and harp
somehow confused themselves
  with China's precious wentletrap.

  Near Life and Time
in their peculiar catacomb,
abalonean gloom
and an intrusive hum
  pervaded the mammoth cast's
small audience room. *(NCP,* 205, ll. 1–17)

Notes: *The Magic Flute*. Colorcast by NBC Opera Theater, January 15, 1956. Line 11: *precious wentletrap*, "wen′tle·trap′ (wen′t'le·trap′), *n.* [D. *wenteltrap* a winding staircase; cf. G. *wendeltreppe*.] Any of numerous elegant, usually white, marine shells of the genus *Epitonium*, or the family Epitoniidae. The shell of *E. pretiosa* was formerly highly valued."—*Webster's New International Dictionary.*[11] (*NCP*, 327)

She stresses that this love story occurs within the precincts of *Life* and *Time* (big concepts, but also popular magazines, headquartered in Rockefeller Center). The poem's speaker, like the opera's hero, follows a difficult path: she goes "up [a] winding stair" (shaped like a wentletrap shell, a name that means "spiral staircase" in Dutch), getting a bit lost in the black marble hallways on her way toward a room thick with "abalonean gloom."[12] The poem's layout spirals too,[13] mimicking what it describes, in another "literal image." Not coincidentally, Rockefeller Center features a similar winding stair, so the poem operates as an architectural ekphrasis and a kind of poème à clef.[14]

The spiral stair also alludes to Masonic lore, specifically the "legend of the winding stairs," which describes a stair in Solomon's temple (1 Kings) leading through three chambers on different levels—the poem offers a visual pun on this, in its three spiral stanzas (*stanza* being Italian for *room*). Masons view the winding stairs as an allegory for the ongoing progress upward toward knowledge that they seek and symbolize in their ceremonies.[15] Images of such stairs recur in Freemasonry books and websites, with each step labeled with a scholarly discipline (Astronomy, Music, Geometry, Arithmetic, Logic, Rhetoric, Grammar) or one of the five senses.

The Masonic path moves from the dark of unreason to the enlightenment of knowledge—but it honors as well the special illogics of music and love, as means toward the overthrow of tyranny and fear; and Mozart's libretto is also known for its illogical plotting. Moore's poem adopts that illogic: the speaker enjoys the "accomplished mishap" of wide-ranging associations that layer figures and concepts from different parts of the brow spectrum. These "hast[il]y hop" together as Moore merges the opera's plot and symbolism, Price's performance, Auden's translation, the renowned building in which it is performed, the trademarks *Life*, *Time*, and NBC, and her own fondness for wentletraps to attract readers of diverse brow levels. Mozart's fellow Masons included many founding fathers, which also suggests Moore in her George Washington costume, and that adds another layer to this poem's engagement with issues of access, democratic principles, and history, and the moral duty to love one's fellow men.[16] Moore situates herself as a character in this poem, playing the role of a spectator/fan present at the occasion of the live broadcast, who also happens to be a celebrity poet and author of this text, whom we observe in performance, actively improvising as she re-forms the operatic material around her own experience.

Indeed, the poem may be read as an opera in itself, mixing multiple artistic media—architecture, sound, myth, movement, color—to achieve a collaborative spectacle. Similar cross-generic effects animate Moore's dance poems, her ekphrases, and her performances delivered in situ. Playing with off- and internal rhymes (lost/ghost/least/waist; stair/where; hop/hap/harp), Moore uses sounds as steps toward enlightenment and connection. Having arrived at the top of the stairs in the first stanza, she speaks briefly in stanza 2 of the "small audience-room" in which the "mammoth cast" performed; she then quickly departs into Rockefeller Center plaza by the skating rink:

> Then out of doors,
> where interlacing pairs
> of skaters raced from rink
> to ramp, a demon roared
> as if down flights of marble stairs:
>
> "'What is love and
> shall I ever have it?'" . . . *(NCP*, 205, ll. 18–24)

Note: Lines 23–24: "*What . . . it?*" *Demon in Love* by Horatio Colony (Cambridge, Massachusetts: Hampshire Press, 1955). (*NCP*, 328)

The demon (figuring Monostatos the Moor) suggests everyone's desperation for love (echoing the old hermit who screams "Love should be put into action!" in Bishop's "Chemin de Fer" [1946]), including that of Moore, the poet character who speaks the only other "I" in the poem to this point. His question is answered in the next line.

> . . . The truth
> is simple. Banish sloth,
> fetter-feigning uncouth
> fraud. . . . *(NCP*, 205, ll. 24–27)

Note: Line 25: *Banish sloth*. "Banish sloth; you have defeated Cupid's bow," Ovid, *Remedia Amoris*. (*NCP*, 328)

Monostatos's rival, Papageno the bird trapper, then appears:

> . . . Trapper Love with noble
> noise, the magic sleuth,

as bird-notes prove—
first telecolor-trove—
illogically wove
what logic can't unweave:
you need not shoulder, need not shove. (*NCP*, 205, ll. 27–33)

The poem asserts that hard work and honesty ("banish sloth . . . [and] fraud]"), a loving heart (like Papageno's), music, and community-affirming (color) television will make things right. At the close we find that illogical Love has woven a text that includes interracial affection, which may be viewed as both individual (as in the plot as enacted in this performance by these artists) and civic (as in the connective social effects of the broadcast), affirming a communal love of and respect for one's fellow viewers and citizens, of all races and status (you need not shoulder, need not shove). The poem's topical material, about love, race, class, and brow interactions, democracy, technology, architectural space, truth, and fandom is enmeshed ("confused") with the literal image of the spiral. Here again Moore features herself as part of the audience, sharing the occasion with the NBC viewers, while also serving as the poem's featured performer and the audience's celebrity guide to exploration of how democracy works.

From the start "Logic" combined accessibility to its immediate audience with complexity, and over time the complexity has increased in some respects, for later readers who don't remember the broadcast. But getting readers to engage with complexity was always part of its point, as with all Moore's work. When it was published six months after the broadcast in *Shenandoah*'s summer issue (after being turned down by the *New Yorker*) and then again in November in Moore's collection *Like a Bulwark* (which sold out its first printing in four months), it spoke to an audience who could recognize many of its signals and, once engaged, develop their own connections and analyses, or just register fleetingly the accessibly "sentimental" cry for love and civility.

Critics at the time varied in their responses to *Like a Bulwark*. Poet Kenneth Koch reviewing it for *Poetry* found the sentiment and the book off-putting,[17] but the anonymous reviewer of the U.K. edition for the *Times Literary Supplement*, enjoying Moore's parsing of the American race-course dialect of Capossela in "Tom Fool," had thoughtful questions about the way the poems worked, which were asked in the name of "the man or woman of ordinary cultivation within whose power it is to make poetry once more widely bought and appreciated": exactly Moore's market. He found Miss Moore's work "the embodiment of wit, of style, of the fantastic and erudite imaginative flight, but [with] something earthy, something Emily Dickinson-like about the epigrams (quotations perhaps, but chosen with what skill) which are placed like cloves of garlic in the exquisite meat of her poems. The eyes under the black cartwheel of a hat are kindly but shrewd."[18]

Dance Political

Like "Logic and 'The Magic Flute,'" Moore's three dance poems—"Style" (1956), "Combat Cultural" (1959), and "Arthur Mitchell" (1962; see Chapter 2)—also combine exploration of politicized performances with highly stylized performances of their own. The first of these blends an anti-Franco argument into an ecstatic recounting of a flamenco performance. Moore saw Vicente Escudero's troupe perform at the Playhouse Theatre in New York on February 26, 1955, with a ticket provided by Louise Crane (1917–1997), Crane Paper heiress, philanthropist, quondam partner of Elizabeth Bishop, and great friend of Moore's from the 1930s on.[19] From 1954 to 1974, Crane published the journal *Ibérica: For a Free Spain*, along with her partner Victoria Kent (1892–1987), an antifascist Spaniard and former member of the pre–civil war Spanish legislature, then living in exile in New York. Moore's politics were informed by their friendship.

"Style" signals its political intention quietly, through brief reference to cellist Pablo Casals's 1940 Letter from Exile, about Spanish Republican refugees in France ("like a letter from / Casals," ll. 11–12). But in draft, the poem spoke more directly: "a kind of bravo / I wish it were a / letter—an invitation to /A free Iberica / A letter to Casals."[20] By 1956 Franco's supporters Mussolini and Hitler had been defeated, but the Spanish dictator remained. As with implicit anti-racism in "Logic and 'The Magic Flute,'" "Style," while making no direct anti-fascist statement, would have conveyed that message to politically alert contemporary readers. Even this indirect statement may have seemed risky in the political environment of the day. Moore first submitted the poem to *Vogue*, for which like "Rosemary" it had been specifically "styled," but she submitted it under the clearly political name "It's Like a Letter to

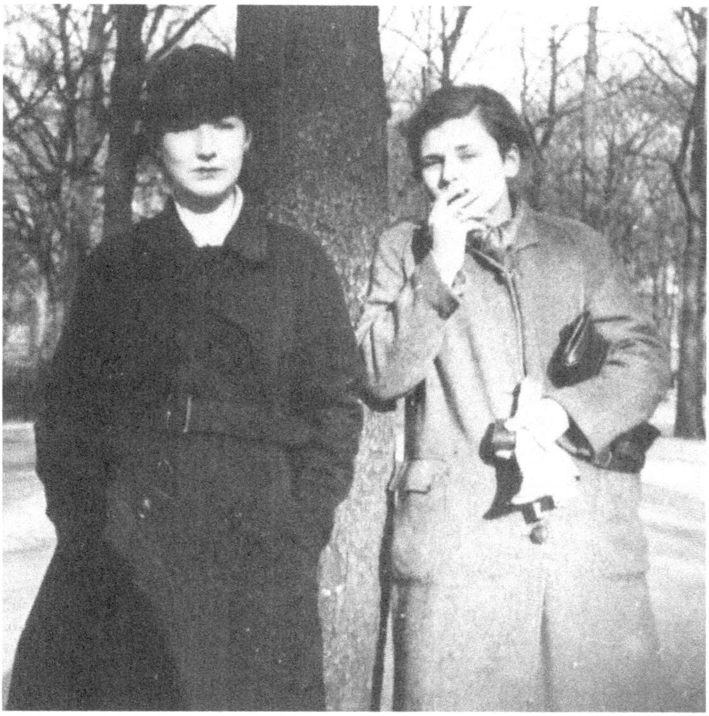

Figure 18. Louise Crane and Elizabeth Bishop, 1937. Louise Crane and Victoria Kent Papers, Yale Collection of American Literature, Beinecke Rare Book and Manuscript Library.

Casals." Though she "admire[d it] enormously," Ms. Talmey turned it down as "really . . . not for us," perhaps because of the politics.[21] Moore next sent it to *Mademoiselle*, which also returned it. Finally, it appeared in the less stylish, more politically committed BBC *Listener*, under the new depoliticized title.[22]

As with the pivot in "Blue Bug," the trailing peacock tail in "Arthur Mitchell," and the whorled shape of "Logic and 'The Magic Flute,'" this poem enacts what it describes. The layout parallels the examples of physical prowess and skills at balancing that the poem treats, looking particularly at examples of flamenco dancers from Franco's Spain, whom Moore compares to skaters and tennis players (mixing arts and sports here too).[23]

Style

revives in Escudero's constant of the plumbline,
axis of the hairfine moon—his counter-camber of the skater.
no more fanatical adjuster
of the tilted hat
than Escudero; of tempos others can't combine.
And we—besides evolving
the classic silhouette, Dick Button whittled slender—

have an Iberian-American champion yet
the deadly Etchebaster. Entranced, were you not, by Solidad?
black-clad solitude that is not sad;
like a letter from
Casals; or perhaps say literal alphabet-
S soundholes in a 'cello
set contradictorily, or should we call her

la lagarta? (*NCP*, 204, ll. 1–15)

Notes: Line 8: *Dick Button*. See photograph, *New York Times*, January 2, 1956.
Line 10: *Etchebaster*. Pierre Etchebaster, a machine-gunner in the First World War; champion of France in chistera (jai alai), pala, and mainnues. He took up court tennis ... retired world champion ... [twelve lines detailing his bio and games, citing *New York Times* articles from 1954, 1955, and 1956].
Line 10: *Solidad*. Danced in America, 1950–1951. (*NCP*, 327)

Like twirling flamenco dancers, the stanzas rotate around a plumbline, with the four seven-line stanzas hanging more toward the left margins, pivoting around a short center line, almost tipping over but "recover[ing,] without a disaster" multiple times. Like the dancers, the syllabic lines of Moore's stanzas (13/16/9/5/13/7/13) combine "tempos others can't combine" and offer what Margaret Holley calls "sensuous sounds" and "syncopated alliteration"[24] in phrases like "counter-camber of the skater," "wrist-rest for a dangling hand," and "suitable simile." Along with mentions of two flamenco dancers (Escudero and Solidad) and a flamenco guitarist (Rosario Escudero), Moore festoons the poem with additional Spanish-linked artistry by citing an "Iberian-American [tennis] champion," Pierre Etchebaster[25] (whose moves Moore likens to Escudero's), and El Greco (the sixteenth-century Spanish painter born in Crete). Then in her own "counter-camber," Moore draws parallels between the Spaniards and artists from elsewhere, with brief references to an American skater (Dick Button, stanza 1) and a sixteenth-century Italian composer (Palestrina, stanza 5), whom Moore imagines portrayed by El Greco.

Though Moore's dance poems often focus on still dance images (in photographs, or as held poses within a dance) rather than on motion (as Aurore Clavier has discussed),[26] this poem maintains a tension between motion and stillness, as its lines simultaneously lie static on the page and range actively across it (through their varied lengths and layouts) while describing an active performance wherein a dancer "can dart down three times and recover / without a disaster" and a guitar player's "dangling hand / [is] suddenly set humming fast fast fast and faster" (Bishop's 1976 poem "One Art" learns something here). "Style" closes with an emphasis on the tension between the author's effort to describe and poetically replicate the embodied-ness of an artistic performance and her inevitable failure to fully capture its ephemeral physicality. Claiming in the final stanza that there is "no suitable simile" for flamenco style, the poem then offers two and a half pretty good ones before giving up at the close and directly apostrophizing the four Iberian artists by name:

> There is no suitable simile. It is as though
> the equidistant three tiny arcs of seeds in a banana
> had been conjoined by Palestrina;
> it is like the eyes,
> or say the face, of Palestrina by El Greco.
> O Escudero, Solidad,
> Rosario Escudero, Etchebaster! (*NCP*, 204, ll. 29–35)

As a performer herself both on the page and in her persona, the poet links art and (small d) democratic politics; and in parallel she makes a case for a free Spain on the basis of the artistic skill of its citizens. In invoking them, Moore also, subtly, invites readers to recognize and endorse the anti-fascist cause as part of their American commitment to democracy.

While "Style" engages with Spanish politics covertly, "Combat Cultural" dances on an overtly political stage. The poem directly alludes to Cold War diplomacy, as Catherine Kodat has demonstrated, and specifically to the arrival of Igor Moiseyev's Soviet folk-dance troupe in New York in 1958, soon after the signing of the first bilateral cultural exchange agreement (a year before the arrival of the elite Bolshoi ballet).[27] Two kinds of cultural combat—the Cold War fight for world domination (via arts with a friendly face here, but with arms struggles in the background) and the competition for audiences between high and popular cultural realms within the United States—overlap integrally here, through descriptions of three of the troupe's dances. Moore literalizes these combats at the poem's close with a description of a comic wrestling match—the troupe's signature piece, which merges (high) ballet with (low) gymnastic clowning.

The détente-inflected context of the Moiseyev performance adds another layer to Moore's demonstration that art (including poetry) is always (though not only) political and situates it very directly in its moment. Kodat notes that Moore's poem does not argue, as some writers of the time did, [28] for an equal and opposite U.S. intervention in an international culture war, or finally for any side. Instead, with the poem's trompe l'oeil close, Moore suggests both that the Cold War adversaries have many similarities (among those, representing a "single phenomenon of aggression") and that political entities cannot dictate the ways an artistic work will be received, which may shift considerably over time.[29]

The troupe was initially scheduled to appear for three weeks at the Metropolitan Opera House from April 14 to May 2, 1958, to be followed by a national tour. When the Met performances sold out, eight more New York performances were added to the end of the (also sold-out) tour, this time at the much bigger Madison Square Garden, over June 20–28, and those performances quickly sold out, too. The troupe then performed for the still-bigger national audience of the *Ed Sullivan Show.* That episode forsook the program's usual variety show format, and the Moiseyev troupe, which included its own kind of variety show of disparate dances from different sectors of the USSR, took over the whole broadcast—first on June 29, 1958, and then by popular demand as an unusual rerun on February 1, 1959.[30] When Moore's poem appeared in the *New Yorker* on June 9, 1959, all her readers would have known something about this hugely successful troupe. Moore's poem piggybacked on the nationwide knowledge of this performance history to power its own performance and reception.[31]

This history of the three New York shows in diverse venues—the elite Met (expensive, limited seating), the popular Madison Square (available to middle- and working-class ticket buyers, huge venue), and the national TV show (free, available to millions)—provides Moore with context for exploring brow dynamics as well as the relationship of politics and art.

Her own experience fed that exploration, since her contacts with the group also occurred across the brow spectrum. Her appointment calendar does not indicate that she saw the show at the Met (she was away or otherwise engaged for most evenings in that period), but she did attend and take notes on a performance at Madison Square Garden on June 20, and her calendar for June 29 indicates that she again watched the troupe on *Ed Sullivan*.[32] On May 3, the day after the final Met performance, she had also participated in a posh lunch at the St. Regis with Moiseyev, where she noted that they, along with her celebrity confrères George Balanchine, Martha Graham, Agnes de Mille, José Limon, Jerome Robbins, Richard Rodgers, and others of the dance and theater elite, ate "turtle borsch, shish kabob charred by flaming cattails, strange sauce, grilled tomatoes, rice, raspberry-vanilla ice [and] scallop shells w tiny jewels full of colored cake."[33] Together these three experiences gave Moore a wide perspective on the troupe and its reception.[34]

"Combat Cultural" (*NCP*, 226) begins with an introductory stanza comparing forms of aerial movement: first with a speeding rook, then trained horses jumping fences, and finally gymnastic dancers ("a team of leapers turned aerial"). The last of these refers to Moiseyev's troupe, and three of their dances are then described. First comes "Partisans" in stanza 2, a danced saber battle between Cossack resistance fighters and Nazis ("a mist / of swords that seemed to sever / heads from bodies—feet stepping as through / harp-strings in a scherzo"). Moore segues in stanza 3 to a dance called "City Quadrille," which she refers to as "the quadrille of Old Russia," in which couples in nineteenth-century garb perform ballroom dances in an old-school manner ("with aimlessly drooping handkerchief / snapped like the crack of a whip"). In stanza 4, the poem moves to what Moore's notes identify as a Nanaian dance[35] from "the frigid north of the Soviet Union"—titled "Two Boys in a Fight."

> . . . Cold Russia
> this time: the prize bunnyhug
> and platform-piece of experts in the
> trip-and-slug of wrestlers in a rug.
>
> "Sacked" and ready for bed apparently—
> with a jab, a kick, pinned to the wall,
> they work toward the edge and stick;
> stagger off, and one is victim of a

flipflop—leg having circled leg as thick. (*NCP*, 226, ll. 17–25)

Though the title "Combat Cultural" might be taken to describe this balletic wrestling match, the next stanza points toward the battle of the brows and Moore's position in it:

Some art, because of high quality,
is unlikely to command high sales;[36]
yes, no doubt; but here, oh no;
not with the frozen North's Nan-ai-ans
of the sack in their tight touch-and-go. (*NCP*, 226, ll. 26–30)

Note: Line 29: *Nan-ai-ans*. The Nanaians inhabit the frigid North of the Soviet Union. (*NCP*, 333)

Here, Moore suggests, is high-quality work that *will* find a big audience in spite of the received knowledge that calls that impossible—the "yes, no doubt" marking the speaker's familiarity with, and the "oh no" her dispute of, the view that "quality," brow level, and low sales numbers are linked.

The poem describes the same sort of meta-intervention for multiple audiences that it enacts: the Russian show (at base a politicized crossover of "folk art" into professional dance) presents lowbrow wrestling within a highbrow dance frame at the Met and then crosses the line again into both broad commercial and diplomatic success.[37] (These dances themselves—accessible online—involve a lot of fast-paced gymnastics mixed with ballet moves and rank as "highbrow" largely due to their ambassadorial context.) Along with its Cold War commentary, Moore's poem offers an artfully self-conscious reflection on the high/low interplay and also makes itself accessible to the wide audience familiar with the dances. And this on the pages of the mixed-brow *New Yorker*, where it reaches a wide national audience. The poem does "a flipflop" of its own, performing a blague on the obscurity of elite poets by demonstrating Moore's skill at wrestling with the high/low dynamics she observed around her, participated in, and intervened to alter. As she had in "England" and "Poetry" four decades earlier, Moore plays here on both sides of the high/low line.

The final stanza explains that, at the end of the dance, "Two Boys in a Fight" reveals itself to have been performed by one person dressed as two:

These battlers, dressed identically—
just one person—may, by seeming twins,
point a moral, should I confess;

we must cement the parts of any
objective symbolic of *sagesse*. (*NCP*, 226, ll. 31–35)

Note: Line 32: *one person*. Lev Golanov: "Two Boys in a Fight." Staged by Igor Moiseyev, Moiseyev Dance Company, presented in New York, 1958, by Sol Hurok. (*NCP*, 333)

This rather obliquely phrased dictum suggests that wisdom (*sagesse*) is best represented through recognition of continuities between apparent opposites—the "two" Nanaian characters in the ballet, the USSR and the United States, the high and the low.

As the poem was going to press, Moore changed the title—which was initially "Cultural Combat"—to further signal the poem's embedded-ness in the high/low debate.[38] By reversing the word order, Moore moves her title into the realm of insistently "high" poetic language (marking it also as foreign; nearly the French *combat culturel*), a gesture that is then undercut by the visual joke in the poem's wrestling-act reveal, which winkingly shows the poem to value the low just as much. In its reverse-order phrasing, the title synopsizes the teasing double-face of all Moore's work around issues of brow and audience. She is comfortable in both worlds and invites her readers from all sectors to recognize that they may be as well.

Spiritual Occasions

While popular artistic events have historically provided one means of connection across classes and brow levels, church services have afforded another—occurring among small groups, but on a national scale. Millions of Americans participated in weekly concerts in their places of worship, Christians of various denominations hearing many of the same songs. Moreover, Christian, Jewish, and Muslim congregations heard some of the same stories. The granddaughter and sister of Presbyterian ministers, Moore attended church twice a week, knew the Bible thoroughly, and deployed religious material in her poetry frequently, including Bible stories, hymns, and rituals that would have been recognizable and attractive to diverse readers of all brows.

Some of Moore's religious references may seem more literary than spiritual to twentieth- and twenty-first-century secular readers. Her retellings of the story of the Fall (as in "An Octopus," "In the Days of Prismatic Color," and "The Steeple-Jack") may be read as allusions to Milton and Blake or to the common cultural store, or as metaphors. Moore took Jonah as a metaphoric self-signifier in poems like "Is Your Town Nineveh?" (1916), "Sojourn in the Whale" (1917), and "Tom Fool at Jamaica" (1953), where he serves as an example of humility learned through trials in concert with the poems' other themes and may be read as simply that. But for believers, such stories also provide access to a world of spiritual grace beyond the literal, literary, or visual, and Moore's belief and strong moral commitment permeate her work.[39] Nonetheless, her work does not merely reiterate the gospels: her borrowings explore and critique the dynamics of authority in the wider cultural field. Moore's early religious teacher, the "believing critic" Rev. Edwin Kellogg, stressed the need to balance faith with intellectual rigor and, as Jennifer Leader puts it, insisted on the importance of "embracing the workings of poetry in order to arrive at a right understanding of the Bible," which was itself inspired poetry.[40]

Blake, as Patricia Willis has shown, served Moore as a key precursor, in both his spiritually inspired poetics and his pairing of poetical with visual means of access to grace.[41] Though Moore did not publish her own drawings, she too emphasized the visual in her often ekphrastic poems, and her work, like Blake's, often suggests a sainted madness, traveling paths sometimes hard for readers to follow.[42] Though she would not have called herself a prophet, she did compare herself at several points to Jonah, who was one, and her long career vibrates with the inspired power of a calling to a poetic ministry not tied to a specific religious doctrine but committed to equity and gusto as spiritual principles; her efforts to reach a wider audience complement those principles. Of course, Bible stories have long communicated across social classes—for centuries the largely illiterate Christian public learned the narratives through sermons, carols and hymns, mystery plays, paintings, and stained glass, and later literate generations added Bible study to the earlier modes. Although a smaller proportion of Americans now attend services than in Moore's day, many still recognize the stories, whether or not they hold them sacred, and Americans of many heritages recognize and celebrate holidays like Christmas and Easter, with or without religious intent.

In the 1950s and 1960s, religious stories and holidays also aided Moore's effort to reach a wide popular audience. Her critique of the commodification of Christmas, which began with "Rosemary" (1954), developed across several poems on related material. The second in the series, "Saint Nicholas," emerged after a detour into another morally inflected fashion poem, about ethically sourced clothing, based on an *Atlantic Monthly* article about a qiviut farm:

THE ARCTIC OX (OR GOAT)

To wear the arctic fox
you have to kill it. Wear
  qiviut—the underwool of the arctic ox—
pulled off it like a sweater;
your coat is warm; your conscience, better. *(NCP*, 221, ll. 1–5)

In this perky piece from September 1958, Moore crosses the line she didn't in *Vogue*, beyond appreciation of the subject matter into outright commerce: the poem asks us to buy qiviut, and we're told in the final stanza that "if you fear that you are / reading an advertisement, / you are." "The Arctic Ox" was Moore's second *New Yorker* poem—appearing five years after "Tom Fool at Jamaica."

Her third, "Saint Nicholas," appeared just three months later (December 27, 1958). It continues the discussion of qiviut from "The Arctic Ox" and repeats many of the holiday tropes of "Rosemary," adding to them a direct gift-giving/buying element, and substituting Saint Nicholas for the Blessed Virgin Mary.[43] The poem invites readers in with a familiar address to St. Nick modeled on a child's Christmas list.[44] This list quickly moves off course, naming things that the poet admires but does not, we quickly come to sense, actually want or expect to possess:

SAINT NICHOLAS,

  might I, if you can find it, be given
a chameleon with tail
that curls like a watch spring; and vertical
on the body—including the face—pale
    tiger-stripes, about seven;
      (the melanin in the skin
      having been shaded from the sun by thin
        bars; the spinal dome
          beaded along the ridge
        as if it were platinum)? *(NCP*, 223, ll. 1–10)

Note: Line 3: *a chameleon*. See photograph in *Life*, September 15, 1958, with a letter from Dr. Doris M. Cochran, curator of reptiles and amphibians, National Museum, Washington, D.C. *(NCP*, 332)

This initial request—not for clothing she might wear but for a beautifully dressed animal—quickly subverts itself. The chameleon's markings provide it with the very camouflage that will make it impossible for Santa to locate ("if you can find it"). After taking pleasure in imagining that evasion, she abandons it ("If you can find no striped chameleon") and transitions to a related request, for clothing made of exotic-sounding fabrics that don't involve harming the source: first a dress or suit made of renewable qiviut hair, then a "drip-dry" "taslon shirt" (a high-tech woven polyester) sewn "by Excello," without collar buttons. Like the "Ox," this stanza full of brand names edges on advertisement, but Moore again rejects the item she describes ("if I can't have the dress"), moving on to more fantasy—turning first to say what she doesn't want ("don't give me . . . / a trip to Greenland, or grim / trip to the moon") and imagining instead clothing made of the moon's shadow (the fabric shadow echoing Bishop's "Man-Moth" [1936]). At last the poem turns to its central desire, "a thing yet more rare." That turns out to be a postcard (not rare in the usual sense) of a painting ("[n]ot the original, of course") of the sanctification of Hubert, an avid hunter whose life was transformed by a vision of Christ on the cross in the tines of a stag (which appeared on a card that Moore had recently received from a friend).[45] After his vision, Hubert, who is credited with the introduction of ethical, compassionate hunting behavior (such as not shooting a doe with young and only shooting when a quick kill is assured), gave his riches to the poor and became a priest (eventually a bishop). Like Saint Hubert, the poem rejects the hunt (for game or presents) from within what would seem to be the hunt's peak moment; it seeks to transform the commercialized holiday from within its advertisement-laden sanctum in the *New Yorker* Christmas issue into a divine moment of transcendence, in which miracle, friendship, beauty, and generosity merge in the poem and require nothing further. By dwelling on Hubert's transformation, the poem reminds the audience that Nicholas (aka Claus) is also sanctified, and as such, not associated with accumulation of material goods but with giving to those in need.

Instead of seeking gifts, the poem itself—including its postcard ekphrasis—becomes the gift, to Moore's readers. Her poem articulates her effort (like that of many artists) to offer something of value that transcends the cost of the magazine in which it's printed and engages the reader in a wider network of cultural and civic meaning. This poem's status as a gift is also supported by its physical artfulness: along with its descriptive portraits, it too presents a "literal image"—the "tail / that curls like a watch spring" in lines 2–3 of the first stanza is echoed in the carefully curled repeating stanza shape. Each ten-line stanza rhymes ABBBACCDED, with many additional internal chimes. The syllable counts repeat exactly in the first two lines of each stanza, and nearly so thereafter. These qualities reinforce the sense of the poem as sculpted object. In invoking Nicholas, Moore calls up the history of saint worship—the millennia-old precursor of celebrity fandom—the influence of which continues resonant even among secular audiences.

"Saint Nicholas" pleased *New Yorker* poetry editor Howard Moss so much that he offered Moore a first-refusal contract that effectively made her a *New Yorker* house poet for the next twelve years.[46] Seven months later, "Leonardo da Vinci's" (July 18, 1959) continued the hagiographic focus.[47] It begins with an ekphrasis of Leonardo's sketch of St. Jerome and the lion (1480), which had recently been reprinted in *Time.*

LEONARDO DA VINCI'S

Saint Jerome and his lion
in that hermitage
of walls half gone,
share sanctuary for a sage—
joint-frame for impassioned ingenious
Jerome versed in language—
and for a lion like one on the skin of which
Hercules' club made no impression. *(NCP,* 227, ll. 1–8)

Note: See *Time,* May 18, 1959, page 73: "Saint Jerome," an unfinished picture by Leonardo da Vinci, in the Vatican; and *The Belles Heures of Jean, Duke of Berry, Prince of France,* with an Introduction by James J. Rorimer (New York: Metropolitan Museum of Art, 1958). (*NCP,* 333)

Having set the scene, Moore continues the story in the next two stanzas: the Saint pulls a thorn from the lion's paw, they recognize one another as friends and equals, the lion proves himself peaceful in contrast to Jerome's expectations (Jerome thinks the lion ate the ass he was set to guard but soon learns otherwise), and, Moore argues, Jerome proves himself leonine (or heroic), apparently through his recognition that animals are not "less" than humans (a view Moore shares).

. . . The vindicated beast and
saint somehow became twinned;

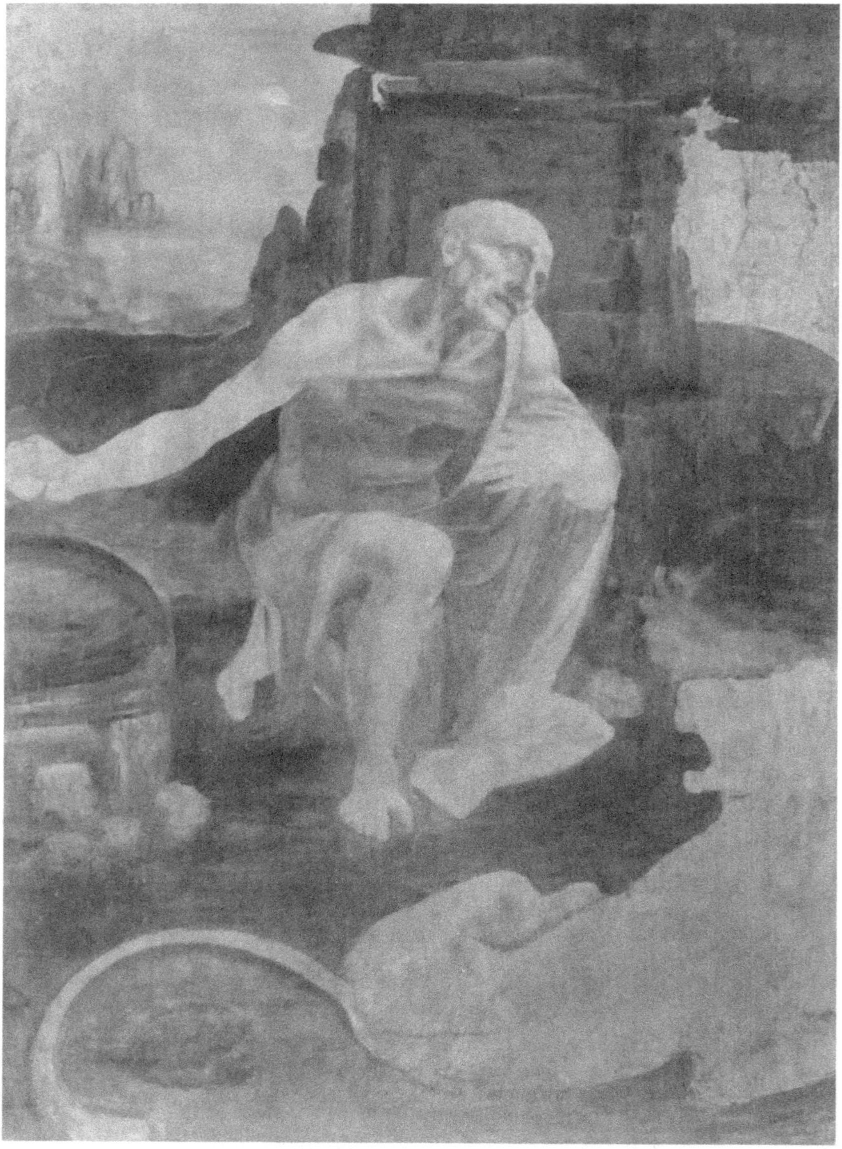

Figure 19. Leonardo Da Vinci, sketch of *St. Jerome and the Lion*, 1480, public domain.

and now, since they behaved and also looked alike,[48]
their lionship seems officialized. (*NCP*, 227, ll. 21–24)

This story bridges the gap between human and animal, and Moore sees a related bridge in Jerome's effort with the Vulgate (his fourth-century translation of the Bible from Hebrew and Greek into Latin to reach wider audiences), one that parallels her own populist efforts. Moore takes Jerome's linguistic dexterity ("versed in language") as basis for an argument made through puns on the word "lion."

Pacific yet passionate—
for if not both, how
could he be great?
Jerome—reduced by what he'd been through—
with tapering waist no matter what he ate,
left us the Vulgate. That in *Leo*,
the Nile's rise grew food checking famine,
made lion's-mouth fountains appropriate,

if not universally,
at least not obscure.
And here, though hardly a summary, astronomy—
or pale paint—makes the golden pair
in Leonardo da Vinci's sketch, seem
sun-dyed. Blaze on, picture,
saint, beast; and Lion Haile Selassie, with household
lions as symbol of sovereignty. (*NCP*, 227–28, ll. 25–40)

Having earlier twinned the lion with Jerome, Moore associates him here with the summertime astrological sign Leo, which also invokes da Vinci's feline forename (making the two men and the lion triplets) while describing the rising of the Nile River in August that occurs under Leo. Due to this timing whereby Leo brings water, Moore claims, fountains are sometimes shaped like lion's mouths, an associative logic she deems "appropriate, / if not universally, / at least not obscure," suggesting that she's making an effort to clarify her logic for readers.

At the close of the poem, the Nile carries the reader to its Ethiopian source and to the Ethiopian Orthodox Christian emperor, Haile Selassie (aka Ras Tafari, and, as the descendant of Solomon, the Lion of Judah), who kept symbolic pet lions and, though sometimes autocratic, was one of the founders of the United Nations. While much religious doctrine is devoted to enforcing static rules and ideas, Moore focuses here on examples of how religion encourages reflection that generates new understanding. In this poem, she depicts Jerome as pushing past received ideas (about lions) to new generative, democratic views that are capable of creating broad-spectrum connection, and thereby accessing the invisible world of grace. She then uses her audience's shared knowledge of Jerome's lion story and his etymological bent to authorize her use of puns on their shared love of lions as a segue to lauding Selassie as a related example of generative thinking, used in his case to expand racial and global equity.

Like celebrity and sports narratives that communicate across class and race lines, this poem about an icon invites reflection and promotes social progress. As analysis of "Leonardo da Vinci's," "Saint Nicholas," and "Rosemary" demonstrates, Moore's use of religious holidays and stories as occasions for bringing together readers who hold them in common was part of her lifelong exploration of democratic means of address. For Moore, as for Blake, religious stories and images were both a private resource and a means of communication with wide audiences, by whom they could be received as familiar, spurring no further reflection; or as challenging or transformative; or yet as something in between—depending on the inclinations of each individual.

Public Occasional Performances

In addition to her poems constructed around shared cultural occasions of various sorts, which made Moore an unofficial populist poet laureate in the 1950s and 1960s, she also twice wrote the kind of formal "occasional poems" intended to debut at and comment on special events, enriching the pomp with their singularity.[49] A particular genre of performative speech act, such occasional poems take on a three-dimensional, embodied quality during their initial performance, which then becomes part of the history of the poem. Although the poet need not be an explicit character in the poem, her or his presence is implied through the occasion: thus, Elizabeth Alexander's "Praise Song for the Day," recited at Barack Obama's first inauguration, includes her in the poem's penumbra as the author and singer of the song on that day worthy of special commemoration. Moore's two in-situ occasional poems take the usual three-dimensional quality of occasional work one step further, by directly including and reflecting upon Moore's own experience around the occasion, as the major subject. Indeed, in both poems Moore is the occasion—different from an inauguration or a monarch's birthday poem, which emphasizes someone other than the author. "In the Public Garden" (1958) and "In Lieu of the Lyre" (1965) both use Moore's celebrity presence to open space for reflection on the occasional poem qua genre and on the effects of fame. They underscore the way all her readings-in-character operate in the context of the self-reflective performance art emerging in the same period—by John Cage, Yoko Ono, and others—as well as the many other kinds of performance active in multiple media in that period. Like those Neo-Dadaists, Moore draws on the Dadaist performance tradition of the 1920s and after, though unlike her younger contemporaries, Moore had also been present at the source. In the 1950s and 1960s, she performs the intersection of art and entertainment.

In the first of these poems, "In the Public Garden," delivered to an audience of five thousand attending the Boston Arts Festival in the Boston Public Garden in 1958, Moore takes the public-ness of its occasion as a springboard to reflection on the process and function of poetry (as Bruce Henderson and Benjamin Johnson have noted).[50] The poem expands on the case for the melting pot's role in democracy that she'd made two years before in "Hometown Piece," through related means.

IN THE PUBLIC GARDEN

    Boston has a festival—
    compositely for all—
and nearby, cupolas of learning
(crimson, blue, and gold)[51] that
    have made education individual.

    My first—an exceptional,
    an almost scriptural—
taxi-driver to Cambridge from Back Bay said
as we went along, "They
    make some fine young men at Harvard." I recall . . .
    (*NCP*, 219, ll. 1–10)

Note: Originally entitled "A Festival." Read at the Boston Arts Festival, June 15, 1958. (*NCP*, 332)

Moore opens by narrating for the "composite" crowd (drawn from many groups and ranks) a brief history of how she came to be there—both literally (by taxi) and figuratively (due to the long poetic career that triggered the invitation).[52] She locates the occasion in the Garden, in Boston, near Harvard. She recalls the weathervane on Faneuil Hall being gilded years before by "a -leafer and -jack" (stanza 3), reminding alert listeners of her 1930s poem about a steeple-jack covering a tilted church spire with gold leaf, which hinted at the inevitability of corruption. As in that poem, she then leads her audience through a spring scene—"a miracle" of pear blossoms and fairy iris and apparently (or perhaps) more innocent than the snake-filled garden in "The Steeple-Jack."

In stanza 6 she steps into a church, again invoking the religious knowledge she had in common with many readers, this time via a hymn:

> let me enter King's Chapel
> to hear them sing: "My work be praise while
> others go and come. No more a stranger
> or a guest but like a child
> at home." . . . (*NCP*, 219, ll. 26–30)

> *Note:* Line 27: "*My work be praise*." Psalm 23—traditional Southern tune, arranged by Virgil Thomson. "President Eisenhower attributed to Clemenceau . . . the observation, 'Freedom is nothing . . . but the opportunity for self-discipline.' . . . 'And that means the work that you yourselves lay out for yourselves is worthwhile doing—doing without hope of reward.'" *New York Times*, May 6, 1958. (*NCP*, 332)

Moore's notebook for 1937 documents that in that year she heard the King's Chapel choir sing Virgil Thomson's arrangement of Isaac Watts's hymn "My Shepherd Will Supply My Need" (based on Psalm 23, "The Lord is my shepherd").[53] That precursor text here supplies Moore's need,[54] when she lets several of Watts's lines (ending: praise / rest / come / guest / home) enter her poem but maps them against the grain of her own lineation (ending: chapel / while / stranger / child / festival), thus creating a counterpoint, as in "Hometown Piece."[55] (See note for discussion of counterpoint in "Melchior Vulpius" [1958].)[56] Her omission of one of Watts's lines unsettles the rhyme scheme of the embedded lyric to create her own reworked praise text. She structures her end rhymes through the rhetorical figure *homeoteleuton* (the trope of like endings), repeating the same sound [*-al*] in lines 1, 2, and 5 of all nine of the poem's five-line stanzas, frequently in creative near-matches.[57]

The poem then links chapels and festivals as both based in the mutual giving that builds community:

... A chapel or a festival

means giving what is mutual,
even if irrational; (*NCP*, 219, ll. 30–32)

We might infer the "irrational" basis for both to have its source in affection or love—not just mutual interest, which would be rational. But the poem then moves directly into what seems like a different kind of irrationally linked set of examples of gifts:

black sturgeon-eggs—a camel
from Hamadan, Iran;[58]
a jewel, or, what is more unusual,

silence—after a word-waterfall of the banal—
as unattainable
as freedom... (*NCP*, 219–20, ll. 33–38)

This seemingly zany display can be read as examples of freedom . . . of association! Citing a recent address on the value of volunteerism by Eisenhower[59] (about whose work ethic and dedication to community Moore had in 1956 written an appreciative poem titled "Blessed Is the Man"), the poem moves on to analysis of democracy:

... And what is freedom for?
For "self-discipline," as our
hardest-working citizen has said—a school;

it is for "freedom to toil"
with a feel for the tool.
Those in the trans-shipment camp must have
a skill. With hope of freedom hanging
by a thread—some gather medicinal

herbs which they can sell.
Ineligible if they ail.
Well? (*NCP*, 220, ll. 38–48)

Linking freedom with self-discipline and the "freedom to toil" (quote unattributed), Moore then segues to refugees seeking to join the composite American community. Her notebooks suggest that several articles about Hungarian refugees in camps provided the poem's spark (though they're not cited).[60] In a context in which Congress was resisting pressures to expand the numbers of immigrants welcomed annually, the poem explains that to be admitted to the United States refugees must have a work skill and be healthy ("ineligible if they ail"), and that some refugees astutely address both of these goals by starting medicinal herb businesses while they wait in "trans-shipment camps." As with the evidence of the value provided by black players in "Hometown Piece," we get evidence here that hardworking immigrants will contribute to the power and skills of the nation, and again that evidence is presented in a context that physically integrates multiple textual "tunes" into harmonic counterpoint. Readers can now recognize these influxes of immigrants (also guided by the "shepherd" to "lie down in green pastures") as the new referent of Watts's phrase "no more a stranger or a guest / but like a child at home." David Herd notes that by placing this poem in Boston, Moore invokes the history of the forced emigrations of the British settlers and the Native Americans they then pushed out,[61] and those summon up as well the flows of immigrants into Boston and the United States since, all of which resonate with the patterns of displacement put in motion across the twentieth century by the world wars. By emphasizing her arrival by taxi (and before that via Back Bay train station), Moore has also marked herself as a variety of immigrant as well.

Thinking about ailing then leads Moore to ask "Well?" in a pun that combines a question about whether the refugees are well (as opposed to ailing) and the more sequential "well, what's next?" The question moves her to cut that stanza short and turn (as with the literal pivot in "Blue Bug") toward a new focus at the close with a self-deprecating reference:

> There are those who will talk for an hour
> without telling you why they have
>   come. And I? This is no madrigal—
>
>   no medieval gradual—[62]
>   but it is a grateful tale.
> Without that radiance which poets
> are supposed to have—
>   unofficial, unprofessional, . . .   (*NCP*, 220, ll. 49–56)

The claim of those last three lines is of course entirely wrong, since the poem has quite professionally, even radiantly, performed exactly what was called for. Along with its artful zaniness, this very professional poem demonstrates its own extraordinary self-disciplines: of homeoteleuton, syllabic metrics, and counterpoint. Moore's performance in the garden both creates and documents an experience—she names the place; associates it with the touch points of her life and career (including her unique and non-banal word-waterfalls) that bring her to the point of celebrity at which she now can be the occasion of this gathering; reflects upon the dynamics of a civic community built by generations of immigrants in the context of a world full of newly displaced populations seeking refuge in democracy; and links that to the community gathered to hear a poem that tells their story. The performance anoints all five thousand of her listeners with a role in the poem, by including them in its project of community building.

The poem concludes with a performative utterance:

. . . still one need not fail

to wish poetry well
where intellect is habitual—
glad that the Muses have a home and swans—
that legend can be factual;
happy that Art, admired in general,
is always actually personal. (*NCP*, 220, ll. 56–62)

Invoking Boston's claim to intellectual capital, Moore echoes her valuation in "Poetry" decades earlier of thoughtful, innovative work. She closes not just by acknowledging the personal references to her past that the poem includes but by marrying poem, performer, and audience through this self-reflectively enacted occasion. The audience members play the necessary role of listeners and interpreters, for whom the poem is now personal as well. Again, as in so much of her poetry, the poem closes with the celebrity poet in the spotlight, but this time that spotlight is on the poet's role as convener of and advocate for the public gathered and constituted as a community in the garden—a community in which all citizens have a personal investment.

Seven years later, Moore was invited back to Boston, this time by Stuart Davis, the president of the *Harvard Advocate* (a student literary magazine),[63] who boldly invited her not only to give a reading but to furnish a poem for publication, on a short turnaround.[64] Though Davis expected she would offer something she had already written,[65] Moore decided to write something new, and the piece she composed—"In Lieu of the Lyre"

(1965)—was colored by this impromptu context. Moore's appointment books indicate that she devoted several days to writing this poem, so its effect of extemporaneous speech was intentionally constructed. That effect continues in the printed poem, which retells the story of its delivery.

Also written for performance, "In Lieu of the Lyre" echoes "In the Public Garden" in multiple ways and operates as a sequel.[66] Like "Style," it performs a balancing act, in this case held together through multiple tension lines that structure Moore's telling of the circumstances that brought her to Harvard. In declaring itself not lyric—not "of the Lyre" but "In Lieu" of it—the title echoes the self-deprecating claim from "Public Garden" that the poem was "unofficial, unprofessional." In this case, however, Moore had legal reasons for the distinction, having signed a contract with the *New Yorker* for first-refusal rights to all new poems. If this text were considered "not a poem," then she could offer it to the *Advocate*. Moore's lifelong habit of claiming not to write poetry served her here, as conveyed by her jovial preamble to this reading, preserved in a recording:

> Mr. Davis invited me to speak to you, and I was delighted to come. And he said "I just, it just occurred to me, this morning, we'd be very grateful if you could give us something to print, something you have to spare." . . .
>
> I was in a frenzy of concocting something, staggering to find out *something that was neither prose nor verse, but might pass for both*. As I explained I have a contract not to offer verse that I write to any but one magazine. So shall I read it first? This is called, very accurately, "In Lieu of the Lyre." L-Y-R-E. [audience laughter][67]

Moore's "In Lieu," also like "Public Garden," narrates its own unfolding within its occasion. Rather than a conventional lyric, Moore offers this poem (ultimately, it is one) as a poetic engineering feat, a metaphorical lyre held together through tension—like the Brooklyn Bridge (as she suggests toward the close), which is also an enormous lyre strung with humming cables. Hart Crane had imagined the bridge as a harp,[68] and this poem (like Moore's "Granite and Steel," written simultaneously and published in 1966; see Chapter 5) is in dialogue with both her old colleague Crane's work and Alan Trachtenberg's 1965 book about the bridge's construction.[69] The first two stanzas set the scene:

In Lieu of the Lyre

One debarred from enrollment at Harvard,
may have seen towers and been shown the Yard—
animated by Madame de Boufflers's choice rhymes:
Sentir avec ardeur: with fire; yes, with passion;
rime-prose revived also by word-wizard Achilles—
Chinese Dr. Fang.

The *Harvard Advocate*'s formal-informal craftly rare
invitation to Harvard made grateful, Brooklyn's (or Mexico's)
ineditos—
one whose "French aspect" was invented by
Professor Levin,
a too outspoken outraged refugee from clichés particularly,
who was proffered redress
by the Lowell House Press—
Vermont Stinehour Press, rather. (No careless statements
to Kirkland House; least of all inexactness in quoting a fact.)
(*NCP*, 252, ll. 1–16)

Notes: Written in response to a request from Stuart Davis, president of the *Advocate*, for a poem.
Line 4: *Sentir avec ardeur*. By Madame Boufflers—Marie-Françoise-Catherine de Beauveau, Marquise de Boufflers (1711–1786). See note by Dr. Achilles Fang, annotating Lu Chi's "Wên Fu" (A.D. 261–303)—his "Rhymeprose on Literature" ("rhyme-prose" from "Reimprosa" of German medievalists): "As far as notes go, I am at one with a contemporary of Rousseau's: '*Il faut dire en deux mots / Ce qu'on veut dire*'; . . . But I cannot claim '*J'ai réussi*,' especially because I broke Mme. de Boufflers's injunction ('*Il faut éviter l'emploi / Du moi, du moi*')." *Harvard Journal of Asiatic Studies*, Volume 14, Number 3, December 1951, page 529 (revised, *New Mexico Quarterly*, September, 1952).
Line 11. *Professor Levin*. Harry Levin, "A Note on Her French Aspect," p. 40, *Festschrift for Marianne Moore's Seventy-Seventh Birthday*, edited by T. Tambimuttu (New York: Tambimuttu and Mass, 1964).
Line 14: Lowell House Press. Referring to a Lowell House separatum: *Occasionem Cognosce* (1963). (*NCP*, 336–37)

The poem opens with an echo of Virginia Woolf's *A Room of One's Own*, as Moore reminds readers that she, like all women, was excluded from Harvard College to that point (female undergrads were admitted in

1977). Whereas the reference to Harvard's "fine young men" in "Public Garden" seemed benign, the wry comment in "In Lieu" suggests a critique, and a tension that shades the gratitude and claims of poetic insufficiency that follow. Nonetheless, she then demonstrates a strong bond with Harvard through Professors Fang and Levin (both of whom may have been present at the performance)[70] and her recent publication of a broadsheet with Lowell House Press. This embedded-ness in anchoring relationships is reinforced by interwoven references to other Moore work, including "Tom Fool at Jamaica" (1953, via Boufflers and Fang), *The Fables of La Fontaine* (1954, via Harry Levin), "Avec Ardeur"[71] (1963, aka "Occasionem Cognosce"), and "Granite and Steel" (1966). All of these links establish this performance poem as part of a network—of texts, and of tensions and dialogues with others—that sustains it, like the anchoring cables of a bridge.

In spite of her exclusion from Harvard, the tricorne-wearing poet assures her audience she is nonetheless grateful (again echoing "In the Public Garden") to be invited:[72]

> To the *Advocate, gratia sum*
> unavoidably lame as I am, verbal pilgrim
> like Thomas Bewick, drinking from his hat-brim,
> drops spilled from a waterfall, denominated later by him
> a crystalline Fons Bandusian miracle. *(NCP,* 252, ll. 17–21)

> *Note:* Line 17: *gratia sum*. Bewick tailpiece, "a trickle of water from a rock, underlined by heart in outline carved on the rock," p. 53, *Memoir of Thomas Bewick Written by Himself* (Centaur Classics). (*NCP,* 337)

Here Moore, a self-labeled lame verbal pilgrim, compares herself to the eighteenth-century English engraver Thomas Bewick (whose works include studies of birds and other creatures as well as illustrations of several editions of Aesop's *Fables*). In the image referred to (Figure 20) Bewick declared himself grateful ("gratia sum" is inscribed at the center) for having stumbled, thirsty, upon a waterfall (another echo of "Public Garden"). Along with their gratitude, Moore and Bewick share status as skilled craftsmen. The poem, like the engraving, also features his hat, highlighting a link to Moore in her tricorne.

Having offered this parallel, Moore declares herself suddenly concerned that the audience may not care about pilgrims or Thomas Bewick and suggests they may prefer engineering facts (fortunately, also a favorite topic of hers):

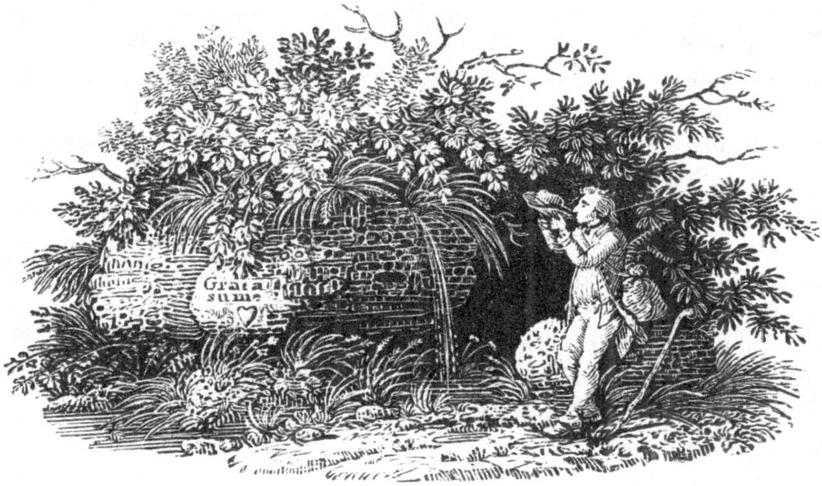

Figure 20. Sir Thomas Bewick, engraved tailpiece, *History of British Birds*, 1797, public domain.

> It occurs to the guest—if someone had confessed it in time—
> that you might have preferred to the waterfall, pilgrim and hat-brim,
> a nutritive axiom such as
> "a force at rest is at rest because balanced by some other force,"
> or "catenary and triangle together hold the span in place"
> (of a bridge),
>
> or a too often forgotten surely relevant thing, that Roebling cable
> was invented by John A. Roebling.
>
> These reflections, Mr. Davis,
> in lieu of the lyre. *(NCP,* 252, ll. 22–31)

Note: Line 27: *a bridge. Brooklyn Bridge: Fact and Symbol,* by Alan Trachtenberg (1965). (*NCP,* 337)

In segueing thus, the poem offers readers both another example of a skilled craftsman in Roebling and another counterbalancing force—establishing a tension among the poem's three realms of craft (engraving, poetry, and bridge-building). Moore's inclusion of engineering axioms gestures also toward the realm of prose, though here, as in Crane's *The Bridge* and Moore's "Granite and Steel," the revelation of the poetry of engineering generates part of the poem's excitement at the same time that it points up the engineering side of poetry, exemplified here. Though the poem had been written beforehand, it is structured to appear extemporaneous ("It occurs to the guest"). When Moore moves to providing engineering axioms, citing Alan Trachtenberg's then-new book on the Brooklyn Bridge, she does not delete the Bewick section as a false start but instead retains it, again suggesting that the poem is written to mimic the performance of a thought process. Playing the character Moore, she narrates her zigzag composition process dressed as George Washington. Zany, perhaps, but in command.[73] Constructed in a relative trice, "In Lieu" plays a delicate counterpoint to the weighty genealogies of "Granite and Steel," its companion piece, as we'll see.

As in "Public Garden," toward the close of "In Lieu" she turns the tables to make the audience part of the poem, too—asking them to recognize their role in shaping what they get, which would include not just what others prepare for them but what they are open to hearing (Bewick or Roebling?). When she spelled out LYRE in her introduction, Moore emphasized the pun on its homonym, Liar, suggesting the manner in which all speech is untrue to any single meaning and, simultaneously, telling the truth about our world—in which everything means multiply, to its various, individual auditors. The poem closes with another return to the personal, reminding us that the individual John A. Roebling[74] invented the cable that holds up the Brooklyn Bridge and repeating the name of her host, the young Mr. [Stuart] Davis, weaving him into the text along with Fang and Levin and all those gathered who became part of the poem by being present at the launch it recounts. Moore's performance on this occasion creates a multilayered, three-dimensional text (with layers including: the recited poem; the poet as author, character, and speaker; the additional "characters" mentioned, some of them present; the immediate audience; the source texts by Bewick, Crane, and Trachtenberg; and Moore's own prior poems referenced), which also serves as a fourth-dimensional bridge between that moment in which these characters were present together and future readers, who are also invited into the poem's community prospectively.

Again Moore, whose celebrity got her invited to this occasion, takes on the role of fan and makes a point of celebrating others and sharing her celebrity with them. (Stuart Davis, now a member of the English Department faculty at Cornell, reports still getting comments about his role in this poem from colleagues [and the occasional phone-interviewer], a form of ongoing literary renown.) The poet who brings this community together is implied as well: in lieu of the lyre/liar (actually quite a lyrical phrase), we get a zany transvestite truth-teller of multiple meanings who engineers the skillful interaction of words, performance, and context, figuring the multidimensional complexity of all human moments. Davis recalled Moore's performance in words that echo the dynamics that I've depicted in the poems. He describes his "sense of her singular personal presence crafted by guardedness and generosity": "It was strategic, or tactical. She offered you a preëmptive deference that left you free to approach, while quietly forestalling incursions and ensuring that the surprises would come from her. You (and other audiences) knew where you stood, but discovered where she stood from moment to moment, which revised your standing. Just good manners?—or good poetics too? Do the poems work that way?"[75] As I hope my readings of these poems in motion have demonstrated, the answer to that last question is a definite *Yes*.

While the poems discussed in this chapter cover a wide range of material, they share a common structure: employing cultural occasions of many kinds to convene diverse communities of readers joined in reflection about the operation of democratic community. As with the sports poems, Moore makes a point of reaching out to readers where they are through poems that appear in the journals they like and that talk about what interests them, which, it turns out, also interests Moore. In Sianne Ngai's analysis, intellectual interest provides the principal motive for human engagement with the world, based in "a feeling of not-yet-knowing" and energized by a libidinized desire to know more, in both nonaesthetic and aesthetic contexts.[76] While seeking knowledge for its own sake may seem self-focused at first, the Interesting also works as a social bonding mechanism: though what's interesting is initially defined by an individual or exclusive group of people "in the know," they then seek to bring more people into the group, by sharing it.[77] This notion of community building through common intellectual interests also serves Moore's audience's political and civic interests (in the sense of direct benefit). It well describes Moore's effort to expand her set of readers across brow levels through engaged reflection on both the widely ranging topics she treats and on the underlying issues of common societal concern that her performance frames (citizenship, racial equality, gendered power, sexual orientation, etc.).

Moore operates in the poems as a comic entertainer in an era both optimistic about the future and fiercely repressive of the effects of the immense losses of the first half of the century and of the ongoing inequities of its only partly realized democratic social structure. Moore's age and her history as a modernist, a feminist, and a war poet mark her as an informed representative of the complexity of the past, bringing forward knowledge of its struggles and strengths and bringing that to bear in the postwar context in the only way admissible to a wide audience—through humorous performance, much of it situational, playing upon the implausibility of her celebrity. These poems also take performance as a topic, exploring who is allowed onstage and why. In the years since her death, much of the work done by these late-phase poems has gone unrecognized, but in returning to them her twenty-first-century audience can determine what can now be heard of their multivalent significations—about our past (Moore's present) and our present, which Moore and her contemporaries helped shape and which her work can now help us to explore.

4

Embracing Affect: Love, Interest, and the Personal

I am in an affectionate frame of mind this year.

—Poetry Notebook (1952)

Neither old age nor lifelong celibacy rhymes with love poetry in standard vocabularies, but Moore only began writing love poems in her late phase, a period in which her unattached status played a featured part in her celebrity. The later Moore was portrayed in countless articles as "a quaint and rather stylish spinster,"[1] or variations thereupon—a characterization she assisted and through which she, as Benjamin Kahan elucidates, "reinvent[ed] the role of the spinster both as a life practice and more performatively as a celibate celebrity."[2] Where in her early career Moore portrayed herself as an observer, a role consistent with the view of the celibate as a cultural bystander, the later Moore used her renown and the attendant fan interest in the details of a celebrity's love life (even if those details included an absence of standard romance) to redefine celibacy as grounded not in lack but in pleasurable activity—including the pleasures of: wrestling with difficulty (in her case with textual complexities that refuse resolution), exploring one's own inventive trains of thought and action among a circle of friends and literary colleagues, and consorting with luminaries in a lively public life.

From the 1940s on Moore's work included poetic celebration of loving friendships, and these evolved in the period of her celebrity celibacy in the 1950s and 1960s into an anomalous authority on love in general. Though she'd declared in "Silence" (1924) that "the deepest feeling" expressed itself obliquely, four late-phase poems venture (variously and non-standardly) into the romance realm. Two were written for Valentine's Day—"For February 14th" (1959) and "Saint Valentine," (1960)—developing on the model of her Christmas-themed pieces; like "Saint Nicholas," both offer lists of gifts and like "Rosemary" they include erotic subtexts. "Love in America?" (1966) takes a political tack, arguing for a democracy of tenderness that includes love of all kinds and sexualities ("whatever the deed," as Moore put it in the *Saturday Evening Post* version). While the fourth poem, "To a Giraffe" (1963), doesn't overtly engage with romance, in it Moore reflects on the role of personal emotion in her own work, in the context both of her relationship with her friend the "impersonal" modernist T. S. Eliot and of the growing influence of confessional poets (who also utilize dynamics of celebrity revelation to engage readers).

Moore's embrace of love as material in her late phase revisits the issues of gendered poetry that she engaged in "Roses Only," "Marriage," and other early poems, and directly contradicts her early phase rejection of the expectation that women would write sentimental poetry. Instead, her later poems fulfill that expectation of sentiment, though in unusual ways. In offering readers emotional access, these late poems also invite in wider audiences—both to reflect on romantic love and to explore diverse manifestations of libidinal energy, the glue that connects humans and undergirds community. Of course, emotion has political dimensions beyond the abstract patriotic love of country. In featuring her own alternative life and love plot in her late-life public persona and poems, Moore also advocates for equity in the realm of sexual politics. The poems open the way to love of fellow citizens of all demographics and to respect for people who love differently.

In engaging directly with love within a framework that includes her own experience, Moore revokes her pledge to the fraternity of Modernist Impersonality, led by her literary comrade T. S. Eliot. In his foundational essay "Tradition and the Individual Talent" (1919), Eliot described the process of writing a poem as "a continual surrender of [the artist] as he is at the moment to something which is more valuable. . . . a continual self-sacrifice; a continual extinction of personality."[3] While an underlying passion still energizes a poem's material in his ideal formula, Eliot concludes that "the emotion of art is impersonal." Both biographical details and sentimental stories about relationships were rejected by followers of this mandate, though failures to relate were sometimes portrayed (e.g., "The Waste Land"). As we've seen, Moore directly engaged with and rejected that formula at the close of "In the Public Garden" (1958), concluding that "Art . . . is always actually personal," and she extends that view into her love poems. Rather than departing from her earlier modernism, however, Moore's later work remains modernist, not only in its form and in its continued obscurity (maintained in tandem with greater accessibility) but also in its exploration of the undercurrents of emotion flowing within modernism.

Andreas Huyssen and others have shown that Eliot's cult of impersonality created special difficulty for women, since it was developed, like Futurist anti-sentimentalism, on purpose to exclude them—or all but the exceptional few. That legacy of gender hierarchy reinforced modernism's elite ranking, through contrast with the feminized mass culture. As we've seen, as a young woman with aspirations to literary recognition and authority, Moore distanced herself from stereotypical femininity, associated with sentiment, bodies, and personal relationships—fashioning for herself instead a more complexly gendered persona combining what Betsy Erkkila describes as "ladylike decorum"[4] with a masculine style of dress and masculine preferred pronouns (among family), scientific and intellectual interests, a life story that rejected traditional gender roles, and a pointedly unsentimental poetic affect. This presentation succeeded so well that Ezra Pound lauded Moore as a practitioner of "logopoeia, or poetry that is akin to nothing but language."[5]

But though her early work seems detached in many respects, personal relationships and references inevitably animated it all along. The poetry's many idiosyncrasies always marked it as deeply personal, with a passion compressed at the core of her stanzas akin to the "cataclysmic torrent of emotion" that, she tells us in "England," lives "compressed in the verbs of the Hebrew language."[6] The personal-qua-biography was long present as well, covertly early on, as in "Marriage";[7] but over the decades she featured biographical elements increasingly. Moore's love poems of the 1950s and 1960s developed out of a series of poems engaging sentiment that began with "The Paper Nautilus" (1940), a paean to maternal love among mollusks, which concludes that "love / is the only fortress / strong enough to trust to." Along with its reference to mothers, including Moore's own, this poem had another directly personal prompt in a gift of a Nautilus shell that Moore had received from her friend Louise Crane in 1937; the loving thoughtfulness of the gift spurred the poem's reflection on the sustaining power of love.[8]

In the context of World War II, Moore reached out to the global community with expressions of patriotic sentiment and ethics in "What Are Years" (1940), "Light Is Speech" (1941), "Nevertheless" (1943), and "In Distrust of Merits" (1943), etc., offering encouragement to the Allies (at home and abroad) to struggle on.[9] That sentiment and her plainer 1940s style afforded readers a new level of access to her work and grew her audience. In this period Moore also wrote poems more explicitly celebrating friends: "The Wood-Weasel" (1942) celebrates Hildegarde Watson[10] (spelled out along the left edge)[11] and closes with a personal affirmation: "Only / WOOD-weasels shall associate with me" (*NCP*, 163). "Voracities and Verities" (1947) thanks an unnamed friend for a "tiger-book" (letters reveal the giver was again Louise Crane), and ends by directly addressing the modernist "sin" of sentiment: "One may be pardoned, yes I know / one may, for love undying" (*NCP*, 182).[12] Such personal expressions of connection ask readers who also have fond attachments (pretty much everyone) to relate to the emotion, the poem, and, potentially, the poet.

In 1947, Moore dealt with the emotional weight of her mother's death in "A Face" (see Appendix). Immediately thereafter, two 1948 poems—"Efforts of Affection" and "By Disposition of Angels"—examined the dynamics of love in Moore's newly independent situation, still from a distance.[13] As the phrase in this chapter's epigraph suggests, as the years progressed Moore grew increasingly overt about affection in her poems. In a note from the same period she disputed modernist claims to unsentimentality:

> We are sentimental when unwary
> about that which we like because
> it is unsentimental.[14]

The quip underscores the sentiment powering both love of impersonality and ardent disdain for overt expression of affection, which puts sentiment's haters (since hate is by definition a sentiment) in the camp of the sentimental, in spite of themselves. Instead of decrying sentiment, Moore now embraces it—as a shared human experience of deep feelings, though the particulars may differ across individuals. Though the later poems emphasize the friendly, filial, communal, and spiritual dimensions of love, romantic love and the libidinized underpinnings of all bondings percolate there too.[15]

While she was a devoted churchgoer and romantically unattached, Moore was not innocent about either romance per se or its non-heterosexual options. In addition to growing up beside her own mother's romance with Mary Norcross, a large proportion of her close friends were gay or bisexual and often in long-term homosexual relationships, including Bryher and H. D., Elizabeth Bishop, Louise Crane and Victoria Kent, Monroe Wheeler and Glenway Wescott, Joseph Cornell, Chester Page, W. H. Auden, Kathrine [*sic*] Jones and Marcia Chamberlain, Lincoln Kirstein, and Clive Driver, as well as many of her less close circle. She had many straight friends as well, but no illusions about the necessity of one romantic path. Moore herself seems to have actively chosen celibacy, or chastity as she called it, and she viewed it as a source of strength.[16] Recently, quite a few critics and readers have taken to calling Moore "queer," using that word to suggest either any non-hetero sexuality, including celibacy or asexuality (Vincent, Kent, Kahan, Arckens, Pollak, etc.), or specifically closeted homosexuality (McCabe). Directly affirming the option to choose against the socially approved grain, Moore's alternative life choices fit Eve Sedgwick's definition of queer as "the open mesh of possibilities, gaps, overlaps, dissonances and resonances, lapses and excesses of meaning when the constituent elements of anyone's gender, of anyone's sexuality aren't made (or can't be made) to signify monolithically."[17] Moore's incongruous masculine federalist persona reinforces that message.

Along with sentiment and affirmation of difference, intellectual interest (or curiosity) may also lead to new bonds (including love) among individuals who share the interest (the multiple meanings of "interested"—to mean attracted, invested, and curious—overlap here). Moore's wide range of poetic topics and forms and her own insistent self-presentation as different from the expected require her readers to embrace difference and new ideas—as distraction or subversion, or both. The speed of movement among her poems' many foci may aid their overall "zany" effect, so the zany and the interesting overlap. Unlike more familiar or conventional work, interesting work requires readers to actively invest more energy to fill in the gaps, and that investment binds, creating a sense of intimacy with the author that introduces another level of attachment (see also Kenneth Burke's analysis, in the Appendix). Interest in the new or unfamiliar is by definition unstable and subject to change—opposite to a kitschy repetition of received ideas that are beloved from the start specifically because they are familiar. Mixing sentiment with pursuit of the interesting, Moore in her late phase creates yet another level of unpredictability to engage readers.

Poems on Love

It was Howard Moss's delight with her Christmas poem "Saint Nicholas" (1958) that spurred him to offer Moore a first-read contract with the *New Yorker* in 1959, but just two months later Moss turned down the first poem she offered him under that deal. In "For February 14th," initially titled "Overture," Moore developed further on the holiday-occasional model she'd employed in both "Saint Nicholas" and "Rosemary" (*Vogue*, 1954), exhibiting a strong sense of her market by expanding the mode to include another gift-linked holiday. As we've seen, the Christmas poems both suggest the greater value of personal connection and ethical action over commodified giving, even though both appeared within magazines full of ads for expensive gifts: the context at once admits Moore's critique and disputes it. "For February 14th" builds on that, layering in further complexity by offering the spinster Moore as a guide to the terrain of romantic love. This poem developed not in response to an invitation—Moore saw the holiday poem parallel and took the initiative to write it for Moss. Addressing Saint Valentine in line 1, Moore reverses the dynamic of asking for gifts *from* Saint Nicholas, instead structuring this one around offering presents *to* the saint of romance.[18] But despite the parallels, Moore's *New Yorker* editors rejected the poem as too obscure, perhaps due to the initial title's not specifically referring to the holiday and the poem's not directly mentioning love.[19] Or perhaps they felt a spinster's views on love unsuitable. Unabashed, Moore revised the text minimally, retitled it "For February 14th," and placed it without problem on page one of the *New York Herald Tribune* on February 13, where it reached a huge audience just in time to be relevant, as had her "Hometown Piece" in 1956.[20]

Eleven months later, *New Yorker* editor Katharine White apparently regretted the rejection and wrote Moore to request, essentially, that she write the same poem. After reading *O to Be a Dragon*, Moore's 1959 collection including "Saint Nicholas" and "For February 14th," White wrote to the poet, "it came to me as an urgent wish that you could *write a companion poem to 'Saint Nicholas'—this one to Saint Valentine, reversing the list of things you'd like to receive to make it a list of things you'd like to send as valentines.* I don't suppose the ideas will appeal to you at all, and you are the last person in the world to be asked to write a poem on a certain subject, but even so I thought I would at least confess my wish or hope."[21] If Moore was puzzled by this request to exactly repeat the structure of her first Valentine poem, and by its entirely inaccurate claim about her unwillingness to write on assignment, she nonetheless obligingly followed White's direction and gave her "Saint Valentine," which, though the details differ, essentially reframes "For February 14th" as White requested, again around themes of eros and gifts. Either Moore's poems, odd as they were, struck White as replicable commodities, even as they attempted to speak beyond predictability—or White had repressed the magazine's bad decision to reject the first one.

Both Valentine poems explore the dynamics of personal connection as enacted through various kinds of gifts, while offering alternatives to conventional love plots. "For February 14th" asks Saint Valentine what gifts he ("you") would like.[22]

For February 14th

Saint Valentine,
although late, would "some interested law
impelled to plod in the poem's cause"
be unwelcome with a line?

Might you have liked a stone
from a De Beers Consolidated Mine?
or badger-neat saber-thronged thistle
of Palestine—the leaves alone

down'd underneath,
worth a touch? or that mimosa-leafed vine
called an "Alexander's armillary
sphere" fanning out in a wreath?

Or did the ark
preserve paradise-birds with jet-black plumes,
whose descendants might serve as presents?
But questioning is the mark

of a pest! Why think
only of animals in connection
with the ark or the wine Noah drank?
but that the ark did not sink. (*NCP*, 225)

Note: Line 2: "some interested law . ." From a poem to M. Moore by Marguerite Harris. (*NCP*, 332)

Moore asks Valentine if he might have liked a series of exotic presents. As in "Saint Nicholas," most of these would be unfamiliar to general readers (a neat and prickly thistle from Palestine, a spherical vine associated with Alexander the Great, a paradise bird from the Garden of Eden) and not things they'd want to capture or touch in person, though they might enjoy their description in the poem. Even the recognizable first gift—a diamond—is presented in alienating terms (as "a stone / from a De Beers Consolidated Mine"), framed to remind us more of the social injustice and the commodification of emotion associated with its production than of the love or beauty that might make it seem desirable. All of the gifts, as Cristanne Miller has noted, are associated with "colonialization, commodification [or] militarism."[23] The poem presents objects readers may admire but don't want, in preparation for the closing swerve to the biblical story of Noah, reminding them perhaps of the sustaining gift of life (given by God in the biblical narrative), both at the time of the flood to those on the ark and since then. This close may also call to mind Saint Valentine's status as a religious martyr, brought to ecstasies not through human mating rituals but through love of the Christian god, whom he is happy to die to join. Valentine's is also a love story, linked to the context in which Moore, also a lifelong celibate and a devoted believer though not a martyr, writes a religious poem for a holiday focused on sexuality—and (implicitly) marriage and procreation (which are also linked to Noah; per the story, he and his unnamed wife, like Adam and Eve, are the common ancestors of all humans).

Like Moore's other holiday poems, "For February 14th" serves as a gift to readers, but her note situates it also as a response to a specific earlier gift—a poem sent as an "overture" (as the initial title had it) from an admirer named Marguerite Harris (1901–1978). Moore's note suggests that the phrase in quotation marks embedded near the start—"would 'some interested law / impelled to plod in the poem's cause' / be unwelcome with a line?"—is borrowed from Harris. This odd characterization of the speaker as an embodied "law" forced into poetry suggests an unusual authority operating within an economic circuit of "interest"-bearing gift exchange (in all three senses of the word—intellectual, romantic, and economic). The gift of Harris's poem spawns Moore's, impelled perhaps by the "law" of reciprocity. "For February 14th" joins the set of Moore's poems written about, and in response to, gifts from friends, this one particularly intended for publication in the *New Yorker*. These poems that are also gifts simultaneously continue that circuit of giving among friends; publicly document Moore's lively network of intimate, loving friendships; and reach out to her audience of readers, who respond positively to the evidence of Moore's personal friendships that the poems document and who pay back Moore's interesting, idiosyncratic poetic gift and its multiple reveals and veils with the gift of their (ongoing, accruing) "interest." At the same time that it responds to the initial giver, the poem creates a relationship with Moore's readers around consideration of how love and gifts work and how they might work otherwise.

While Harris's poem is referenced in the note, the "quotation" that note appears to document seems to be Moore's own construction—only the word "plod" survives from Harris's poem "The Risk," which was enclosed with her letter to Moore of January 18, 1958.[24] Apparently Harris's gift (and the will to community it bespeaks) spurs Moore's new poem about gifts—more than Harris's words themselves. Harris's poem suggests that it may have been offered in apology for boldly coming up to Moore at a poetry event while tipsy, and it specifically asks Moore's forgiveness and love (both Harris's intrusion and the poem about it were efforts to connect).[25] Later collected in a volume called *The Risk of the Vine* (1965), "The Risk," dedicated "For Marianne Moore," claims a value in intoxication, because it spurs talk that risks offense but jars doors open:

> The risk of the vine . . .
> Is holy, not folly, and all
>
> All, plies and plods
> To ineluctable good.[26]

Moore, not a big drinker, extrapolates from Harris's topic to Noah (subject of another Bible tale about alcohol that many in her audience would know), and her poem takes off in directions beyond Harris's, but still linked to both the gift poem and its topic.

As critic Elizabeth Wilson has noted, Moore's reference in the poem to the story of Noah's drinking may, via the sexuality inherent in the Valentine theme, invoke the events that follow it in Genesis 9, including his nakedness and its reminder of his "animal" passion, as well as Ham's sexual shame for his father, and Noah's anger at Ham's "disrespectful" looking. A dense allusion! In Br'er Rabbit mode, Moore's request that we not think of animals and Noah's drunkenness has the opposite effect.[27]

The oblique reference to Noah's nakedness serves as yet another "reveal and veil [of a] peacock tail" that in context, Wilson keenly argues, suggests Moore's reflection upon her own history of choices around sexuality as well.[28] Wilson interprets the poem's closing affirmation of Noah's skilled construction of the ark (which stayed afloat) as an endorsement of Moore's own choice to devote herself to skillful poetic construction, in honor of God and in place of romance. I submit that insofar as they succeed in engaging committed readers (including but not limited to Moore's friends) in the process of constructing new meanings *with* the poet, the poems themselves constitute a place of libidinized literary connection, animated across time and space by shared interest. Though middlebrow readers may be drawn into the poem by Moore's celebrity and the recognizable Valentine's theme, thinking they'll find familiar narratives—perhaps kitschy commentaries on the heterosexual romance plot—they quickly learn otherwise. Along with its challenging storyline, "For February 14th" utilizes readers' fan-knowledge of Moore's personal history as an anomalous spinster-performer to prompt them to risk further extrapolations about and engagement with alternative plots and alternative-ness per se.

As Katharine White requested, Moore's second Valentine poem mimics many elements of the first.

SAINT VALENTINE,

permitted to assist you, let me see . . .
  If those remembered by you
are to think of you and not me,
  it seems to me that the memento
  or compliment you bestow
should have a name beginning with "V,"

such as Vera, El Greco's only
  daughter (though it has never been
proved that he had one), her starchy
  veil, inside chiffon; the stone in her
  ring, like her eyes; one hand on
her snow-leopard wrap, the fur widely

dotted with black. It could be a vignette—
  a replica, framed oval—
bordered by a vine or vinelet.

Or give a mere flower, said to mean the
love of truth or truth of
love—in other words, a violet.

Verse—unabashedly bold—is appropriate;
and always it should be as neat
as the most careful writer's "8."
Any valentine that is *written*
is as the *vendange* to the vine.
Might verse not best confuse itself with fate? (*NCP*, 258)

This poem's title wryly repeats (down to the comma) the first line of "For February 14th," and its own first line situates itself as a direct sequel by also entering into Valentine's realm, in order to assist him with gifts. This time instead of gifts to Valentine, Moore imagines things to give to others on his behalf for Valentine's Day (the recipients go unnamed), assuming those things should all begin with V (*literal* gifts) to mark them as gifts reflective of him, even though she is doing the (imaginary) shopping. Moore explores a *vignette* (a framed image) and a *violet* as options, then settles on *verse*, again making the poem itself the gift it seeks to identify.

But before suggesting these three, Moore suggests a rather spectral gift of ambiguous physical status, sidestepping through ekphrasis into an exploration of the relation of art and truth, as they connect with the poem's implicit Valentine's Day focus on love. Invoking an El Greco painting believed by some to portray Jeronima de las Cuevas, his companion and the mother of his son (Figure 21), Moore cites (without attribution) an issue of the *Illustrated London News* that included both that image and an explanation that it was "long known as 'The Artist's Daughter,' although it has never been fully established that he had one."[29]

Though the article assigns her no name, Moore calls her (imaginatively) Vera (*truth*), immediately tainting everything that follows as allegory, and as at least partially untrue. Vera, described as wearing both a veil and a fur (not an ermine but a spotted "snow leopard"), suggests hidden truths and another Moore-ish self-revelation,[30] inviting readers to investigate. Here again, Moore both acknowledges the complexity of love (invoking its filial, godly, romantic, and intellectual forms through the poem's references to the daughter, the Saint, the love holiday, and verse's implied dialogue with its audience) and affirms her own choice of a life devoted to "verse"—her "fate"—rather than to standard romance.

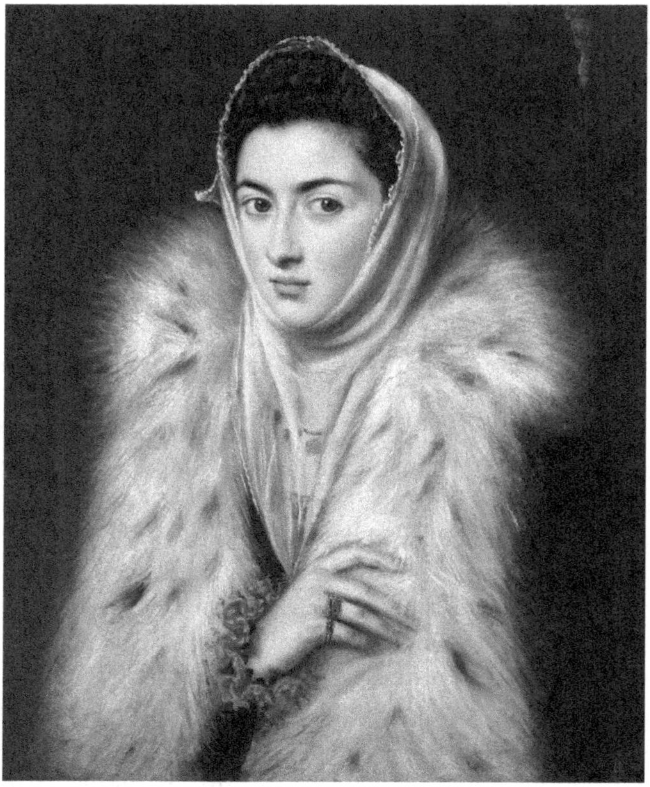

Figure 21. El Greco, *Lady in a Fur Wrap* (1577–79). Pollok House, Glasgow. © CSG CIC Glasgow Museums and Libraries Collection. Reprinted by permission.

But she also hints that a woman defined (chastely) as a daughter (a fictional character created, perhaps ironically, by the *Illustrated London News*, whom Moore, herself well known as a daughter and a spinster, then hijacks into her poem) might also have lived other lives—perhaps as a lover, we may infer since this is a Valentine's Day poem, or in many other roles.

Whether or not Moore knew Jeronima's name, her arch parenthesis and vivid description certainly provide reasons to doubt that this astounding image of a woman in spotted furs was a portrait of the artist's daughter. The byplay jars the door to erotic awareness that the poem's title opens, even as Moore's failure to speak directly of romance may appear to shut it. Instead the hijacked image becomes a triangulated "self-portrait," in the Mannerist mode that Moore particularly favored in her photographic portraits[31] (the portrait's unknown subject now includes Moore in its realm of potential reference ["Vera" too wears a pinky ring]).

"Saint Valentine," also continues Moore's private circuit of personal relationship, through another allusion to Harris's gift of the "Risk of the Vine" in the last two stanzas' discussion of *vine* and *vendange*. And though the speaker claims to want to turn readers' attention away from "me" and toward Valentine with all the V words, the idiosyncrasy of the enterprise only reinforces the sense of Moore's presence, contradicting the claim to seek to honor Valentine, or him alone.[32] "Saint Valentine," invites the reader to engage with Moore around the poem's condensed gift: of a violet-encircled vignette of Vera rendered in verse, the layered complexity of which can only signify the endlessly supplemental "Moore."

In both Valentine poems Moore takes the occasion created by the confluence of her *New Yorker* contract with the ongoing demand for occasional poems by her, qua celebrity, as well as with the special interest that her celebrity had created in her status as spinster, both in spite of and because of its perceived anomaly. She reveals and veils herself yet again, a flickering and splendid apparition within this ekphrasis, as in them all. These two poems—along with "Rosemary" and "Saint Nicholas," the other palimpsestic holiday gift poems—explore the connections among erotic, friendly, familial, heavenly, and intellectual love, and all four advocate for exchanges of affection and of ideas, within communities created through the poems. As John Emil Vincent notes, the revealing and veiled dynamic around multiple meanings in Moore's texts creates a "stubborn and unsettling oscillation [that] is itself erotic."[33] Moore's multivalent, libidinized texts work to bind readers in community—an enterprise and effect she understands to be based in love.

Saturday Evening Post editor Thomas Congdon doubtless had this aspect of Moore's work in mind when he invited her to submit a poem for a special issue devoted to "Love in America." By 1966 Moore had a reputation for love poetry, for patriotism, and for thematic occasional work, so her being invited to opine on love for this end-of-year issue would not be surprising to the *Post* audience, though they would expect something divergent. The magazine collected work from six poets: "five leading American poets [who] address[ed] the human heart" in a section called "Voices of Love," and the "celebrated" celibate poet Marianne Moore, whose submission appeared as part of the concluding editorial and claimed a wider, more political, reference.[34] Where the other poets lauded standard romance in poems with titles like "Leaving the Motel" and "New Love," Moore, the only female poet included and one who publicly and consistently performed the rejection of standard romance, took her title from the special issue, adding a question mark.[35] Blending Passion and Patriotism, the poem serves as a reply to the title's implied questions: "What Is Love in America Like?" and "Is There Love in America?"

Love in America?

Whatever it is, it's a passion—
a benign dementia that should be
engulfing America, fed in a way
    the opposite of the way
in which the Minotaur was fed.
It's a Midas of tenderness;
    from the heart;
nothing else. From one with ability
to bear being misunderstood—
    take the blame, with "nobility
    that is action," identifying itself with
    pioneer unperfunctoriness

    without brazenness or
    bigness of overgrown
    undergrown shallowness.

Whatever the deed, let it be without
    affectation.

Yes, yes, yes, *yes*. (*Saturday Evening Post*)[36]

Notes: Line 5: The Minotaur demanded a virgin to devour once a year.
Line 6: Midas, who had the golden touch, was inconvenienced when eating or picking things up.
Lines 10–11: Unamuno said that what we need as a cure for unruly youth is "nobility that is action."
Lines 13–15: *without brazenness or bigness* . . . Winston Churchill: "Modesty becomes a man." (*NCP*, 338)

Though it appeared at New Year's and doesn't discuss presents, "Love in America?" follows in the pattern of the four holiday gift poems, as a direct treatment of love at holiday time, for a wide audience. This poem begins by rejecting the assumption that there is a common and limited definition of love; the *Saturday Evening Post* version refers to love inclusively in line 1 as "Whatever it is" and then in line 16 as "Whatever the deed"—pointedly opening this affirmative poem to lovers of all kinds and orientations (in the *Complete Poems* version the phrase in line 16 is altered to repress the initial forthrightness, repeating the phrase from line 1). Moore does, however, characterize love in America as passionate, benign, and demented (perhaps in the sense of love crazy). Though the version she initially submitted to the *Post* had four additional stanzas at the start (focused on art), the published version cuts those[37] and begins with a series of negative definitions of love, in tension with the four *Yeses* in the closing stanza.

While this poem does not mention gifts directly, gifts of love are implied in the "opposite" of virgin sacrifice to the Minotaur. Love's value, the poem asserts, lies in being tendered from the heart and spread widely, not as (Midas's) gold or (the Minotaur's) power but as passion. Though love may not yet actually be engulfing America, the poem declares that it should be—another instance of Moore's advocacy for community connection and noble action, including presumably the love for one's fellow humans that Moore advocates in her anti-racist and pro-refugee poems, and love for friends, family, romantic partners, and fellow citizens. The qualities associated with love in lines 10–15 are virtues—at once civic and interpersonal: responsibility, noble action, directness, and modesty; and all the situations that the poem references with notes involve political structures. The initial two notes reference problematic monarchies (of Minos and Midas), while the remaining two imagine right rule, the first through a challenger to political extremism in Spain (Unamuno) and the second through a British defender of Democracy (Churchill).

Moore again figures herself in the center of this politics of love, as "one with ability / to bear being misunderstood"—a (virgin) speaker who risks misunderstanding (a form of *self*-sacrifice) in order to connect. Like a poem, the risky business of love often begins with a conversation through which one hopes to interest the other, without a guarantee of response. But taking the risk of showing yourself (the risk of the poem, to adapt Harris) is essential to a good outcome, in romance, friendship, or community, and Moore takes that risk over and over in her late work, where she refuses to limit herself to the impersonal or unemotional. The love poems of this period are interactive performance pieces, interesting readers through Moore's celebrity and through their mapping of her processes of association and emotional circuits, which stage new meetings of minds and hearts, across brow levels, with each poetic encounter.

Toward this poem's close, Moore reiterates her mandate of outreach to the people without off-putting elitism, fulfilled here both in the middlebrow context of the *Saturday Evening Post* and in the poem's message: punningly, instead of the snobbish fakery of "affectation," she endorses building national community across all sectors, through democratic affection. The fourfold "Yes!" at the poem's close exuberantly affirms that, indeed, there is love in America, and plenty.[38] Given the political lens that I've suggested the poem asks us to view it through, the three roman Yeses, followed by the summary italic *Yes*, can read as a vote count—all three ballots are cast in the affirmative, adding up to the final announcement of the result: *Yes*! Whatever Love is, whatever the deed involved, Moore endorses its rule, and the poem affirms its victory as the law of the land.

Is the Personal Fatal?

> I specialize in giraffes; is the paddock ever over-crowded?
>
> —Moore to W. R. Benét, July 28, 1933[39]

Moore's expanded expression of personal feelings in her late poems and her celebritized performance of a public persona directly linked to that poetry both built on propensities she had evolved over decades. Beginning in the 1950s, these propensities overlapped with the emergence of a new generation of poets, including Allen Ginsberg, Robert Lowell, Sylvia Plath, and Anne Sexton. Their "confessional" school of poetry developed in direct reaction against the modernist cult of "impersonality" and as a means of offering readers at least the impression of intimate access to the poet, along lines similar to the "inside stories" about celebrities' lives that filled fan magazines of the day. Beginning with Ginsberg's "Howl" in 1955, confessional poets, most of whom had been analyzed, utilized the psychoanalytic method of unfettered talk about one's thoughts and feelings (fairly new to the United States). This work has deeply influenced poetry since then, opening up the possibility of moments of detailed personal "sharing" in every mode. At the same time, it has often been looked down upon by critics as an outpouring of unedited data from the world of experience ("mere confessionalism" and too "real").

The confessional poets quickly became celebrities themselves and served their moment by articulating the anxieties both personal and communal of their readers and fans. Simultaneously, they explored the next phase of the same questions about the gendering of authority that Moore had engaged with early on and that she continued to explore in new ways as her career progressed. Where the "impersonal" modernist paradigm had been gendered "masculine," both male and female confessionals stressed their "feminine" side, admitting to having emotional needs and a body with weaknesses.[40] Much confessional work involved a disclosure of something scandalous—not just gossip-rag misbehavior but often the internal struggles explored on the psychiatrist's couch, including murderous, suicidal, or incestuous wishes. Underlying those scandals defined through action or desire were framework social scandals—about identity, about who is worthy to speak, and about who and what can be heard. The basic scandal to which Plath and Sexton confess is that they are women, in a world where femininity involves something shameful per se, and where women's speech appears particularly dubious. Their struggles toward authority built directly on Moore's, which was also inherently scandalous in its day, though that scandal was defanged by Moore's rejection of the realm of the standard feminine. The confessionals embrace that realm, speaking in detail about the physical powers and experience of their bodies, as well as their psychic struggles, in language much more straightforward than Moore's. Where Eliot and the early Moore had rejected "personal" (feminine) speech, the confessionals turned bold speech about the forbidden feminine realm into an authority claim, challenging the terms of its censure. Women's confessional poetry represented a scandalous activity in itself, and it opened that to scrutiny. Male poets' confession to personal weaknesses, associated by definition with femininity, in itself constituted a related scandal for them.

As an elder poet called on to serve the younger generation as an advisor, a contest judge, and a recommender, Moore made it clear to both Ginsberg and Plath that while she admired their skills, she disliked their material. Responding to the manuscript of Ginsberg's *Empty Mirror*, Moore complained (as she had about Elizabeth Bishop's naming of a water closet in "Roosters" in 1941): "In the opening piece . . . you say, 'I wandered off in search of a toilet.' And I go with you, remember. Do

I have to?" About his "Archetype Poem," which begins "Joe Blow has decided / he will no longer / be a fairy," and then goes on to portray him forcing himself to sleep with a woman, Moore wondered, "Are you for this? Is there any 'universal principle' to be deduced?"[41] Her concern was not that the material was shocking but whether there was anything uplifting to take away from the struggles the poem portrayed.

Ginsberg took Moore's critique in stride, but her censure upset Plath, whose work Moore had judged the co-winner of a college contest in 1955 and who hoped Moore would serve her as a mentor and patron. As Vivian Pollak has documented in her exploration of their interactions, when Moore advised Plath in 1958 to make her poems less "grisly" and "unrelenting"[42] (including "Mussel Hunter at Rock Harbor," a poem in which Plath had imitated Moore's syllabics and the argument of her poem "A Grave"), Plath took it hard. In 1961, though she began by noting that "I do like to like a book, especially anything by Sylvia Plath," Moore still counseled the Guggenheim Foundation to deny Plath an award because her application indicated that she planned to write from the experience of motherhood. Moore felt she shouldn't be funded to have children (or to write about that), though she then went on to recommend that Plath's husband, Ted Hughes, who had also just had the same children, be funded in Plath's stead.[43] When Plath learned of Moore's views of her work from her agent in 1962, she documented her fury in a poem.[44] While Moore was rejecting her own "impersonal" past in the postwar period and moving toward a more "feminine" expression of personal feelings, she still could not see the value in Plath's very different, next-generation approach to material and voice. Despite that failure, in her late phase Moore did engage the confessional mode directly, sometimes espousing confessional tendencies (as in her "Public Garden" claim that "Art . . . is always actually personal") and at other times employing her own forms of "scandalous" confession, to explore and activate that aspect of celebrity culture as a point of interaction with ordinary folk. Where Plath's scandals sprang from her outright treatment of female physical and psychological experience, Moore's scandals (of a different order) arose when she as a modernist spoke about the personal or sentimental at all and (as we'll see in Chapter 5) from her continued presence on the world stage as an elderly woman.

She directly addresses the question of the place of emotion and personal reference in poetry in "To a Giraffe" (1963), a late poem that augments its argument with personal inflections—some overt, some submerged. The poem thoughtfully and humorously explores the issue of gendered authority through specific engagement with her authoritative friend T. S. Eliot, chief among the "impersonal" poets—though his own claim to keeping his work free of personal reference was dubious.[45] Eliot did acknowledge that poets' emotional experience formed a necessary background to the power of their work, though he discouraged its direct representation. In "To a Giraffe" Moore teasingly explores the operation of personal emotion in the poetic environment of the 1960s in which she composed it. Though it differs from her more explicitly love-focused poems discussed above, this too is a species of love poem.

To a Giraffe

If it is unpermissible, in fact fatal
to be personal and undesirable

to be literal—detrimental as well
if the eye is not innocent—does it mean that

one can live only on top leaves that are small
reachable only by a beast that is tall?—

of which the giraffe is the best example—
the unconversational animal.

When plagued by the psychological
a creature can be unbearable

that could have been irresistible;
or to be exact exceptional

since less conversational
than some emotionally-tied-in-knots animal.

After all
consolations of the metaphysical
can be profound. In Homer, existence

is flawed; transcendence, conditional;
the journey from sin to redemption, perpetual. (*NCP*, 239)

Note: Ennis Rees summarizes the *Odyssey*, I feel, when he finds expressed in it, the conditional nature of existence, the consolations of the metaphysical: the journey from sin to redemption. (*NCP*, 334)

Written over 1961–62 and published in 1963, "To a Giraffe" was commissioned by Steuben Glass, which asked thirty-one poets selected by the Poetry Society of America (including W. H. Auden, Louise Bogan, and William Carlos Williams) to write poems on topics of their choice. Steuben artists and glass designers then made glass statues to "capture the theme or spirit of each poem in crystal"[46] (ekphrasis in reverse), to be photographed and included as side-by-side illustrations.[47] From the start Moore's poem was to have a "real," three-dimensional aspect augmenting the text on the page, as well as a broad, nonliterary audience.

Giraffes had long been among Moore's favorite animals, both in themselves and as part of her menagerie of animal names for friends and family members.[48] She submitted a draft of the poem to Steuben Glass in June 1961. In the coming months she revised substantially and resubmitted, characterizing the earlier version as too informal.[49] Over the same period, Moore was corresponding about the poem with Eliot, who was also her U.K. editor, and who wanted to include it in Moore's next Faber and Faber collection. Although their letters don't indicate that Eliot understood the poem to be directed to him, Moore's archive suggests that it was, as Ruth Carrington has documented.[50] The poem expresses feelings around friendship, love, and collaboration, while simultaneously exploring the role of personal feelings and experience in poetry, the complexities of gendered age and sexual fluidity, and the dynamics of a poem's relation with its audience.

If, as the first line states, being personal is fatal, then there's good reason to refrain—but the claim also raises questions about why that would be so, and the initial "if" makes it at least arguable. The phrase "*If* it is unpermissible" posits that possibility without affirming it—and in what follows Moore debates the point. The source of the view on the fatal aspect of the personal in poetry is close at hand in this poem addressed to a giraffe, since Moore's correspondence with Eliot and with his Faber and Faber colleague Frank Vigor Morley documents that the principal giraffe in Moore's personal menagerie was Eliot. Morley (1899–1985), a Rhodes scholar and brother of American novelist Christopher Morley, had first come to know Moore in 1934 when he visited her about the British publication of her *Selected Poems*, and the two continued to correspond.

In 1946, when Morley wrote to inform Moore that Eliot was in the States and hoped to see her, he characterized Eliot's New York digs as

"Our giraffe house at 131 East 66th Street"—meaning, as Morley's relatives confirm, the Morley family duplex, which had a two-story living room, the balcony of which reminded his six-year-old daughter Peregrine of the raised manger in the Central Park Zoo's giraffe house.[51] Morley's animated phrase led Moore to rhapsodize in her reply, using the Arabic and Latin words for male and female giraffe and the Latin species name to designate Morley, his wife and kids, and their guest: "What is there in New York so enticing as the giraffe house and its remarkable giraffes, Zaraf F. Vigor, Zarafa Christina (now and then spelled Regina), Camelopardus Oliver, Camelopardia Susanna, and their 'remarkable visitor in the shape of' Zaraf San Tomás?"[52] Five months later in November, Moore extended the joke into her correspondence with Eliot. After an initial exchange in which they both referred to Moore as a "gosling,"[53] Moore told Eliot that Morley had classified him as a Giraffe—though actually Moore had made that connection. Eliot continued the animal game in his response: "But it was very mischievous of [Morley] to classify me under Giraffes, unless anybody is a Giraffe who has dwelt in the Giraffe House: my proper classification is under Elephants." Moore replies, "An elephant, surely. (Tremendously Sage Elephant in any scientific classification)," capitalizing the initials T S E.[54] Although their correspondence continued for some years without reference to giraffes, the discussion had increased their level of intimacy, and during this period they moved from Miss Moore and Mr. Eliot to first-name friends.

Friendship between these two seems natural, particularly since they had a great deal of shared and parallel history, such that they practically constitute a twin study on the effects of gender difference on career. The two were born within a few miles and a few months of one another: she in the St. Louis suburb of Kirkwood in November 1887, and he in St. Louis proper in September 1888. Both were the grandchildren of prominent local ministers (hers Presbyterian, his Unitarian), and for high school Moore's mother had attended the academically rigorous Mary Institute, founded by Eliot's grandfather. Though Moore's family moved away in 1894 when she was six, the two poets connected in the 1910s and 1920s, particularly through Scofield Thayer's *Dial*, which awarded Eliot the Dial Prize for *The Waste Land* in 1922 and in 1924 gave it to Moore for *Observations*. (Thayer was Eliot's friend at Harvard and introduced him to his first wife; he was also Moore's sponsor and employer and perhaps at one point her suitor.)[55] Poetically, the two shared a habit of disjunction as well as a tendency to quotation; Ezra Pound's notes on *The Waste Land* manuscript suggest that Eliot adopted this method from Moore.[56] Moore reviewed Eliot's *Prufrock and Other Observations* (*Poetry*, 1918), praising his lack of sentimentality,[57] and *The Sacred Wood* (*The Dial*, 1921); Eliot reviewed Moore's work in the *Others Anthology* (*Egoist*, 1918) and her *Poems* and "Marriage" together (*The Dial*, 1923). All these reviews were very positive.

Both were also active editors, Moore at the *Dial* and Eliot at the *Egoist* and the *Criterion* magazines as well as at Faber and Faber, and they solicited reviews and poems from one another. In 1921 Eliot asked to publish a volume of Moore's work in the U.K., just three months before H. D. and Bryher did so without Moore's knowledge.[58] In 1935, Eliot actively intervened in Moore's career when he edited and introduced her *Selected Poems*, bringing the weight of his by then firmly established poetic authority to bear in support of her work's "genuineness." But though the two poets were significantly connected, they also maintained a formality in their relation until the 1940s. It wasn't the giraffe talk alone that brought them closer: Eliot visited Moore and her mother in Brooklyn in 1946 after Morley's letter,[59] and thereafter they continued to exchange visits and professional and personal correspondence. After a dinner in New York in May 1956, Eliot sent Moore a variety of valentine—a hand-drawn heart with an arrow through it, addressed to Moore from a "grateful anonymous admirer."[60] But their connection suffered a blow in January 1957, when Eliot eloped with his thirty-year-old secretary, Valerie Fletcher. Moore learned of the marriage through the news and didn't write to Eliot for six months. When she did, she explained she hadn't wanted to intrude with felicitations; he replied that no friends had known in advance.[61] They then continued as friends, visiting as a trio and corresponding regularly. This explanation does not entirely fit with the account of Moore's housekeeper Gladys Berry, who considered that "Marianne Moore really loved T. S. Eliot" and that "she felt quite bad about" his marriage.[62] Secondhand accounts of emotional display may radically distort cause, but it seems reasonable that Moore had an emotional investment in Eliot, her longtime friend and advocate, a fellow Missourian, and one of the few people by whom she felt understood, both poetically and personally.[63]

"To a Giraffe" augments the possibility that Eliot is the addressee by taking on material linked to him. Eliot was the source of the proposition under consideration, that "it is unpermissible, in fact fatal / to be personal and undesirable / to be literal." Moore appears to acquiesce here to this doctrine (around a variation of which she had shaped her early career) at the same time that she contradicts it in the present, not least by basing her poem in their (personal) relationship.[64] Her poem clearly debates two positions regarding speech and poetry: she portrays the giraffe as an "unconversational animal"—and opposes it to gabbier creatures who also delve into emotions and psychologize. In 1963, there's plenty of room to read these others as confessional poets, who shared details about their lives and passions and whose working doctrine counters Eliot's directly.[65] But though Moore sympathizes with the unemotional, non-confessional poet, contrasting him to the "unbearable" psychological poet, she also questions the understanding that all good poets must match this description. "If it is unpermissible . . . to be personal," the poem asks, "does it mean that // one can live only on top leaves that are small / reachable only by a beast that is tall?" The question equates impersonal-ism with top-leaf eating and implies a negative answer (there are other ways of sustaining oneself as a poet). Yet the poem closes with a refusal to choose either position; there is no one right way ("existence / is flawed; transcendence, conditional"). While some poets just can't reach those high leaves that the giraffe likes, we can infer that they find leaves at other levels, appropriate to non-giraffes, who may also be good poets. Does Moore include herself among the non-giraffes? The poem's two-sided sympathies open that possibility, even *without* the evidence of her personal connection that contradicts the argument against "personal" poetry. Readers of the day could have recognized Eliot in the impersonal giraffe, and the poem as published gives readers permission—urges them even—to look for the personal in Moore's work, as I have here.

Earlier drafts of the poem, which speak much more directly and emotionally, also reflect its personal dimension.[66] Moore submitted the following text to Steuben Glass in June 1961 and immediately thereafter to Eliot for consideration for inclusion in *The Arctic Ox*:

To a Giraffe [June 1961 draft]

uncatchable by me at all
events—who am unsucculent and small—

they say it is not permissible
to be personal; or desirable

to be literal. Animal,
creatures can't help being personal.

"Let me feel thy fair large ears." Recall
Titania and Bottom? Little

masterpiece, it can be fatal
if the eye is not innocent. Regal

beast, if you are favorable to a sequel—
thinking of some people—

"consolations of the metaphorical" [*sic*]
can be profound. Homer, for example:

"existence is conditional;
and the road from sin to redemption, perpetual."*
* Ennis Rees

This draft shortens the version Moore had been working with in May, which included an additional four couplets:

When plagued by the psychological
a creature becomes objectionable

that could be irresistible;
or speaking exactly, exceptional—

whereas if mute and more humble—
or if not mute, less conversational,

it could be really lovable;
if I daren't say giraffecal.

In these earlier drafts, the poem opens with a first-person speaker (the "me" in the first line) who describes herself as a leaf unattractive to giraffes because she is "unsucculent and small," in contrast to the "treetop leaves" (also small, but juicy) in the published version that do catch its interest. Moore, who described her elderly self in 1969 as "all bone . . . just solid pure bone," thus sets up a contrast between herself and more "succulent" types.[67] On the other hand, "succulent" pretty perfectly describes the then thirty-five-year-old Valerie Eliot. In context, Figure 22 demonstrates that age means differently for women and men, and it suggests the humorous eye with which Moore, recognizing this difference, viewed the world.

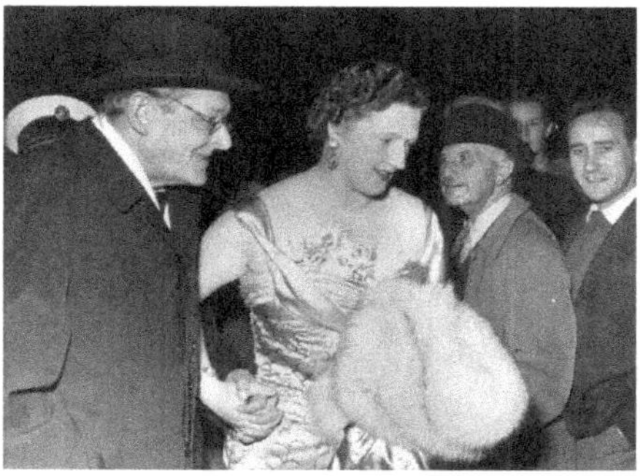

Figure 22. T. S. Eliot and Valerie Eliot, London, 1958. Photographer: *Evening Standard* via Getty Images. Reprinted by permission.

Though no "confessional" poem can be read as a direct personal statement, this draft plays wittily with personal reference in the confessional vein.

The second stanza of this earlier draft moves from a first-person account to third-person rule-giving. "They say it is not permissible" in line 3 distances the speaker from the claim more clearly than the "If it is not permissible" of the published version, by distinguishing "them" from the "me" of line 1. And in being emphatically personal, the "me" of stanza 1 directly contradicts what "they say" in stanza 2. The third stanza furthers the speaker's distancing from "their" views by affirming that "animal, / creatures can't help being personal." Though this line may seem to distinguish people from beasts (if animals can't help it, perhaps people can), in Moore's poetry, where animals often stand in for aspects of the human, the distinction is not firm (and people are also animals). The line also recalls the claim in "In the Public Garden" that "Art . . . is always actually personal."

The fourth stanza jumps directly into the realm of animal-human interaction and equivalence, with the phrase "Let me feel thy fair large ears," set in quotation marks and followed by a direct attribution of the quote (another rarity for Moore). By asking if we "Recall Titania and Bottom?" Moore invites us to remember the source of the quote in the love scene between the queen of the faeries and a man-turned-ass in *A Midsummer Night's Dream*, apparently as an example of interspecies love.[68] The reference to the source text also asks us to recognize the change Moore has introduced: in the original, immured in their hallucinatory bower, the doting Titania invites Bottom, her new darling, to

> Come, sit thee down upon this flowery bed,
> While I thy amiable cheeks do coy,

> And stick musk-roses in thy sleek smooth head,
> And kiss thy fair large ears, my gentle joy. (Act IV, scene 1)

Moore substitutes the friendly "feel" for the more directly erotic "kiss," making her poem more discreet, but the elided kisses become part of the poem too via the reference, lingering in the background and expanding the frame to include romance—and comedy. Stanza 5 emphasizes the comedy, telling readers to take the analogy innocently (or risk a fatality—or just a very bad reading of the poem). Stanza 6 addresses the giraffe again ("Regal/beast") and invites him to repeat the Titania/Bottom affair in a sequel—a parallel that casts the poem's speaker as Titania. By drawing a parallel between the giraffe and Bottom, the poem further suggests that the beloved beast is actually a person transformed—through a magic spell or, more mundanely, through metaphor.[69]

By choosing to delete the final four lines of the May draft (the preceding four were also cut in May but made their way into the final poem), with their humorously self-contradictory last line ("If I daren't say giraffecal"), Moore may seem to enact the very failure to dare that she undermines when she initially "says," or writes, the word *giraffecal* (or the riskier words, "really lovable," which are also deleted).[70] Yet in so doing, she also affirms the humble and less conversational (but not mute) role that the poem as a whole seems to endorse. In this way, "To a Giraffe" shares concerns with "Silence," the poem written forty years earlier that opines on how best to express "the deepest feelings"; and as in that poem, this poem's structure participates in its argument. "Silence" makes the case for "not . . . silence, but restraint" by framing itself almost entirely as a quotation, suggesting that its poet has been silent (though the notes then belie that suggestion). "To a Giraffe," on the other hand, represents feelings fairly overtly in the early versions—with some personal basis emphasized—but then pares that away over sequent drafts in a context of reflection on the relative virtues of direct statement and restraint—a self-narrating exercise in active repression of the personal, documented across the drafts.

This poem's drafts participate in building the poem's argument, over time and versions—in ways related to the time lapse in the versions of "A Face" (discussed in the Appendix). "To a Giraffe" is unusual in its initially fairly direct treatment of an aspect of Moore's own emotional life (her bemused affection for her friend Eliot, some years after he ran off with Miss Fletcher)[71] as the case study for this multilayered reflection on what Moore can say in a poem in a post-Modern world (hers was, after all, a very special position in this regard—as a poet with a history and as an elderly, celibate, cross-dressing celebrity considering her options). Eliot seems not to have engaged with these dynamics, other than to endorse the poem. At one point, Moore submitted a new draft of the "Giraffe" to him saying, rather fiercely, "If you don't like it, please say and we can kill it."[72] Although they didn't put an end to it, she did bury its original lively suggestiveness in layers of abstraction.

But do the buried drafts matter to the final poem? If the draft expresses love and emotion, does the cutting of the more overt phrases mean the final poem does not? Eliot complained in a letter about an early draft of "Little Gidding" that "the defect of the whole poem, I feel, is the lack of some acute personal reminiscence (never to be explicated of course, but to give power from well below the surface) and I can perhaps supply this in Part II."[73] Moore's poem also draws on the power not just of personal reminiscence of emotions past but of emotions near to hand—including affection and anxiety, as well as humor. It draws too on her personal history of interaction with rules, both poetic and social, about what emotions may and may not, should or should not, be expressed and by whom, and that resonates in the final text. As a group, the series of drafts performs a poetic ritual, of creating through repression or condensing of affect, and it narrates the process across the versions. Though the final version may be read to conclude on the side of restraint, the poem's history and structure, part of a dialogue with a personal friend on multiple levels, also together make the opposite case: in favor of at least some expression of personal and literal material. Moore creates a Blakean paradox where "contrarieties [are] equally true,"[74] and she argues both sides. Given their demonstrative relation to the poem's argument, these unpublished drafts could well be considered part of an accretive version of the final poem—a palimpsestic text in which all the layers signify, as steps in the poetry-writing process that is the poem's topic.

The poem activates emotional dynamics as well when its personal energy engages its audience, inviting all its readers (including but not limited to Eliot) to be personal, to operate in relationship, making meaning together, in spite of all the prohibitions. This is a poem about breaking rules—yet another fortunate fall. Even the word Moore employs to mark the prohibition—"unpermissible"—breaks the rules of standard usage (rather than "impermissible" or the "not permissible" employed in an early draft).[75] Finally the poem engages all its readers in a literary version of a personal relationship, with a poet whose questions about emotion, poetry, and authority echo across decades.

So, is the personal fatal? While in 1918 Moore may have felt it would have been for her, by 1963 the situation had changed for women writers. Insofar as her evolving role as a leading female modernist had contributed to the expanded acceptance of authoritative female poets of the 1950s, Moore had herself played a role in effecting that change, so that in her later phase she could participate, if restrainedly, in the confessional sequel to her own early battles over gendered authority. In her latter days, Moore could embrace the sentimentality that she had earlier actively repressed, recognizing that proud claims to a lack of sentimentality are always bogus, since, "unwarily," they demonstrate strong sentiment about being "unsentimental."[76] Like her poems spurred by gifts from Louise Crane, Hildegarde Watson, Barbara Church, and Marguerite Harris and by conversations with Philip Rahv and Stuart Davis, Moore's poem to Eliot circulates within a witty community of friends and colleagues, for whom the personal and sentimental were not just not fatal but vital elements of the work.

Moore's love poems manage to be at once apparently innocent of and effectively engaged with and critical of the sexual and poetic politics of their day. Her critique evolves the one she offers in "Marriage," a poem that Hilton Kramer described as full of "sexual preening . . . mercilessly satirized" and "infused with an acute sexual tension. . . . in which the erotic is everywhere subsumed in a struggle for power and domination." Kramer bemoans Moore's late-phase transformation into a "cultural celebrity" whose late aesthetic he views as opposed to the "stringent and unyielding vision of her best writing." He notes the "withering and hilarious irony" of the early work, which "both freezes the blood and makes one laugh"—work he calls the "most astonishing" of Moore's distinguished generation "for its radical innovations in poetic discourse."[77] I argue here that Moore redeploys that same acute mind in the late work, in a new context, in less withering but also radically innovative ways, for wider audiences—this time embracing affect as a means of engaging millions and affirming the feminine realm of emotion while still modeling critique of the standardized, limiting emotional and sexual circuits allowed acknowledgment in her day. In our own day, the energy of the poems' explorations of democratic means of poetic engagement across a wide spectrum of readers remains to be tapped by new audiences, ready to recognize and embrace her challenges to received ideas then and now, yet another manifestation of the Moore-ish supplement.

5

"Still Leafing": Age, Activism, Immortality

> "No man may him hyde
> From Deth, holow eyed"
>
> —"'Sun!'" (1916, *Becoming*, 177)

Moore led a vigorous public life in her final years, full of performances and engagements that were covered enthusiastically by the media. The poems, the persona, and the events fed one another and her project of outreach and inclusion. But that energetic activity operated in tension with her advancing age, and the contrast provided yet another form of unexpectedness in her presentation in the late 1960s. The increasingly elderly Moore performed both her mortal frailty and her resistance to it for a wide audience of all ages, who were drawn to her by (among other things) the universal scandal of our shared impending end. Moore's example balanced that frailty with an ongoing vitality and a will to be part of the scene. Aging provided yet another point of democratic commonality and access, and Moore explored her responses to it from many directions in her late poems.

The eighteen poems of Moore's last individual volume, *Tell Me, Tell Me: Granite, Steel, and Other Topics* (1966), cover a variety of subjects, as the title indicates.[1] But while their overt themes differ, many of these and the nine additional poems Moore published after 1966 have in common an underlying and increasing concern with aging and legacy.[2] Many of these poems playfully experiment with the operations of time and its bridging of past and future, while others explore her responses to encroaching mortality and her poetry's origins and afterlife, in ways directly engaged with her friend Wallace Stevens's related concerns. Though individually fairly short, these poems function as a linked set of reflections. Their inward-facing dynamic was balanced by an expanded outreach, and at several points Moore put her late-phase popularity to work in the world as celebrity activism.[3] Her spirited performance of elderly feminine authority continued until late 1969 when strokes ended her writing and her public appearances. But in these last poems, while continuing her established patterns of self-flaunting, ekphrasis, and obliquity mixed with accessibility, she also continued to innovate, both structurally and topically, to engage with her poetic precursors, and to anticipate her successors, with remarkable wit and skill.

Tell Me, Tell Me

Signification through structure had always played an important part in Moore's poetry, as we've seen, and in *Tell Me, Tell Me* she extends that method of signifying to the book as a whole. Developing on the pattern Eliot had used in Moore's *Selected Poems* of putting her most recent work near the front, in this volume she sets all the poems in reverse order of their initial publication, as Benjamin Kahan has documented.[4] She opens with "Granite and Steel" (1966), moves backward chronologically across fifteen poems and four essays to the penultimate "Saint Valentine" (1960), and then hops across five decades to the final poem, "Sun," written in 1911 and first published in 1916. Moore draws attention to her retrospective approach by listing the initial publication date and venue of each poem in the notes (the only such treatment). This method echoes the eponymous poem's claim to being a "told-backward biography," and reverberates in the many poems of this period that reflect on history and legacy.

Moore's reversal of the book's chronology may be fruitfully read, as Kahan has done, as sign of an anachronistic queer or celibate sensibility that critiques mindlessly procreative, future-focused worldviews and teleology and prefers complex knots of signification to decoded, explicitly summarizable content. But though the poems feature celibates (like Beatrix Potter, Henry James, and Emily Dickinson) as well as sexually active gay people (like Hart Crane, Jean Cocteau, and, arguably, Walt Whitman) whose alternative sexual and social choices Moore affirms, they also, knottily, engage deeply with ideas about bridging the past and the future, from the point of view of an elderly poet aware of her own coming death and concerned with her poetry's future influence and place in the pantheon.[5]

The poem "Tell Me, Tell Me" describes a collaborative method of construction that parallels Moore's own.

Tell Me, Tell Me

      where might there be a refuge for me
      from egocentricity
and its propensity to bisect,
misstate, misunderstand,
      and obliterate continuity?   (*NCP*, 241, ll. 1–5)

The speaker invites advice, then finds the refuge she seeks via Potter's *Tailor of Gloucester*, also a story of collaboration—about mice who aid the tailor who released them from his cat's clutches, by stitching together the pieces of the waistcoat that he had cut previously but is now too ill to sew himself. In addition, they embroider it beautifully, and the final garment makes the tailor's fortune. Moore's collaborations extend beyond her dialogue with her readers (enjoined to "Tell Me") to the many writers past and future with whose work hers is also in dialogue, and with whom she refused from the beginning of her career to "obliterate continuity."[6] Likewise, many of the other poems in the book emphasize intertextual and historical connections. In featuring such dialogues with the writers of the past she also models her own work's future dialogues with poets to come.

Although the book begins with "Granite and Steel," the volume's final but earliest piece provides an important framework. "Sun," a poem about time and mortality written when Moore was twenty-four but already interested in immortality, begins by acknowledging that "Deth" is unavoidable for all (citing fifteenth-century poet John Skelton, also a figure for death via his name), but the speakers (Hope and Fear) then attempt to avoid "this inconvenient truth" anyway.[7]

Sun

Hope and Fear accost him
            "No man may him hyde
            From Deth holow-eyed";
      For us, this inconvenient truth does not suffice.
   You are not male nor female, but a plan
   deep-set within the heart of man.
Splendid with splendor hid you come, from your Arab abode,
a fiery topaz smothered in the hand of a great prince who rode

before you, Sun—whom you outran,
piercing his caravan.

O Sun, you shall stay
with us; holiday,
consuming wrath, be wound in a device
of Moorish gorgeousness, round glasses spun
to flame as hemispheres of one
great hour-glass dwindling to a stem. Consume hostility;
employ your weapon in this meeting-place of surging enmity!
Insurgent feet shall not outrun
multiplied flames, O Sun. (*TMTM*, 49; *CP*, 234)

Hope and Fear (warring aspects of Everyman) are the speakers of the poem ("us") and seek to evade death (and Skelton's motto) by making the Sun ("you") stand still (stay, take a holiday).[8] They aim to stall it with a stop-time "device / of Moorish gorgeousness" (a portmanteau timepiece, combining an hourglass shape with the winding mechanism of a watch). The poem echoes the hourglass shape (another "literal" image) and did so even more emphatically in its initial, centered version.[9] "Sun" offers itself as exactly such a "Moore-ish" device—a vehicle of immortality for its ambitious young author and an early instance of the self-figuring that paves the way for Moore's late-phase celebrity performance. The speakers close by asking the sun to consume their (and all) hostilities or battles in flames. Given that Skelton does live on in his quotation despite his claim about the inevitability of demise, the poem suggests the *hope* that Moore might also overcome death through this "gorgeous" poetic stratagem. Yet the *fear* that she might not is suggested as well at the close, where the poem's "insurgent feet" are consumed by the multiplied flames of the Sun. That fear is itself mitigated, however, since the closing image echoes the image of being outraced by the Sun on the road to eternity in Dickinson's poem 479, "Because I could not stop for Death."[10] Dickinson (whom Moore studied in her course on imitative writing)[11] survives in Moore's allusion (more organically than Skelton in the quotation), affirming the possibility of Moore's poetic survival as well, as part of an ongoing relay of renown through dialogue.[12]

This poem, actively blurring the lines of sex and race (the Sun is neither "male nor female" and perhaps the speaker too, and the "Moor[e]" is an Arab) as well as of mortality, features perhaps the most overt of Moore's appearances in her poems, and asserts her ambitions. But her decision to cut it from her canon for more than thirty years, between its 1924 appearance and its republication in 1957 in the *Mentor Book of Religious Verse*, itself becomes part of the poem's revelatory story, adapting the veil-and-reveal dynamic active in so much of Moore's work. After 1957 she repeatedly drew attention to "Sun," reprinting it in 1961 and 1964 as well as in this 1966 volume, where she positions it where it cannot be ignored. By including this poem about evading death, which most readers of *Tell Me, Tell Me* would take to be recent work by a poet of advanced age since she explicitly and inaccurately states that it was "first published in . . . 1957" in the notes, Moore reframes it as part of her late-phase concern with aging.[13] But longtime readers who remembered the poem would recognize that she had always had immortality in mind.[14] By including a (variously dated) early poem and running her poems backward, *Tell Me, Tell Me* condenses time, creating a thick simultaneity—a kairotic moment outside chronological time, in which all periods of one's life appear to occur at once, similar to the ecstatic temporality of "The Past Is the Present" (1915). Moore's peculiar history of ongoing revision also pertains here: she regarded all her poems as never finished, always susceptible to revision, operating in a continuous present and in dialogue among themselves. The inclusion of "Sun" near the close as well as the start of her published oeuvre underscores this sense of temporal simultaneity and gestures at the transcendent everlastingness it pursues.

Though "Granite and Steel," the first poem in the volume, begins in the present (1966) with a description of the Brooklyn Bridge and the Statue of Liberty in the bay, like "Sun" it quickly invokes the past, through language that directly engages Hart Crane and material that from the start connects readers to Moore's suffragist history and her commitment to principles of democracy and freedom:

GRANITE AND STEEL

Enfranchising cable, silvered by the sea,
  of woven wire, grayed by the mist,
  and Liberty dominate the Bay—
  her feet as one on shattered chains, 5
  once whole links wrought by Tyranny.

  Caged Circe of steel and stone, 7
  her parent German ingenuity.
  "O catenary curve" from tower to pier, 9

implacable enemy of the mind's deformity,
of man's uncompunctious greed,
his crass love of crass priority,
just recently
obstructing acquiescent feet
about to step ashore when darkness fell
without a cause,
as if probity had not joined our cities
in the sea.

"O path amid the stars
crossed by the seagull's wing!"
"O radiance that doth inherit me!"
—affirming inter-acting harmony!

Untried expedient, untried; then tried;
sublime elliptic two-fold egg—
way out; way in; romantic passageway
first seen by the eye of the mind,
then by the eye. O steel! O stone!
Climactic ornament, double rainbow,
as if inverted by French perspicacity,
John Roebling's monument,
German tenacity's also;
composite span—an actuality. *(NCP*, 251)

Notes: See *Brooklyn Bridge: Fact and Symbol* by Alan Trachtenberg (New York: Oxford University Press, 1965). [Moore counts the title as first line here.]
Line 7: *Caged Circe.* See Meyer Berger's story (retold in *Brooklyn Bridge: Fact and Symbol*) of a young reporter who in the 1870s was unaccountably drawn to climb one of the cables to the top of the bridge's Manhattan tower, became spellbound, couldn't come down, and cried for help; none came till morning.
Line 9: *O catenary curve.* The curve formed by a rope or cable hanging freely between two fixed points of support. "Engineering problems of the greatest strength, greatest economy, greatest safety . . . are all solved by the same curve," John Roebling said. (Trachtenberg, p. 69.) *(NCP*, 336)

Moore's title cites "Atlantis," the closing section of Crane's *The Bridge* (1930):

Through the bound cable strands, the arching path
Upward, veering with light, the flight of strings,— . . .

> Up the index of night, granite and steel— . . .
> Sibylline voices flicker, waveringly stream
> As though a god were issue of the strings. ("Atlantis," ll. 1–2, 5, 7–8)

From the title on, Moore's poem is in dialogue (or "inter-acting harmony") with Crane, taking over his visionary diction and rephrasing lines from his multipart epic poem about the same site, at the junction of the Upper Bay and the East River.[15] A comparison of Moore's poem with the first two stanzas of Crane's initial section, "To Brooklyn Bridge," sustains this connection:

> How many dawns, chill from his rippling rest
> The seagull's wings shall dip and pivot him,
> Shedding white rings of tumult, building high
> Over the chained bay waters Liberty—
>
> Then, with inviolate curve, forsake our eyes
> As apparitional as sails that cross
> Some page of figures to be filed away;
> —Till elevators drop us from our day . . .
> ("To Brooklyn Bridge," ll. 1–8)

Her first stanza reworks his "chained bay waters Liberty," and her other near-quotations similarly borrow his tone in slightly altered phrasings. Where in the 1920s as *Dial* editor Moore famously rewrote Crane's poem "The Wine Menagerie" into her own vocabulary and vision,[16] here she submits her poem to his diction and sweep, which carry with them big emotional weight.

The emotional center of Moore's poem is a patriotic vision of asylum for all those fleeing oppression, a deeply American topic that Crane also explored, as "Migrations that must needs void memory." Continuing in the more political vein of her suffrage work in the early part of the century, in this poem Moore seeks "enfranchisement" for all, and not only in the form of the vote but in full citizenship, without hierarchies enforced by birth or privileged identity. Moore's allusions to Liberty, the shattered chains at her feet, and the poem on the Statue's pedestal all reinforce this.

"Granite and Steel" also affirms the "enfranchising" effect on the poet of a cable of poetic connection to precursors, which in this poem extends backward through Crane to Emma Lazarus (author of the pedestal poem) and to Whitman, who before the bridge was built had also crucially documented this exact place of passage—between Brooklyn and Manhattan and on into the American continent—in "Crossing Brooklyn Ferry" (1856). Crane's poem about passage across the bay directly invokes Whitman and creates a queer, American genealogy as underpinning and motor of his poem. In her stage in this genealogy, Moore overtly invokes Crane (and Whitman-through-Crane) as part of that queer history, but she also invokes Whitman per se, having shared his democratic impulse all along, in spite of her purported distaste for him.[17] Moore also affirms an "enfranchising" chain of artistic/engineering connection—to Roebling and Bartholdi, the visionary builders, respectively, of the iconic bridge (1883) and statue in the bay (1886) that emblematize the American promises of liberty and ingenuity (also features of its poetry). Whitman's Brooklyn poem invoked the people of the future much more directly than either Crane's or Moore's poem does, calling out that "you that shall cross from shore to shore years hence are more to me, and more in my meditations, than you might suppose." But by putting their poems in dialogue with Whitman's they enact the futurity he invokes (becoming Whitman's heirs "who look back on me because I look'd forward to them)" and invite their own sequels. Like the bridge that carries traffic in two directions ("way out, way in"), in her poem Moore reaches out to the past and the future at once when she borrows from the past (with slight alteration) Crane's words invoking poetic descendants to come ("O Thou whose radiance doth inherit me"). Elizabeth Bishop's 1955 "Invitation to Miss Marianne Moore," which asks her to "come flying" across the Brooklyn Bridge, also resonates here, embodying in the more complex relationship of contemporaries both a precursor and an heir at once.

Whitman also offers an apt model for Moore's many celebrations of herself, often in disguise but always in dialogue with her readers. Her unblanching affirmation of and pride in her own peculiarities and differences is arguably the most irresistible part of Moore's performance, perhaps because that evidence of self-acceptance and self-respect communicates to others that Moore, like Whitman, will extend a similarly generous love of and respect to them and their differences. Like many other Moore poems, this one also features a figure who, like the ermine or Li Siau Than (and even though veiled in Crane's language), may be read to represent her: this time it's Bartholdi's Statue of Liberty (dominating the bay). Lady Liberty, who also appears in "Light Is Speech" and "Is Your Town Nineveh?" invokes

Marianne, the symbol of France's democratic revolution upon whom it may have been modeled; as Kahan notes, the common name connects Moore and the statue (two American icons of varying wattage). Moore also shares the statue's concern for the world's refugees, as expressed in Lazarus's 1883 sonnet about it, the final five lines of which are engraved on Liberty's base:

THE NEW COLOSSUS

Not like the brazen giant of Greek fame,
With conquering limbs astride from land to land;
Here at our sea-washed, sunset gates shall stand
A mighty woman with a torch, whose flame
Is the imprisoned lightning, and her name
Mother of Exiles. From her beacon-hand
Glows world-wide welcome; her mild eyes command
The air-bridged harbor that twin cities frame.[18]
"Keep, ancient lands, your storied pomp!" cries she
With silent lips. "Give me your tired, your poor,
Your huddled masses yearning to breathe free,
The wretched refuse of your teeming shore.
Send these, the homeless, tempest-tost to me,
I lift my lamp beside the golden door!"[19]

This emblematically American feminist precursor text galvanizes Moore's poem as does Crane's, though she invokes his language more overtly. Moore reiterates the concern for refugees that she shares with Lazarus by reminding readers of their plight, and of the role of the United States as a place of asylum, a recurrent theme in several Moore poems of this period.[20] But though Liberty's pedestal welcomes refugees and her feet stand on their shattered chains, in "Granite and Steel" lines 10–18 seem to refer to refugees refused entry. This is likely an allusion to Congressman Francis Walter's refusal to expand immigration quotas after the Hungarian Revolution in 1956 but may invoke any governmental failure of welcome—thus recent anti-immigration efforts reinforce the poem's resonance.[21] Moore asks the United States to live up to the credo on the statue's base and provide both a place of refuge in the global community and a model of democracy for the world's citizens ("Untried expedient, untried; then tried; / sublime"). "Granite and Steel" continues Moore's efforts to reach a wider audience, and as the opening piece in *Tell Me, Tell Me*, it sets the stage for the volume. The poem's overt allusions to Crane's well-known poem make it easily accessible to literary readers, and as an overtly patriotic text it welcomes non-literary readers as well.

Tell Me, Tell Me also includes four prose pieces (interleaved with the poems, also in reverse chronological order of publication), which punctuate the spaces between poems as commentary might at a reading. The first of these, a brief essay titled "A Burning Desire to Be Explicit" (first published in January 1966 in the *Christian Science Monitor*), follows right after "Granite and Steel" and continues the outreach to readers by directly describing Moore's long struggle to write poems that explore and represent the complexity of experience but that also engage middlebrow readers, by allowing them some reassurance that they will encounter a clear story. That's a tightrope, since in the best cases the process of wrestling with a difficult poem moves readers beyond cliché into new territories of phrasing, thought, and plot—the opposite of reassuring. Moore recounts being asked to clarify a poetic phrase:

> In a reading of my verse for a women's club, I included these lines from "Tell me, tell me":
>
> I vow, rescued tailor
> of Gloucester, I am going
>
> to flee: by engineering strategy—
> the viper's traffic-knot—flee
> to metaphysical newmown hay,
> honeysuckle or woods fragrance. . . .
>
> After the program, a strikingly well-dressed member of the audience, with equally positive manner, inquired, "*What* is metaphysical newmown hay?"
>
> I said, "Oh, something like a sudden whiff of fragrance in contrast with the doggedly continuous opposition to spontaneous conversation that had gone before."
>
> "Then why don't you *say* so?" the impressive lady rejoined. (*TMTM*, 5)

The lady exemplifies exactly the dogged resistance to the new that Moore seeks to escape, so the example is ironic. But the poet is also sympathetic to the lady's confusion, noting next that "Although prepared for an 'element of the riddle' in any poem, an even somewhat experienced person is not irked by clues to meaning" and then cites artists' comments on their paintings that helped her better understand their work (*TMTM*, 5–6).[22] This piece, which essentially repeats in prose the credo of "Values in Use" (1956), reassures readers that the poet is on their side and encourages them to engage, in spite of potential difficulties. But her method remains that of "engineering strategy—the viper's traffic-knot," which can only lead travelers to unexpected places by destabilizing their received ideas; here again Moore performs a balancing act of democratic outreach and provocation.

Moore's elderly status provides another point of connection to a wide readership—since everyone ages, and in that process many reflect on time, ancestors, and those to come. Moore's late work includes poems that make these issues immediately accessible to all, as well as others that operate more subtly, through literary allusions that will be recognized by a more restricted readership. Like "Granite and Steel" and "Sun," quite a few of the other poems in *Tell Me, Tell Me* explore temporal dynamics and often portray unusual relations or transitions between past and present. The moods and the amount of reflection and complexity they involve vary widely. For instance, in "Dream" (1965), written in response to a comment about how university faculty positions function as a modern form of art patronage, Moore jumps Bach forward two centuries to take a position in the present as an artist-in-residence at Northwestern. This poem-qua-time-travel-comedy engages with issues of legacy across centuries, imagining Bach as a fellow producer of art on demand ("Expected to create for university / occasions"), who along with Haydn (who "begged Prince Esterházy to lend him to Yale") reintroduces counterpoint and fugue to the contemporary music scene ("Master-mode expert fugue-al forms since, prevail"). Although the poem is not itself a fugue (or contrapuntal like others we've examined), Moore suggests that history and influence may be—as the reanimated composers (and the felicity they create) are "Repeated fugue-like, all of it, to infinity" (*NCP*, 254).

"Old Amusement Park" (1964) also involves time travel, this time within an ekphrasis of a photo representing the entertainment space that once operated where LaGuardia Airport stands now, into which readers are transported. The first three lines evoke the hectic modern traveler's life in the airport of the present, but as readers are drawn into the familiar context, the ground quickly shifts beneath our feet, carrying us across time to 1892 by line 4.

Hurry, worry, unwary
visitor, never vary
the pressure till nearly bat-blind.
A predicament so dire could not
occur in this rare spot— (*NCP*, 255, ll. 1–5)

Note: A Port Authority photograph given to me by Brendan Gill. (*NCP*, 337)

Our hurried schedules are figured as unimaginable to the relaxed nineteenth-century denizens of Gala Park, whose world resurfaces in the lines that follow. The scene features an elephant lying down, a furry pony, a "never-ending / Ferris-wheel ascending," and a "pony-paddock boy . . . [who,] limber-slouched against a post, / . . . tells a friend what matters least" (ll. 16–17, 19, 24–25). This poem seeks not to preserve old things in the present but to access them in their (slower-paced) pastness directly, through the time travel of memory and of poetry, spurred by the image.

In several cases in *Tell Me, Tell Me*, pairs or groups of Moore's poems address related issues of aging and legacy from different angles. For instance, "An Expedient—Leonardo da Vinci's—and a Query" (1964) directly represents a negative response to aging: in spite of his genius for analysis and his great "memory making past present," Leonardo apparently fell into a late-life depression. Moore, who admired da Vinci, retroactively wishes for him an optimism that would have allowed him to accept and move on from a disproof of his faith in mathematics' universally positive effects. Instead, she suggests, he enacts the devolution he fears through his own negativity:

Peerless, venerated
by all, he succumbed

to dejection. Could not
the Leda with face matchless minutely—
have lightened the blow?
"Sad" . . . Could not Leonardo
have said, "I agree; proof refutes me.
If all is mobility,
mathematics won't do":
instead of, "Tell me if any thing
at all has been done?" (*NCP*, 247, ll. 26–36)

Notes: See Sir Kenneth Clark: *Leonardo da Vinci: An Account of His Development as an Artist.* "Continuous energy. If everything was continuous in movement it could not be controlled by mathematics in which Leonardo had placed his faith." . . .

Lines 31–36: *"Sad"* . . . *"Tell me if anything at all has been done?"* Dr. Henry W. Noss, Associate Professor of History, New York University, quoting Leonardo da Vinci in a lecture. (*CP*, 295)

The draft of this da Vinci poem entwines with that of "W. S. Landor"[23] (also 1964), wherein, in contrast to da Vinci's depression, Moore endorses unceasing energy in the face of mortality, like that of Walter Savage Landor ("*There* / is someone I can bear"). This hotheaded, long-lived poet and essayist (1775–1864) was most well known for *Imaginary Conversations*, in which he has fantasized conversations with literati from the past (much like what Moore does here), keeping them alive through dialogue. Briefly summarizing his story with quotations from Havelock Ellis's introduction to Landor's *Imaginary Conversations*, Moore focuses at the close on Landor's refusal to settle on any one explanation of time or mortality:

. . . —considering meanwhile
infinity and eternity,
he could only say, "I'll
talk about them when I understand them."[24]
(*NCP*, 256, ll. 12–15)

The paired poems represent contrary responses to later life channeled through these representative men, but they needn't be the possession of separate individuals—one person might feel both at different times. Presaging age-studies scholar Margaret Gullette's argument in *Declining to Decline*, in both poems Moore actively rejects narratives of dejection in age (while also, in the da Vinci case, blaming the victim).

But a year later (1965) she offers yet another counterstory, seeming to embrace depression, rejecting a story of transcendence:

The mind, intractable thing

even with its own ax to grind, sometimes
helps others. Why can't it help me? (*NCP*, 253, ll. 1–2)

Moore addresses a figure called "imagnifico" (invoking Wallace Stevens via his "Metaphors of a Magnifico"), a "wizard in words" to whom she attributes ability "to deal / with pent-up emotion, a ballad, witchcraft / . . . [and] disparagers, death, dejection." In contrast, though she chases two

Stevensian birds representing perhaps the hope of profound insight into life's depths (a road runner and a cuckoo), she claims to be unable and afraid to catch them in her poem ("craft with which I don't know how to deal")—though of course the birds do alight herein. She belies the poem's own evidences of skill and insight, in elegiac obeisance to her friend Stevens, ten years after his death; but we needn't take her at her word given the context. She directly portrays the dejection and self-questioning that are often part of the process of invention and of aging (as they were with da Vinci). In an essay tracking the interactions of Moore's late work with that of her friend Stevens, whose work she knew intimately,[25] Charles Berger thoughtfully discusses several poems in which Moore does reflect on legacy and mortality, in a late "effort to write the mind at its end." Though he details these poems' successes, he frames the discussion within an assumption of Moore's lack of sustained serious output in her latter decades, and of her limited engagement with these issues. Including the more accessible work in critical consideration creates a bigger pool of reference; and viewing all these poems as a connected set demonstrates Moore's persistent concern with mortality and forms of farewell.

While it resonates with the "Expedient"/"Landor" pair, the "Intractable" poem also has a more direct partner—in the like-titled "The Mind Is an Enchanting Thing" written two decades earlier (1943). Both "Mind" poems explore that organ's inner workings, which are also portrayed through example in the many Moore poems that track associative connections. Where "Intractable" represents the speaker's mind as incapable, "Enchanting" represented the mind as able to handle multitudes of inputs:

The Mind Is an Enchanting Thing

is an enchanted thing
    like the glaze on a
katydid-wing
        subdivided by sun
        till the nettings are legion. . . .

        Like the gyroscope's fall,
        truly unequivocal
because trued by regnant certainty,

it is a power of
    strong enchantment. (*NCP*, 169, ll. 1–5, 16–20)

Whereas the Enchanted Mind "takes apart / dejection," the Intractable Mind claims inability to do so. The difference in attitude might be attributed to the twenty-year difference in Moore's age at their composition; but again, "Intractable" is contemporaneous with and opposite in mood to the da Vinci and Landor poems, and in the same volume where "Intractable" expresses the speaker's sense of poetic insufficiency, quite a few poems demonstrate enormous poetic expertise. Together these poems engage complexly with encroaching mortality, and the volume as a whole responds, through reflection on the entwined forms of renown, celebrity, and poetic legacy.

Given the by-definition activist nature of her presence as an authoritative woman writer on the modernist scene, Moore's legacy would always have involved activism, though of an indirect kind. But in her latter days her celebrity gave her activism new force. Her 1940s poetry had had a public dimension—both in her war interventions and in poems like "He 'Digesteth Harde Yron'" (1941), which made a case against species extinction (with particular reference to ostriches) as part of a reflection on ethics, war, and violence. Her 1958 poem "The Arctic Ox (or Goat)" makes a related preservationist argument but playfully (see discussion in Chapter 3). This poem jumps the boundaries between poetry, advocacy, and advertisement to sell readers a musk-ox hair product called qiviut, underscoring the transgression:

> If you fear that you are
> reading an advertisement,
>   you are. If we can't be cordial
> to these creatures' fleece,
> I think that we deserve to freeze. (*NCP*, 222, ll. 66–70)

Having plugged her own celebrity into qiviut's promotional circuit with "Arctic Ox," Moore followed up in *Tell Me, Tell Me* with two poems on the uses of celebrity for specific near-term causes.

Her celebrations of violinist Isaac Stern's preservationist action in "Carnegie Hall: Rescued" (1960, originally titled "Glory") and of actor Yul Brynner's intervention on behalf of Hungarian refugees in "Rescue with Yul Brynner" (1961),[26] both based on news stories, explore the way an artist's "star" status may be utilized for public good. To make this clear in Stern's case, Moore underlines the pun in the German etymology of his name ("our spearhead, Mr. Star"). Borrowing from language in an April *New Yorker* Talk of the Town piece, also titled "Glory," Moore represents Stern as a brilliant general leading the preservation campaign, even as she also calls him "Saint Diogenes," for his lack of interest in the kind of wealth expressed by the real estate mogul who sought to raze the concert hall in order to build something more profitable:

> Stern . . .
>
> rescuer of a music hall
> menaced by the "cannibal
> of real estate"—bulldozing potentate,
> land-grabber, the human crab
> left cowering like a neonate. (*NCP*, 245, ll. 21, 25–29)

Mr. Star's skillful use of his celebrity—his "glittering"—ensured his success in preserving the Carnegie Hall legacy ("our music stronghold") for the generations of musicians and listeners to come, bridging past, present, and future. In so doing he creates a legacy of community commitment of his own, which Moore expands through her celebration of his activism on behalf of the group.

In the case of Brynner, most famous for his role in *The King and I* on stage and screen, Moore puns in "Rescue with Yul Brynner" on the way his choice to downplay his shining celebrity ("His neat cloth hat / has nothing like the glitter reflected on the face / of milkweed-witch seed-brown dominating a palace") demonstrates his true majesty ("His deliberate pace / is a king's, however") (*NCP*, 244). In both poems, Moore features the star's heroic off-stage performance, using his star power for civic good—in Brynner's case, to aid refugees. The poems laud these stars and their modeling of real-world positive effects that celebrity may create, an effect that Moore then emulates in a poem published the year after *Tell Me, Tell Me.*

"The Camperdown Elm"

To honor the one-hundredth anniversary of Brooklyn's Prospect Park in 1967, Moore was invited to write a poem; she used that opportunity to make an argument for parks as civic centers that bring together citizens of all ranks in celebration of their shared connection to nature. "The Camperdown Elm" invokes the community-minded action through which these centers of democratic value evolved, reminding readers of the American tradition of poets and artists as environmental advocates and requesting aid for an ailing tree—a metaphor for the same community she appeals to for its support.

The Camperdown Elm

Gift of Mr. A. G. Burgess to Prospect Park, Brooklyn, 1872.

I think, in connection with this weeping elm,
of "Kindred Spirits" at the edge of a rockledge
overlooking a stream:
Thanatopsis-invoking tree-loving Bryant
conversing with Thomas Cole
in Asher Durand's painting of them
under the filigree of an elm overhead.

No doubt they had seen other trees—lindens,
maples and sycamores, oaks and the Paris
street-tree, the horse-chestnut; but imagine
their rapture, had they come on the Camperdown elm's
massiveness and "the intricate patterns of its branches,"
arching high, curving low, in its mist of fine twigs.
The Bartlett tree-cavity specialist saw it
and thrust his arm the whole length of the hollowness
of its torso and there were six small cavities also.

Props are needed and tree-food. It is still leafing;
still there. *Mortal* though. We must save it. It is
our crowning curio. (*CP*, 242; *NCP*, 265)[27]

Moore focused quite a few of her late poems on trees, and this poem revolves around an unusual one still growing in Prospect Park, planted from a cutting of a mutant elm in 1872. The elm fell ill in the 1960s, but the city, in economic decline, had no funds to treat it. First published in the *New Yorker*, the poem demanded a real-world monetary response from its initial readers, while more broadly asking sequent readers to support their parks and environmentalism generally. Moore backed up the poem's call with an even more direct request for donations in an op-ed in the *New York Times*.[28]

Line 4 invokes one of Moore's nineteenth-century poetic precursors—the "tree-loving [William Cullen] Bryant" (1794–1878)—and it operates as a sequel to Bryant's well-known "The Planting of the Apple

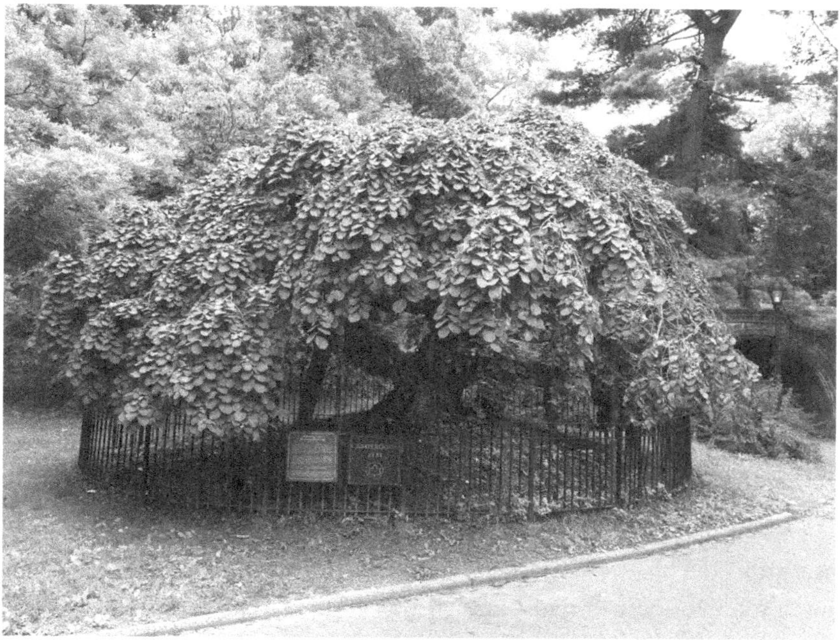

Figure 23. Camperdown Elm, 2018. *Brooklyn Eagle* photo by Lore Croghan. Reprinted by kind permission.

Tree" (1851), which tells the life story of an apple tree, from its planting in the "greensward" until its waning days.[29] Moore's poem picks up Bryant's story at the point of the tree's decline, morphing it from apple to elm (a form of graft) via the allusion to Asher Brown Durand's painting of Bryant (with his friend, painter Thomas Cole) under an elm; as the apple becomes an elm, so that poem's author, Bryant, transforms into this poem's author, Moore, who then directly intervenes in the world to effect the transformed tree's survival—carrying it forward into its second hundred years.[30] Like her elderly physiognomy, Moore's allusions also testify to her age. Having outlived many of her contemporaries, she serves as a relic not only of modernism but also of the generations of readers (including many modernist poets in their youthful days) who knew and loved the work of poets like Bryant (whose star shines in contemporary consciousness most brightly in relation to Bryant Park, the thriving greenspace behind the central branch of the New York Public

Library). Moore's age serves her here, allowing her to see connections across one hundred fifty years of American poetry (though she wasn't that old, she grew up reading the full nineteenth-century canon) and to herself become a bridge joining the American literary past, present, and future.

In addition to their mutual love of trees, Moore and Bryant shared an affection for parks. Bryant, a longtime editor of what is now the *New York Post*, wrote an important editorial himself in 1844, in which he proposed the idea for an enormous public park, to "give our vast population an extensive pleasure ground for shade and recreation in these sultry afternoons."[31] This led to the creation of Central Park in Manhattan in 1857 and then to Prospect Park in Brooklyn ten years after (both designed by Frederick Law Olmsted), a major contribution to the experience of a democratic community, in which people of all classes can relax.[32] These parks remain places of idyllic recreation to this day. In recognition of his advocacy, the poet was honored with the smaller park in his name in 1884. Twenty-seven years later in 1911, merging his literary and environmental interests, the library's main branch was completed next to Bryant Park, and the Durand painting, donated to the library by Bryant's daughter, was hung in the Main Reading Room, a powerful reminder of the history of the place (it remained there until 2005 when the city sold it to the Walmart Museum in Arkansas). Fifty-four years yet further on, in 1965, Marianne Moore, a frequent visitor to the Reading Room, was appointed the first president of the New York Greensward Foundation (formed "to foster and promote public appreciation of Central and Prospect Parks").[33]

Having introduced her public persona directly into the poem ("I think . . . We must save it"), while also, arguably, reincarnating Bryant, Moore further multiplies her operative identities by drawing a parallel between herself and the Camperdown Elm. The closing phrase "our crowning curio" describes the unusual Moore and her odd poems as aptly as it does the elm.[34] And like the tree, she too is mortal and, at eighty, frail and old enough to expect that her own death is fairly near. Though it is hard to read the poem as a request on Moore's part for direct medical assistance for herself, it certainly invites reflection upon the mechanisms of artistic and personal survival—across a career, a life, and the posthumous future.

Her invocation in line 3 of "Thanatopsis" (ca. 1811), Bryant's most famous poem, asks readers to recall that meditation on mortality. Written when Bryant was a teenager, "Thanatopsis" counsels readers not to fear death but to look forward to it as the opportunity to "[lie] down to pleasant dreams" in nature ("the great tomb of man"), with all the kings of the past and the billions of others who have lived and died on earth. Expanding considerably on Wordsworth's "A Slumber Did My Spirit Steal" (1798), Bryant presents death as a rejoining with nature[35] and anticipates it with the cheerful view that, as his contemporary Hazlitt noted, only the very young for whom death is yet a fable can take.[36] "Thanatopsis" utilizes a recycling model—for life and for literary influence—when it pictures a corpse reduced to its elements providing nourishment to an oak tree. Moore's early poem "A Grave" (written 1917) engages similar material—speaking of the sea as a grave to millions. When it appeared in print in 1921, readers' memories of boats sunk in the recent war were still strong, and "A Grave" views death as rather more predatory than Bryant's poem does. Almost half a century later, "The Camperdown Elm" modulates this theme, combining a cheerful attitude as in "Thanatopsis" with a rejection of that poem's acceptance of death. Though it begins by situating its eponym as a figure of sorrow (the weeping elm), the poem quickly becomes a fond portrait of dead artists past, giving evidence of their continued beneficent influence. The focus shifts toward arboreal science in the middle, then shifts back to contemplation of mortality as the poem closes, acknowledging the tree's fragility ("*mortal* though") but rejecting the inevitability of its death when the speaker enjoins readers not to let the elm die but to save it.[37]

Moore builds upon her opening invocation of "Thanatopsis" with her ekphrasis of Asher Brown Durand's well-known painting *Kindred Spirits*, in which Durand portrays Bryant and his then-recently deceased friend, the landscape painter Thomas Cole of the Hudson River School, on a rock ledge by a stream in the Catskills, with an elm tree in the foreground. Durand's painting was commissioned as a gift for Bryant in 1849 in response to Bryant's eulogy for Cole, who had just died of pneumonia at forty-seven.[38] The painting serves as a monument to Cole's artistic genius, by his friend and mentee Durand, who in carrying Cole's teachings forward in this image enacts his victory over death. Cole lives on in his own work, in this portrait, and in all the work of those who learned from him, be they painters, poets, or preservationists. Like "Thanatopsis," the painting represents a recycling—of death into new life, this time not as a new organic entity but as art.

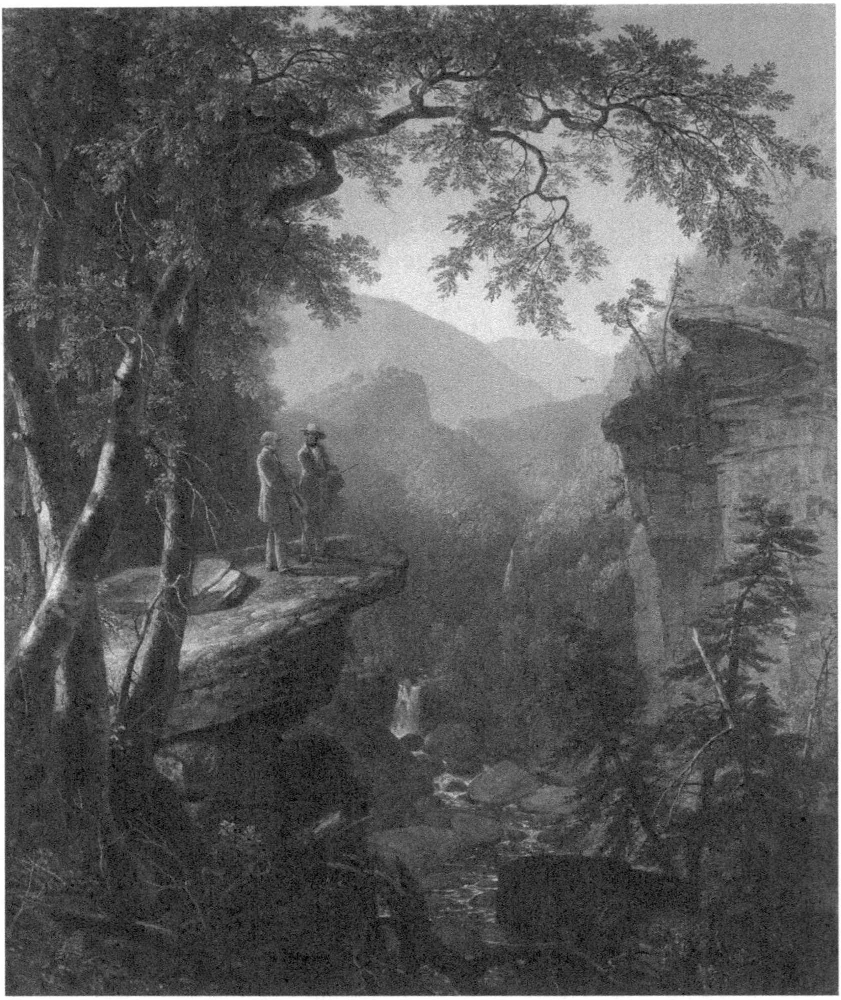

Figure 24. Asher Brown Durand, *Kindred Spirits*, 1849. Oil on canvas, 44 x 36 in. Courtesy Crystal Bridges Museum of American Art, Bentonville, Arkansas, 2010.106. Photography by the Metropolitan Museum of Art. Go online for full color view.

As a real ekphrastic object that invokes the fleetingness of life, Durand's painting on Cole's death per se figures the reality of death—a memento mori.[39] Durand took the painting's name from the sonnet "O Solitude," the first published poem of Keats (another short-lived genius of long influence), which also features friends in sweet converse in a natural scene. The painting creates a nexus of interwoven literary and artistic explorations of nature, mortality, friendship, and artistic lineage, to which Moore's poem adds more strands, thereby placing her poetic plea on behalf of the Camperdown Elm in the context of activist writers and artists who had likewise drawn attention to the value and beauties of nature, leading to the American conservation and parks movements. From its opening lines the poem underscores the connections among art, poetry, and wilderness by creating its own literal image of a rock ledge in line 2, which overlooks the stream of text in line 3:

> I think, in connection with this weeping elm,
> of "Kindred Spirits" at the edge of a rockledge
> overlooking a stream: (*CP*, 242; *NCP*, 265)

Building on the painting's evocation of a world of mutually influential friendships, Moore's poem also reflects on the operations of influence in the present, including the influence exerted by the famous upon their public. Moore uses her good name to influence her readers to assist the elm, utilizing their sense that she is a kindred spirit to provoke their action. Following the examples of celebrity rescues in "Carnegie Hall: Rescued" and "Rescue with Yul Brynner," Moore effects a rescue of her own.[40]

In Keats's sonnet, "kindred spirits" names an intimate relationship among friends—an electric meeting of harmonious minds that is "the highest bliss of human-kind." The phrase also describes the poem's relationship with its ideal audience—the meeting of minds that may provide readers with material for reflection and perhaps with the impetus to join the conversation with creations of their own. As with "Granite and Steel," the genealogy of poets traced in "The Camperdown Elm" (from Keats to Bryant to Moore) anticipates the continued forward relay of poetic lineage, as does the poem's eagerness for the tree's survival.

But satisfying though the hope for posthumous influence might be in prospect, its consolations prove inadequate here. "The Camperdown Elm" clings ardently to life in the moment. At eighty, Moore reflects on death from a rather different position than the teenaged Bryant did in "Thanatopsis," and the poem's conclusion suggests she feels herself too close to the grave to celebrate its effects ("We must save it"). Like the tree, Moore moved into her latter years "still leafing" (activating the Whitmanic pun on book *leaves* there—Whitman having been another Brooklyn poetic parks advocate and a founder of Fort Greene Park [1847] in Moore's neighborhood)—still producing poems that respond to and engage the world multiply. But, also like the tree, she advanced under threat: from the ravages of age per se and, in her case, from the added pressures to be silent faced by older women, variants on those she had battled in youth in poems like "Silence" and "Marriage."

In this poem, she thwarts mortality for the elm and for herself not by transcending it but by defying it. To accomplish that, she turns her focus to action and relationship in the present. This begins in stanza 2, where she parallels the dynamic of the pony moving around in the fine print in "Blue Bug" by liberating Cole and Bryant from their frozen stance in the painting, walking them through a forest of diverse trees and into Prospect Park, part of their legacy, where they find and admire the massive elm.

> No doubt they had seen other trees—lindens,
> maples and sycamores, oaks and the Paris
> street-tree, the horse-chestnut; but imagine
> their rapture, had they come on the Camperdown elm's
> massiveness and "the intricate patterns of its branches,"
> arching high, curving low, in its mist of fine twigs.
> (*CP*, 242; *NCP*, 265)

Although they encounter the elm in the past subjunctive ("had they come"), the tree lives in the park (and the poem) of the present, where the men join Moore and her readers, who participate in their revivification by imagining them rapturous. In the closing lines Moore acknowledges the eventual mortality of the elm but calls on her readers to join her in saving it from death now, an effect only their collaborative action can (and soon thereafter did) achieve: thus the poem creates both a community and a cure. Not only must we save the tree, the poem argues, but only *we* (through community action) can save it. The poem utilizes Moore's celebrity to extend her democratic outreach into community-building effects in the real world; aiding the tree aids the community that helps the tree, sustaining both through that joint action. The poem reminds us that we are all defined and sustained by the wider set of relationships—with people (living, dead, and yet to come), with art, and with nature—through which we construct our worlds. Though in its initial moment "The Camperdown Elm" actively refused to be an elegy for the tree, after Moore's death, the lines become a "self-elegy," still performing a denial of death for the (still thriving) tree but claiming for Moore the immortality that all elegies claim for their subjects, sustained by the community of her readers.

"Enough: 1969," "The Magician's Retreat," and "Tippoo's Tiger"

Moore suffered a first stroke in 1958, and though she recovered, over the ensuing years her health deteriorated. In 1967, when she was eighty, her family relocated her from Brooklyn to an apartment on 9th Street in Manhattan, with a niece nearby, her longtime housekeeper in regularly, and twenty-four-hour nurses available if needed. But she continued to make appearances and to write through 1969, when a series of strokes confined her to bed and ended her poetry production. Following up on "The Camperdown Elm," Moore's two final published poems, "Enough: 1969" and "The Magician's Retreat" (both completed in spring 1969 though published in 1970), make brief but direct statements about death, art, and power in terms that recap key dynamics of her oeuvre and continue her active dialogue with writers past.[41] "Enough: 1969" echoes back to Moore's 1957 poem "Enough: Jamestown, 1607–1957," written for the 350th anniversary, which explores the harms done *by* the initial British settlers (the forced repression of the Natives, the importation of tobacco to Europe, and the introduction of slavery to the colony to grow the crop) and *to* them ("maddened men in starving time"), though it ends up affirming the settlers' efforts, half-heartedly, as "enough" to endure—"if present faith mend partial proof."

The 1969 poem portrays a different but also historical scene: the first words echo those of "Baseball and Writing," and the poem then turns from the world of contemporary enthusiasms to dialogue with two immortals, Plato and Ben Jonson, first in a place of philosophy and relaxation in Athens.

Enough

Am I a fanatic? The opposite.
    And where would I like to be?

Sitting under Plato's olive tree
or propped against its thick old trunk,

away from controversy
or anyone choleric. (*NCP*, 268, ll. 1–6)

Moore then pivots on the "tree" link to Ben Jonson's commonplace book *Timber: Discoveries Made upon Men and Matter* (1640), in which he develops ideas and phrases he has taken from ancient writers. Moore cites what seem to be guidelines for constructing walls:

If you would see stones set right, unthreatened
by mortar (masons say "mud"),
squared and smooth, let them rise as they should,
Ben Jonson said, or he implied.

In "Discoveries" he then said,
"Stand for truth, and 'tis enough." (*NCP*, 268, ll. 7–12)

On closer inspection of the source, however, these turn out to be guidelines for building sentences (which Jonson develops from Tacitus, Suetonius, Seneca, and Fabianus): "The brief style is that which expresseth much in little; the concise style, which expresseth not enough, but leaves somewhat to be understood; the abrupt style, which hath many breaches, and doth not seem to end, but fall. The congruent and harmonious fitting of parts in a sentence hath almost the fastening and force of knitting and connection; as in stones well squared, which will rise strong a great way without mortar."[42] Moore borrows from Jonson to compactly summarize what Roger Gilbert calls her "disjunctive practices," concatenating what seem initially to be miscellaneous, disconnected items, joined by no conjunctive mortar, but which "in the end prove to be deeply ordered by what 'To a Snail' calls 'the principle that is hid.'"[43] The Truth in all these versions turns out to be full of and even sustained by gaps in its expression, which readers may fill in and which will evolve over time. Any of the three styles might describe Moore's method here. She ends quite emphatically with a maxim, again with a Jonsonian source: "Stand for truth, and 'tis enough" expresses much in little and certainly sounds compelling and simple, but nonetheless "leaves somewhat to be understood." Again the source text adds complexity. Jonson offers the advice Moore quotes within a nuanced exploration of canonicity, viewing the history of writing as a community effort to build on one another's work in order to construct a group Truth:

> I do not desire to be equal to those that went before; but to have my reason examined with theirs, and so much faith to be given them, or me, as those shall evict. I am neither author nor fautor [patron] of any sect. I will have no man addict himself to me; but if I have anything right, defend it as Truth's, not mine, save as it conduceth to a common good. It profits not me to have any man fence or fight for me, to flourish, or take my side. Stand for truth, and 'tis enough.[44]

Standing for truth proves not simple, since only with examination can we determine what constitutes truth, even as in this analysis. Through her allusion to Jonson, Moore invites posterity's fair weighing of her work and recognition of its discoveries and truths insofar as they are useful contributions to the human community's ongoing analysis of what matters.

Part of the difficulty Moore's critics have demonstrated in recognizing these late poems' concern with legacy and age seems based in failure to acknowledge Moore's strong poetic ego. This may be due to her modest presentation (though that was always countered by a flaunting of difference that simultaneously demanded attention) and to the relative shortness of the individual poems, and was likely reinforced by the critics' own gendered expectations, which often seem to block recognition of Moore's enormous ambition, skill, and daring. A few lines later in his *Discoveries*, Jonson describes Immortality as his goal, noting that "If divers men seek Fame, or Honour, by divers ways; so both bee honest, neither is to be blam'd; but they that seek Immortality, are not onely worthy of leave, but of praise." This goal too Moore shares with Jonson. She invites us to read her work, fill in the connections, and heed the company she dialogues with. For Moore as for Jonson, age is conquered not by mortality but by immortality.

Moore's final published poem, "The Magician's Retreat," continues the method of dialogue with artists past, this time with visual artists, and adds to that an active structural dynamic that builds into this poem a remarkable, ongoing liveliness. In this at once plain and visionary poem, Moore directly claims for herself the wizardry she disclaimed in "The Mind, Intractable Thing." Moore's notes tell us that the poem involves a double ekphrasis: the title comes from the design of "visionary architect" Jean-Jacques Lequeu (1757–1826) for a "Repaire des Magiciens" (The Magicians' Retreat) (Figure 25), while the body of the poem describes

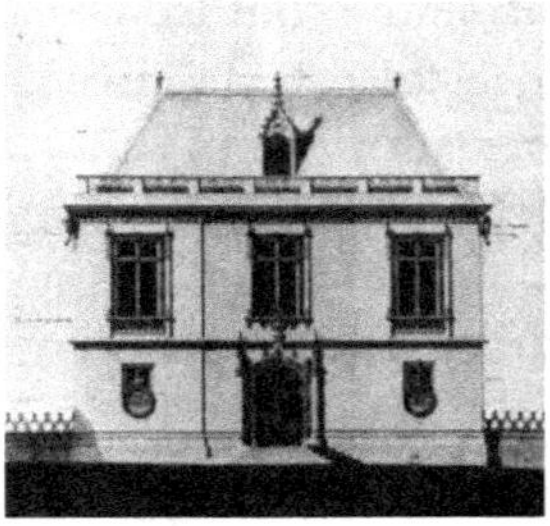

Figure 25. Jean-Jacques Lequeu, "Repaire des Magiciens" (The Magicians' Retreat), late eighteenth century, public domain.

one of René Magritte's (1898–1967) series of paintings called *L'Empire des lumières* (Empire of Light) (Figure 26).

Lequeu's revolutionary building designs combine wild varieties of architectural elements parallel to Moore's poems' combinations of diverse materials, and (as the article about his work that Moore cites underscores) his mysterious image of a sorcerers' lair suggests something and someone are hidden within. The Magritte image also presents a building in a natural but odd context, in which day and night seem to occur simultaneously—contrarieties equally true. This house too seems to brim with magical secrets, veiled and revealed at once, spurring curiosity.

In examining this poem as part of his exploration of Moore's late pattern of unusual closural techniques, John Emil Vincent argues convincingly that its title (altered to refer to a single magician) also serves as the penultimate line,[45] as part of the poet's sleight-of-hand demonstration of her wizardry—at both formal innovation and discreet signification. As Vincent notes, the first stanza ends with a triplet rhyme, and the second with a couplet, suggesting that something's missing near the end:

The Magician's Retreat

of moderate height,
(I have seen it)
cloudy but bright inside
like a moonstone,
while a yellow glow
from a shutter-crack shone,
and a blue glow from the lamppost
close to the front door.
It left nothing of which to complain,
nothing more to obtain,

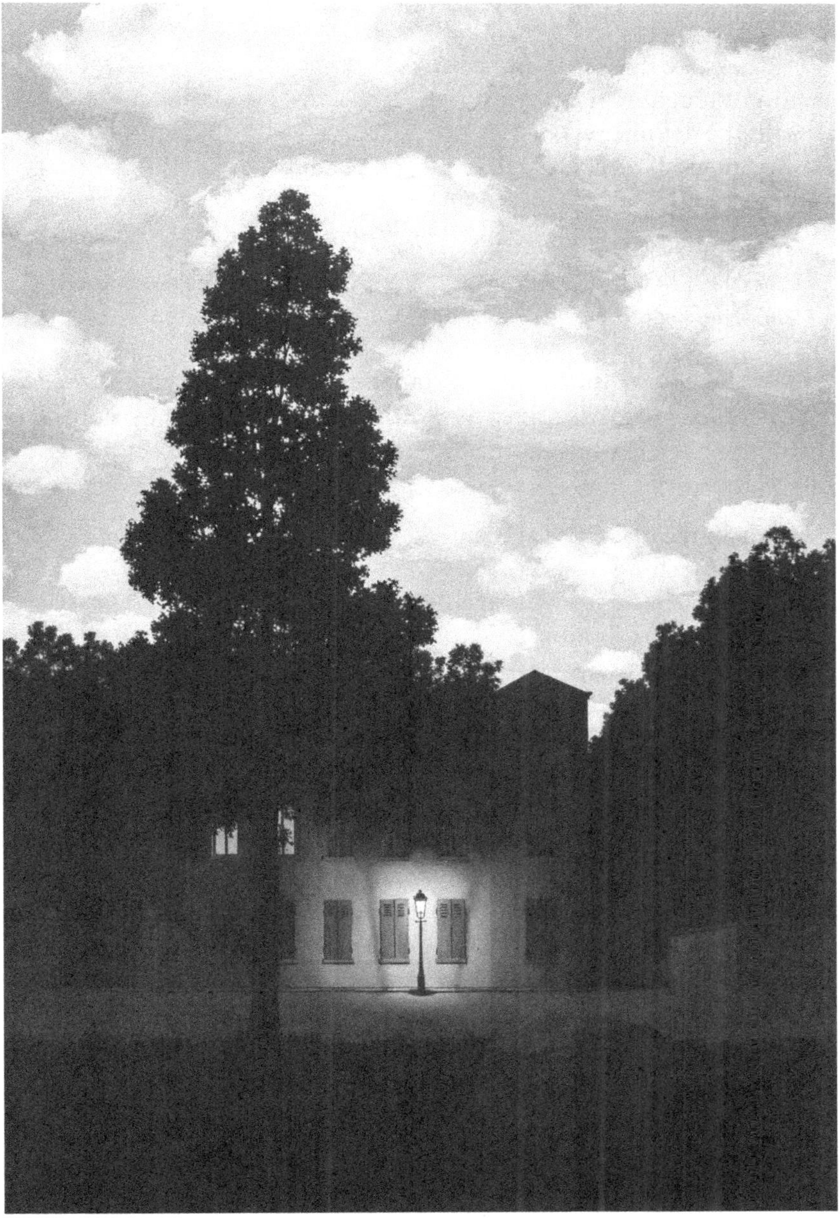

Figure 26. René Magritte, *L'Empire des lumières* (Empire of Light), 1953–54. Oil on canvas, 195.4 x 131.2 cm. (Peggy Guggenheim Collection, Venice 76.2553 PG 102). Original in color. Reprinted by permission.

consummately plain.

A black tree mass rose at the back
almost touching the eaves
with the definiteness of Magritte,
was above all discreet. (*CP*, 246; *NCP*, 269)[46]

Notes: Drawing by Jean-Jacques Lequeu (1757–1825), *Arts Magazine*, December/January 1967–68.
Line 14: René Magritte, Domain of Lights, 1953–54. *New York Times Magazine*, January 19, 1969, p. 69. (*CP*, 297; *NCP*, 339)

As Vincent shows, the sense that stanza 2 lacks a line is emphasized by a gap in the logic of its sentence, which is neatly supplied by slotting in the title as the next-to-last line, where it becomes the subject ruling the final clause:

A black tree mass rose at the back
almost touching the eaves
with the definiteness of Magritte,
[*the Magician's Retreat*]
was above all discreet.

This poem's structural play both reveals and veils the poet/wizard, who operates in surprising ways here (as in so many of Moore's poems), this time putting the poetry in motion literally—of a piece with the movement of Moore's name into final line position in "Blue Bug," and in a manner that "rhymes" with the structural signification of her time traveling across the pages of *Tell Me, Tell Me*, of the thorn prick in "Roses Only," of the breaking of the glass across versions of "A Face," and of the many other ways in which she inhabits and activates unexpected structural aspects of her poems.

Beyond formal closural play, Moore explores issues of personal closure here—of her own death and immortality—as she does in many other poems of this period. The poem conjures a magician making something disappear: the prestidigitator performing this disappearing act is the poet Moore, but she is also the vanishing girl. As in "Sun," she hides herself in plain view with a homophone—in line 10, where there is "nothing more to obtain." The poem puts her in motion and performs her exit. As much as the title rushes down to fill in the missing penultimate line, as Vincent suggests, I'll add that that line also rushes away, ascending to the position "above all" in the title, which, situated above the text as it is, also serves (punningly, via Magritte's painting) as the sunny heaven above the dark tree mass in the poem, the place of immortality to which Moore the magician actively retreats here, sitting on high both discreetly and in plain view.[47] Though this particular reveal-and-veil takes on a special resonance because this turned out to be her last published poem, "The Magician's Retreat" bespeaks Moore's career-long interest in immortality and it hints at returns and departures to come, through endless readerly encounters with this lively poem and with the rest of her oeuvre, as well as with the works of those influenced by her many innovations and insights.

The late poem "Tippoo's Tiger" (1967) also explores poetic immortality, addressing explicitly the need for heirs. After detailing the story of the emperor Tippoo's identification with tigers (his name means *tiger*, his throne has tiger's feet, he dresses his soldiers in tiger stripes, collects hunting cats, and he has constructed an automaton that reenacts the murder by a tiger of his British enemy's son), the poem concludes:

> This ballad still awaits a tiger-hearted bard.
>   Great losses for the enemy
> cannot make one's own loss less hard. (*NCP*, 264, ll. 21–23)[48]

While the poem offers various ways of reading the enemy, the "tiger-hearted bard" would seem to have its source outside the story of Tippoo, in Moore's own generation narrative. As Patricia Willis has demonstrated, at least seventeen of Moore's early poems focus on or invoke William Blake, a key precursor.[49] Blake's poem "The Tyger" extolling the daring makers, both divine and poetic, who take the risk of creating the new and challenging, is invoked here as part of Moore's invitation to the next generation.[50] In Blake's poem, the bold Tyger figures both the creature and the creator, and in Moore's poem the tiger figures Blake while Tippoo figures her, at least in some respects. Like Tippoo (or Tipu, the poem uses both) "the tiger was [her] prototype," and the escape of Tippoo's great polecat ferret in lines 11–14 foretells *her* death to come in the future just as it does his in the past. In looking forward to her own heirs, Moore imagines poets and artists who will share and carry forward her Blakean energy, modified by its passage through Moore's own passion and vision. Such future poets and artists would inevitably be quite different from Moore in many respects, as Moore is from Blake, but linked to Moore in more and less subterranean ways.

The richest of those heirs will follow her in activating all aspects of the text to signify collectively.

In 1942 Randall Jarrell beautifully encapsulated the interactive abundance of Moore's formal effects, in terms that proleptically admit the many additional techniques that came later. Jarrell also intuits her connection to Blake and anticipates the subjects of several poems to come:

> She not only can, but has to, make poetry out of everything and anything: she is like Midas, or Mozart purposely choosing unpromising themes, or the princess whom a wizard forces to manufacture sheets out of nettles—if the princess were herself the wizard. . . . Her forms have the absurd mathematical extravagance of snowflakes; they seem to one arbitrary as the prohibitions in fairy tales; but they work as dangerously as those—disregard them and everything goes to pieces. Her forms, tricks and all, are like the aria of the Queen of the Night: the intricate and artificial elaboration not only does not conflict with the emotion but is its vehicle. And her machinery—bestiary, rather—fits both the form and final content of her poems as queerly and completely as if all three were pieces of some extraordinary puzzle. . . . [The things Moore describes] *are* what Miss Moore wants to say, and express her as naturally and satisfactorily as the Lamb and Tyger did God.[51]

The Moore-ish supplement triggers the gorgeous devices, the curious machines that are her poems, signifying multiply and democratically, with "something for everyone," inviting all readers in to discover their own insights and capacities through the dialogue.

Moore's latter years were stunningly busy on multiple fronts. She continued to engage her public through her trademark performances until her strokes sidelined her, and even then to the young scholar Pat Willis, who met Moore at her home when she could no longer speak but could nonetheless communicate, she appeared "radiant, even joyous."[52] Up to that point, as her many letters, notebooks, drafts, and appointment calendars document, she led a life of great energy and productivity—dedicated to a multimedia democratic discourse, through poetry, prose, lectures, letter writing, appearances, and social interactions. A splendid and engaging apparition wherever she went, she flew in the face of the bias and limited expectations prevalent in her day about elderly women, unmarried women, cross-dressers, or anyone who publicly performed a nonconformist or nonhegemonic identity.

Whereas her early poems enacted authority through an elite position even as they questioned the hierarchies that position rested upon, her later poems continued that questioning from a popular position that allowed her to advance a democratic agenda through a performance that combined comedy with serious cultural reflection. Moore utilized her celebrity and the sense of intimacy it afforded to make "personal" contact with fellow citizens and kindred spirits, through diverse points of access, as we've seen, creating a cross-brow conversation about issues of moment to their personal and communal lives. In so doing she continued to push the boundaries of who could be heard and by whom. Whether sitting under the Durand in the New York Public Library Reading Room in sweet converse with admirers, throwing out the first ball at Yankee Stadium, welcoming guests at Gracie Mansion with Mayor Lindsay, trading rhymes at Toots Shor's with Muhammad Ali, attending leading-edge performances with Louise Crane, or staying up late with Auden and Capote, Marianne Moore was an active player in the civic and cultural scene of her day, performing seniority as one more productive stage in a life committed to advancing democracy by speaking her mind innovatively. And she was clearly having fun—old, mortal, but still laughing too.

Epilogue: "Correspondances"—Ma-Ray-Andy

Always avant-garde, Moore in her late work engaged with popular culture and celebrity in innovative ways directly related to visual as well as literary arts. Artists Ray Johnson and Andy Warhol, two of Moore's younger contemporaries in the 1950s and 1960s arts scene, can helpfully contextualize her late-phase methods;[1] though their media differ, her deep ekphrastic impulse connects them. I offer these two "correspondances" (borrowing a pun from Johnson) to emphasize the importance for criticism going forward of viewing Moore's work in this period in relation not just to work she'd done previously but also to the work of her younger contemporaries, to track similarities as well as mutual influence.

Though Moore was anomalous in many respects, she had much in common with these two younger artists, who inhabited New York with her for twenty-three years and whose art, like hers, crossed lines—of class, sexuality, media, and brow. All three operated outside the standard romance plots, sharing an awareness of self and society as constructs, built around received cultural scripts that could be imagined otherwise. All three made art both invested in and critical of contemporary valuation of celebrity. Though Moore (who arrived in New York in 1918) was decades older than Johnson and Warhol (both of whom arrived in 1949), their work shares much.

Warhol, by far the most famous of the three currently, performed an iconic public persona that was in many ways similar to Moore's. His white wig (not far from federalist fashion) and her tricorne and cape

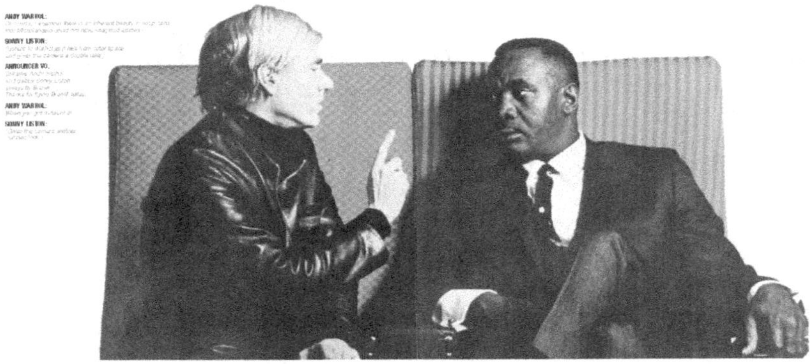

Figure 27. Andy Warhol and Sonny Liston in advertisement for Braniff Airlines, 1969. Reprinted by kind permission.

both functioned as camouflage that allowed these shy people to hide in plain view, participating in the celebrity and popular culture worlds out of which both made art and engaging a public that otherwise might not feel comfortable with them either. Like Moore, Warhol also appeared in the 1969 Braniff Airlines ad campaign that paired "high" art stars with popular celebrities—Moore with Mickey Spillane and Warhol with Sonny Liston, both uttering the tag line "When you got it, flaunt it."[2]

Both were charismatic self-flaunters in life and in art—the two were major contributors to the history of unexpected juxtaposition of fine art with lower-brow realms (including those of sports and advertising), within which the Braniff ads resonated. Both frequently quoted prior texts in their art—mining both high and low references, pointing to the embeddedness of these realms, challenging hierarchies based on their distinction, and tracing the speedy evolution of the processes of meaning-making in the postwar scene. The work of both creates a simultaneous pleasure in and critique of the celebrity-patrolled commodity-capitalist system.

The biographies of these two big personalities also had anomalous similarity,[3] and, coincidentally, the December 1954 *Vogue* issue in which Moore's "Rosemary" appeared also included Warhol's first *Vogue* advertisement, for Palizzio shoes. As a skilled and inventive draftsman, Warhol managed the rare feat of combining commercial and fine-art careers by blurring the line between the two, making ads that gestured beyond standard sales mode (with disorienting spatial relations and a provocative tone) and art that remarked on his commercial connections. His witty and sexualized shoe images carried him up the ladder of glamour and art-world success—self-fashioning, in the couturier mode. The work intersects with the persona to tell a story of social rank and self-transformation, a basic American story of self-making extended to include all those excluded from the "top," including the queer, the dark-skinned, the feminine, the working class, and the "lowbrow." Like Moore, Warhol explores the workings of democracy, emphasizing liminality to mark simultaneously points of exclusion and of possible crossing of barriers.

Ray Johnson, less well known than the others, was a Conceptual artist and collagist, and if not a national celebrity in his day certainly an anomalous personality well known in the New York art scene who was obsessed with, among many other things, Marianne Moore. Johnson invented Mail Art—later more formally and punningly titled the "New York Correspondance School of Art" (a system of art postcards bearing a drawing of his silhouette that invited artistic interventions from their many recipients with the phrase "Please add to & return to Ray Johnson").[4] As it was for his friend Andy Warhol, celebrity was part of what Johnson explored artistically at the same time that he sought it, guardedly. Simultaneous to her performance of celebrity, Moore also performed the role of fan in public, doubling the role of her own fans, many of whom were also fans of the popular figures she wrote about. Johnson does something similar in his collages—which take fan art to an early height, exhibiting it in art spaces and adding a critical dimension that asks questions about what celebrity is and where value inheres.

Johnson made quite a few collages involving Moore, and his short poetical essay "Is Marianne Moore Marianne Moore?" (1966), like much of his visual work, runs on a punning logic very like that motoring many Moore poems.

> . . . I clipped a page from Life magazine show-
> ing Marilyn Monroe's tomb stone which read
> Em Em 1926–1962. I was impressed by her
> dates. Like Joe. (Joe D.). Joe De Em.
> Joe Death. A playing card figure this way
> also that way. The card part of the Cardin-
> als, a baseball team. . . .

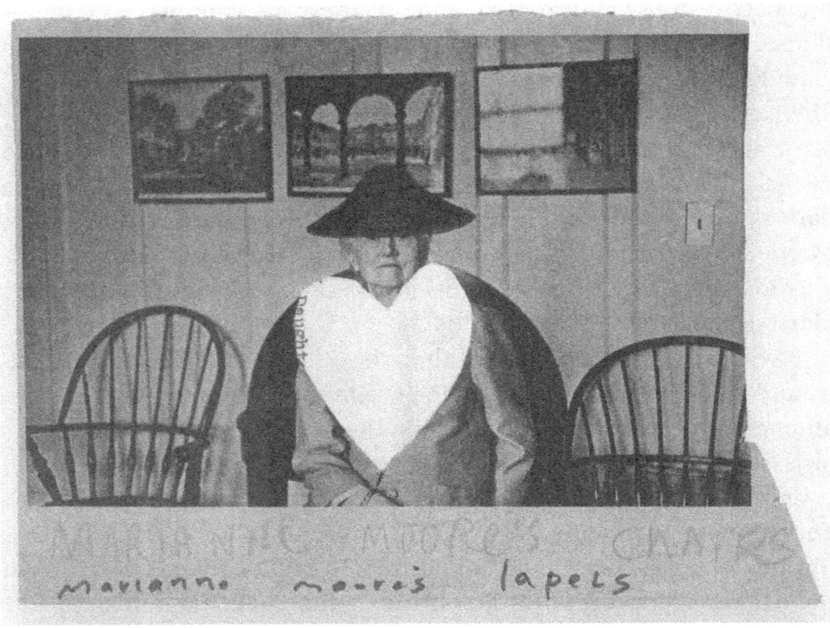

Figure 28. Ray Johnson, "Marianne Moore's Lapels," collage, date unknown. © The Ray Johnson Estate. Reprinted by kind permission.

> Marianne Moore certainly is not Marilyn
> Monroe. In collage, Marilyn's head could
> be put on Marianne's body. One could pretend
> to be someone one is not. Children's play.
> I'll be you and you be me. Be my valentine.
> Ray Johnson wearing Marianne Moore's hat. . . . [5]

Comparing Moore to Marilyn Monroe (connected via their shared initials—"Em Em"—and perhaps via their shared relation to baseball, Monroe's connection being her ex-husband Yankee center fielder Joe DiMaggio), Johnson suggests that in spite of their apparent differences—around sexuality, age, culture level, and so on—they, and all people, share many similarities. While celebrities are the valorized self transmogrified, in another story or set of circumstances we could all be them; or we could adopt entirely different roles from those that are currently

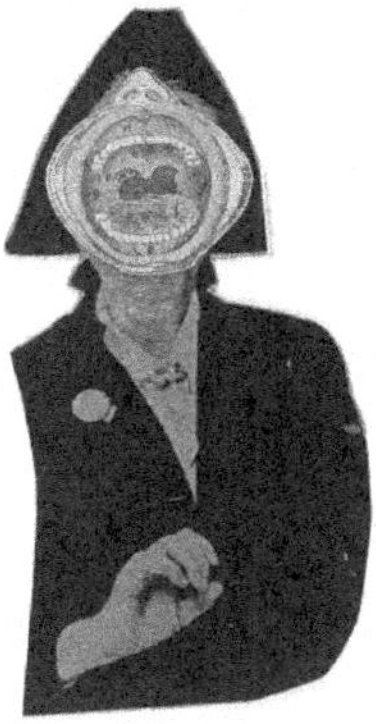

Figure 29. Ray Johnson, "Marianne Moore," collage, 1963. © The Ray Johnson Estate. Reprinted by kind permission.

on offer, were we so brave or imaginative. Moore in her black tricorne seems to function for Johnson as an example of a bold self-fashioner and a model for his own explorations.

Both Johnson and Moore require the active participation of their audiences in the construction of the meaning of their texts—by making them impossible to read without that and/or by directly calling for input from the audience in making the work. This dialogue creates an anti-hegemonic model not just for the art but also for the participants, who have to move out of their fixed positions into the process of making. Both model subversive celebrity, not as fixed or idealized icons but as collaboration. Johnson's images of Moore may read as both fond (Figure 26) and, arguably, critical (Figure 27), but the interest and sympathy flow consistently.

Moore's lifelong performance of alternative art and life styles was part of the history that set the frame within which artists like Warhol and Johnson, and poets like John Ashbery,[6] Elizabeth Bishop, Gwendolyn Brooks, Allen Ginsberg, Langston Hughes, Robert Lowell,[7] Frank O'Hara, Yoko Ono, Sylvia Plath, and others, made sense in their turn, even if Moore herself didn't always endorse their product. Her work then gained further energy from their work in the 1950s and 1960s, as they all pursued what were in many respects linked agendas of critique and innovation, which opened the path later for Language poets like Lyn Hejinian and Susan Howe, American Oulipian poets like Harryette Mullen—and more!

Appendix: The Retrospect, Moore's Shifting Texts, and Her Archive

The Retrospect

Early Days

Since Moore's later work builds on what came before, I offer here some brief context for those less familiar with her early oeuvre. Understanding of Moore's biography helpfully informs reading of her work, its gestures toward "impersonality" notwithstanding. The narrative of the "spinster" Moore as an asexual naïf has been reframed by biographer Linda Leavell's account of her unusual upbringing. Moore spent her teen years in what we could now call a lesbian household (though no such concept existed then), and, notably, her unapologetic mother and her partner were also passionately Christian. Mary Warner Moore had left her Bible-mad husband while pregnant with their second child (the nascent Marianne)[1] and never looked back—moving first to her minister father's manse and then, upon his death seven years later, to Pennsylvania, where in the small city of Carlisle she supported the family through teaching and frugal living.[2] She constructed a special family language and naming system with her son and daughter (Moore was called Ratty, Weasel, and Fangs, among other sobriquets) and a mythos of uniqueness that bound the three in a lifelong, extraordinarily tight unit, which expanded only once—but for a formative eleven years—to include Mary Warner's romantic partner, Mary Norcross, the daughter of the family's pastor.

Marianne herself was gender fluid from early days—acknowledged as female in sex but at her request called "brother" and with male pronouns at home.

At Bryn Mawr College, Moore, like many others in her peer group, had girl crushes—but they did not last. Through most of her life she seems not to have seriously considered romance with either sex,[3] and she was apparently a lifelong celibate. But as her poems' fiercely connective energy demonstrates, she was not asexual. Her *Dial* colleague Kenneth Burke remarked that "I never saw a more sexual woman, who was remote from all those things. Every damn thing was turned into little twists and turns"[4] (his phrasing suggests how the intimacy of shared attention may become sexualized). Nor was she sexually judgmental or obtuse: many of her close friends were lesbians and gay men, many in long-term relationships. Though a lifelong and staunch Republican by family inheritance, Moore was, as Leavell notes, "arguably the most liberal-minded of the modernists."[5] Instead of investing in a romantic partnership, Moore spent her first sixty years (excepting college [1905–9] and two months in 1911) living with her mother, until Mary Warner's death in 1947. Though Moore excluded her mother from some aspects of her world, she also loved and respected her, and sometimes quoted her in poems. Her Navy chaplain brother was also a household constant, though he often traveled for work and lived at a distance—at his jealous wife's insistence. The arrangement allowed Moore to devote herself to her poetry, uninterrupted by the demands of coupledom or children. Her poem "Marriage" (1923) conveys her sense of that institution's limitations, which it took "all one's criminal ingenuity / to avoid," and of the very different freedoms available to women who took themselves out of ordinary sexual circulation, embracing celibacy as a means of rejecting male power and redefining life options.

Moore's upbringing directly shaped the ways she could engage the world—both in poems and in life, allowing her to refuse standard narratives and to imagine the world radically otherwise. So did the avant-garde and little magazine cultures that encouraged her innovation and enabled her first forays into public performance and renown. Her work combines oblique but canny social and aesthetic commentary with her own highly original prosody (including syllabic meter;[6] extensive use of quotations to signal borrowing, irony, dialogue, and/or mottos; internal/"light" rhyme; disjunctive line breaks; interplay between poems and their notes; etc.) that allowed her to say new things, yet remain in dialogue with the forms she altered and their history.[7] The obscurity that insistently characterized much of Moore's work served her multiply: much beyond excluding her mother from full access, it offered Moore a way to explore issues forbidden overt statement in the political and social environment of the day; a way to claim authority as a female poet in a context in which that was rare; and a way to represent the world's fast-evolving complexity, allowing readers to construct their own innovative analyses in collaboration with the poet.

Literal Imagery

Among Moore's prosodic innovations, her habit of activating a poem's shape as part of its signification system has gone unrecognized to date. Several of Moore's later poems feature this technique but Moore employed it as early as 1924, in the second version she published of the precisely syllabic "Roses Only" (a poem she retired from her canon after 1935).

Roses Only

You do not seem to realize that beauty is a liability rather than
  an asset—that in view of the fact that spirit creates form we are justified in supposing
    that you must have brains. For you, a symbol of the unit, stiff and sharp,
  conscious of surpassing by dint of native superiority and liking for everything
self-dependent, anything an

ambitious civilization might produce: for you, unaided to attempt through sheer
  reserve, to confute presumptions resulting from observation, is idle. You cannot make us
    think you a delightful happen-so. But rose, if you are brilliant, it
  is not because your petals are the without-which-nothing of pre-eminence. You would, minus thorns,
look like a what-is-this, a mere

peculiarity. They are not proof against a worm, the elements, or mildew
  but what about the predatory hand? What is brilliance without co-ordination? Guarding the
    infinitesimal pieces of your mind, compelling audience to
  the remark that it is better to be forgotten than to be remembered too violently,
your thorns are the best part of you. (*Observations* 39)

This sharp poem intervenes in the tradition of poetic rose symbolism, asserting the need for women (like men) to coordinate their physical being with evidence of mental skills, in a world where "beauty is a liability."[8] The poem supports its case with evidence of both mental and physical strengths. Each stanza's lines measure 21/24/17/24/8 syllables, with an ABCBA rhyme scheme, which is skewed only in stanza 2, where the second line's end rhyme ("make us") finds its anticipated rhyme two lines later not with the end word but with the word before it ("minus").[9] In full-size type, the long line 9 requires a wraparound:[10]

> is not because your petals are the without-which-nothing of
> pre-eminence. You would, minus thorns (*NCP*, 37)

But when it is set as a single line, as with the smaller type above, the poem turns into an abstracted image of a rosebush, with "thorns" sticking out (dangerously) both in sound (through the lack of rhyme) and on the page. Moore knew that her wittily protracted line would not be visible to readers, but she labored to build it in nonetheless.[11] Even as the poem's "point" lies in affirming the rose's (and the poet's) wit and skill, this repression balances that with an additional dose of humility, veiling the poet's skill even as she displays it.[12] Many aspects of Moore's poems across her career perform similarly generative combinations of shyness and self-flaunting.

As with the "shape poems" of George Herbert, Moore's poems sometimes become "literal images," making pictures out of letters (often imprecise but evocative, as with the rosebush)—the flip side of the ekphrases that undergird many Moore poems.[13] The literal images join Moore's pattern of activating as signifiers many more of a poem's physical characteristics than usual (a precursor to the Concrete and Visual Poetry of the 1950s and after). In "Roses Only," the literal image activates the physical body of the poem so that it performs the coordinated relation of the rose's physical and cerebral aspects that the poem treats. The spelling pun in the phrase "writes errror with four /r's" in "The Pangolin" (1936) offers a related simultaneously physical and mental performance.[14] The unusual two-dimensional visual displays in the early work lay the groundwork for Moore's later addition of three-dimensional performances to her postwar poetry.

The poetic intersection with the visual also had a spiritual connection for Moore, one that directly connects to her love of William Blake, whose inspired, interactive texts and images Moore invokes in (at least) seventeen of her very early poems (1914–19), as Patricia Willis has shown, and from whom Moore derived her habit of balancing "contrarieties equally true."[15] As with Blake, the multimedia aspect of Moore's poems celebrates the many dimensions of creation.

Evolving Populism

Moore's 1924 collection *Observations* was well received, and her subsequent role as *Dial* editor in the late 1920s increased her renown and authority in modernist circles. In 1935, her reputation as a highbrow, challenging poet was solidified by the publication of her *Selected Poems*, and in particular by T. S. Eliot's introduction to that book, in which he deployed his authority as guarantor of hers.[16] Larded with quotable phrases,[17] Eliot's essay has been cited ever since by Moore's reviewers, relieving them of the task of accounting for her difficult work themselves (the *Newsweek* review cited in my Introduction invokes Eliot in line 2). But Moore came to question the value of modernism's "highbrow" mode: increasingly through the Depression and World War II she found that obliquity didn't serve her desire to connect to and express support for her fellow humans in times of hunger and need, or to aid the steeling of souls against the depredations of hatred. The further changes of the 1950s and 1960s continue an evolutionary pattern of democratization always active in Moore's work.

In his essay on Moore's "Democratic Taste," Patrick Redding tracks her negotiation of divided interests, from college through the 1920s: she makes a "distinction" between genuine (innovative) and derivative (ordinary) poetry, and prefers the genuine, while also acknowledging the value in common and often derivative objects ("business documents and // schoolbooks" ["Poetry," 1919, *NCP*, 27]) and in attracting ordinary citizens as readers.[18] Contra the conventional wisdom that pairs democracy and anti-intellectualism, Moore all along viewed intellectual engagement as essential to democracy—for teaching tolerance and equality, which both depend on the "persistent use of the 'mind' in the struggle for democratic justice."[19] But engaging all readers within a democracy through poetry required that the work be widely accessible, at least in some degree—even if levels of complexity also remained. Moore's tour-de-force poem "Poetry" explores and enacts through its odd prosody the means of "striving to hold quality and equality in a single thought."[20] But after including it in the first edition of her 1924 volume *Observations*, by 1925 Moore was already radically simplifying and cutting this poem for the second edition, out of concern that it was too difficult to engage many readers. (The simplification didn't satisfy, however, and close variants of the 1924 text reappeared in her 1935 and 1951 collections, only to be radically reduced [from 36 to 3 lines] in the 1967 *Complete Poems.*) Responding to critic Herbert Gorman's critique of *Observations* as difficult and therefore "undemocratic," Moore's 1925 revision of both the poem's argument for democratic poetry and its structure is multiply ironic, at the same time that it continues the struggle to balance aesthetic skill with accessibility. Luke Carson and Odile Harter have explored Moore's conflicted allegiances in the post-*Dial* 1930s where her investment in elite artistic excellence achieved through hard intellectual work and superior skills was countered by her equally strong need to respond ethically to the great economic suffering of the Depression; they demonstrate that her poetry of the 1930s became more accessible than that of the decade prior.

As with "Poetry," Moore felt free to evolve all her poems with each republication and even in individual copies of books that she'd been given to autograph, keeping them all in an ongoing draft process in her head. Her published poems also remained in constant dialogue with her new work. Issues that arise in a poem of the 1920s appear again years later in new poems that take up the conversation as though only moments had passed, though reframed to fit the style Moore had come to consider most fruitful for reaching her audience at the later point. This shifting approach to prosody, material, and audience mirrors the multiple interpretations that readers may bring to Moore's work, endorsed through its active refusal to be specific. ("I will never be entirely certain of what 'it' is in 'The Fish,'" noted John Ashbery some years later—spotlighting Moore's method of obscured reference, which might be said to have generated his entire oeuvre.)[21]

In seeking to accommodate the economic and political climate of the 1930s, Moore adopted a more narrative style and focused on broad themes—including America's history of tension between freedom struggles and racist oppression ("Virginia Britannia," "The Hero") and the ethical and emotional dynamics of creaturely existence ("The Pangolin," "Pigeons," "Bird Witted"). In response to the upheaval of World War II, Moore's poetry again shifted in topic, attitude, and form, aiming to reach a yet wider audience.[22] Anticipating Paulo Freire's pedagogy of the oppressed (who for Moore included middlebrow citizens), her 1940s poems were, per Margaret Holley, "more comfortable to the general reader . . . and probably [therefore] on the whole more moving and memorable . . . without sacrificing Moore's distinctive signature."[23] For *What Are Years* (October 1941), she greatly revised poems she'd written in the 1930s to match the style of the more recent poems they were republished with. Heather Cass White reads this simplifying revision as a sign of Moore having lost faith in her audience's ability to deal with ambiguity and complexity. But her revisionary practice served her effort to move beyond her coterie audience in pursuit of new, wider publics—with less time for or interest in contemplation. "I rekkonize my trouble, as being too oblique & obscure," Moore noted in a January 1941 letter to her brother, in which she also discusses the remaindering of her 1935 *Selected Poems*.[24] Her 1940s poems are Moore's most anthologized.

Though most critics to date have read the 1940s poems as over-sentimental and under-artful, Cristanne Miller argues that Moore's drafts demonstrate that she thoughtfully developed an "emotional register to construct a simultaneously political and spiritual exploration of the ethics of individual response to the issues raised by international genocide and world war." Miller looks in particular at "In Distrust of Merits" (1943), which turns to compassion and love as antidotes to the ambient violence and hatred, and views personal ethical choices as the basis for national ones. The final stanza concludes thus:

> Hate-hardened heart, O heart of iron,
> iron is iron till it is rust.
> There never was a war that was
> not inward; I must
> fight till I have conquered in myself what
> causes war, but I would not believe it.
> I inwardly did nothing.
> O Iscariotlike crime!
> Beauty is everlasting
> and dust is for a time. (*NCP*, 172, ll. 71–80)

Here Moore espouses a doctrine of individual responsibility for all the world's harms, in a language of direct emotional appeal,[25] employing a first-person speaker who represents the public in conversation with itself.[26] All the poems of her 1940s *Nation* phase[27] presented her as an affective poet, directly addressing America's patriotism, misery, and hopes, and affirming a global human ethics. Her war work's success laid the groundwork for her late-career renown. In the postwar years, Moore recasts this affective nexus, moving from the patriotic group level back to a more personal level, but maintaining an emotional circuit between group and individual feelings.

While her war poems were loved by many, some disagreed: Randall Jarrell took particular exception. He had reviewed Moore's *What Are Years* with profuse praise in 1942—calling her "the greatest living woman poet," admiring her minute animals and moralized exotica, celebrating her skills in making the most of her restricted universe ("Miss Moore *has* her limitations—her work is one long triumph of them"). He praises her for succeeding in the realm he considers appropriate to old women. Three years later, reviewing *Nevertheless* (1944), he savages the same world he'd praised—famously lambasting Moore for "sen[ding] postcards to only the nicer animals." "In Distrust" particularly angered him: "For this poem Miss Moore has given up her usual method, because of the emotion and generality that have overwhelmed her. I wish that she had—as the world has—taken her little animals, her bric-a-brac with all their moral and aesthetic qualities, her individuals with their scrupulous virtues, and shown them smashed willy-nilly, tortured, prostituted, driven crazy—and not for a while but forever; that is, till the day they died."[28] A rather violent response to a poem that actually does notice misery ("The world's an orphans' home. Shall / we never have peace without sorrow?"), while looking for some lesson to draw from the huge loss of life. One source of his strong response seems to lie in her movement out of bounds—into the masculine realm of war, which he feels she thoroughly misunderstands.

Despite Jarrell's implication, however, Moore did know something about loss: the stresses of the war both general and individual (her brother served as Admiral Nimitz's chaplain in the South Pacific) and her own illnesses, along with her care for her sick mother, all devastated Moore in the 1940s and reinforced the emotional quality of her work. The six poems of *Nevertheless* comprised a tiny but powerful volume in that moment, laden with memorable, encouraging maxims ("What sap / went through that little thread / to make the cherry red!" "Nevertheless" [*NCP*, 162]) and deeply felt considerations of experience ("he / is not here to worship and he is too wise / to mourn,—a life prisoner but reconciled," "Elephants" [*NCP*, 165]). *Nevertheless* continued Moore's ongoing effort at integration of a wide audience with committed democratic, ethical thought.[29] Jarrell's disciplinary, misogynistic review, which works to push Moore and her affective concerns out of the main poetic arena, could only have exacerbated an already painful time, but it didn't sway her.[30]

Two years later in 1947, Moore's mother's death further affected and altered her work. Mary Warner Moore had served her daughter as source of poetic material, as critic, as inspiring companion, and (per Leavell) as a spur to her obscure style. The poem "A Face" (1947), written just after Mary Warner's death, pays quiet tribute—moving Moore's work into the personal realm:

A Face

"I am not treacherous, callous, jealous, superstitious,
supercilious, venomous, or absolutely hideous":
    studying and studying its expression,
    exasperated desperation
        though at no real impasse,
        would gladly break the glass;

when love of order, ardor, uncircuitous simplicity,
with an expression of inquiry, are all one needs to be!
    Certain faces, a few, one or two—or one
    face photographed by recollection—
        to my mind, to my sight,
        must remain a delight. (*Collected Poems*, 141)

The poem offers an expressive glimpse of strong emotion about the loss of the "one / face photographed by recollection." A later version of the poem added a performative element, enacting the desire to break things that was expressed at the end of stanza 1, by substituting "mirror" for "glass" and thus breaking the rhyme scheme and the poetic fourth wall. This dialogic dynamic across the two versions combines direct violent expression of emotion (in the rhyme break) with representation of the passage of time (via the revision), and through those it suggests a lifetime of love as well as the ongoing process of mourning.[31] This performative quality recurs in diverse ways in many later poems.

After Moore's *Collected Poems* piled up prizes and she became famous to millions, she extended her habit of evolving her poetic techniques to meet the current cultural context, morphing them further to engage and respond to the popular culture of the 1950s, in which she had new status as a celebrity of the new postwar type.

Moore's Shifting Texts

Understanding of Moore's career arc has been complicated by her revisions of poems over years and her omissions of many early poems from her later collections. Her famously incomplete *Complete Poems* (1967; 1981) contains fewer than two-thirds of her published poems, some in versions greatly changed from their initially published texts. These transformations created both confusion and a gap in the historic record, since unwitting new readers couldn't tell that the poems differed greatly from what their first readers had encountered. It makes some sense that fans of the early work would feel uncharitably toward her later self for this obstructionism, at the same time that many of them, without considering the context, view the later work negatively precisely for being so accessible, since an important element of engagement with the early work often involves pleasures associated with rigorous effort. Taking seriously *Complete Poems*' emphatic epigraph "Omissions are not accidents," we can recognize that she made these changes as part of her wider effort to retool her oeuvre for her new public, even while we may lament that the revisions and cuts long impeded full understanding and appreciation of her early accomplishment. Since 2000, six new editions of Moore's work have appeared in print, all of them seeking to provide a fuller sense of various aspects of the work. My ideal volume would include all the books Moore published, in sequence[32]—providing readers with the evolving history and context of each poem's presentation. While Moore's post-1951 revisions of earlier poems are themselves arguably part of her late-phase oeuvre, this volume focuses on the new work first produced in this period.

Moore's Archive

Many of the later poems' ephemeral cultural references that would have been obvious to their initial readers are inevitably less clear to readers decades after. Usefully, Moore provided endnotes to many of her poems, which fill in some gaps for later readers.[33] In addition, she made and actively preserved an enormous cache of documentation, including: 122 handwritten notebooks (divided into three sets: notes toward poems, reading notes, and notes on conversations); decades worth of detail-filled daily appointment calendars (1931–69); extensive correspondence with hundreds of friends, family members, literary peers, editors, and so on;

and multiple typescript drafts of many poems. My understanding of the poems' concerns and evolution, developed within an effective literary critical vacuum, has benefited greatly from reviewing and cross-referencing as much of all of these forms of documentation as I could, but the material is so voluminous that I haven't been able to read through it all on numerous visits to Moore's archive in Philadelphia. As a result, in addition to interpretative differences, future researchers will likely find factual holes to fill in my arguments (omissions here may well be accidental!) and outright errors. But I have discovered quite a bit that should be of interest to Moore scholars and fans, and I am happy to be part of reintroducing to critical discussion and analysis this wonderful body of poetry and the astonishing archives that support it. The Marianne Moore Digital Archive team led by Cristanne Miller, of which I am also pleased to be a part, is in the process of transcribing the notebooks and calendars and putting them online so that readers around the world can access them easily in future.

Moore's active self-archiving—holding on to so many pages for decades in small apartments and eventually selling them to the Rosenbach Museum and Library in Philadelphia—suggests that she intended them as scholarly aids, and occasionally she makes comments in the notebooks that directly address scholars to come (see, for instance, the epigraphs to Chapter 1). Indeed they are very helpful—not because they tell us the "right" meanings but because they allow us to track her associative writing processes, her multifarious sources, and some of the connections among her work, her life, and the artistic and social issues in play at the time of the poems' birth—all of which offer significant insights for our reading in the present. More than most poets, Moore seems to have regarded all her poems and their various iterations as parts of one palimpsestic oeuvre in progress.

In this volume, I draw where relevant on source texts that Moore quotes from or invokes; poem drafts; poems' histories of revision across publications; Moore's notes and letters; and personal and public current events to which she refers. Though Moore scholars have long referenced materials from her archive, this study does more of that than usual, in an effort both to track the associative processes that connect elements within the poems (documenting Moore's own associations, and associations contemporary readers might also have made) and to explore Moore's edits and the logic behind them (particularly in relation to her evolving sense of audience) as they played out across versions of the work, which I read as aspects of the total poem-in-process. My method inevitably raises questions about what constitutes a poem, questions that Moore pointedly refuses to allow us to easily answer. I hope readers will find the method fruitful and enlightening, as well as, sometimes, destabilizing.

Permissions

Given that there are many editions and versions of the poems and that these vary, please note that throughout I cite the *New Collected Poems* (*NCP*, 2017) text, as the most complete, correct, judicious, and consistent of the several volumes of Moore's published work available, with exceptions as indicated.

Elements of this book have appeared previously in *Discourse*, *Journal of Modern Literature*, *Modernism/modernity*, *Critics and Poets on Marianne Moore: "A Right Good Salvo of Barks,"* and *Twenty-First Century Marianne Moore: Essays from a Critical Renaissance.*

Notes

Abbreviations

Becoming	*Becoming Marianne Moore: The Early Poems, 1907–1924*. Edited by Robin G. Schulze. Berkeley: University of California Press, 2002.
CP	*The Complete Poems of Marianne Moore*. Rev. ed. New York: Macmillan/Viking, 1981.
CPr	*The Complete Prose of Marianne Moore*. Edited by Patricia C. Willis. New York: Viking, 1986.
CRMM	*The Critical Response to Marianne Moore*. Edited by Elizabeth Gregory. Westport, CT: Praeger, 2003.
Holding On	*Holding On Upside Down: The Life and Work of Marianne Moore*. By Linda Leavell. New York: Farrar, Straus and Giroux, 2013.
NCP	*New Collected Poems of Marianne Moore*. Edited by Heather Cass White. New York: Farrar, Straus and Giroux, 2017.
PMM	*The Poetry of Marianne Moore: A Study in Voice and Value*. By Margaret Holley. Cambridge: Cambridge University Press, 1987.
RML	Marianne Moore Collection, Rosenbach Museum and Library, of the Free Library of Philadelphia. Philadelphia, Pennsylvania.
SelLet	*The Selected Letters of Marianne Moore*. Edited by Bonnie Costello, Celeste Goodridge, and Cristanne Miller. New York: Alfred A. Knopf, 1997.
TFCMM	*Twenty-First Century Marianne Moore: Essays from a Critical Renaissance*. Edited by Elizabeth Gregory and Stacy Carson Hubbard. New York: Palgrave, 2017.
TMTM	*Tell Me, Tell Me: Granite, Steel, and Other Topics*. By Marianne Moore. New York: Viking, 1966.

Introduction

1. "Best Living Poet." Emphasis added.

2. Aldington, "Review of *Observations*."

3. Such judgment fuels this cavalier roasting of the later Moore by a poet who admires her early work: "It is difficult to understand how Moore, so strictly 'abstinent,' could, late in life, have become such a spectacle. In the bizarre eye blink of her celebrity, when she showed up in *Seventeen* and *Ladies Home Journal*, on the *Tonight Show* and at the Polo Grounds, she became (to borrow a phrase from Randall Jarrell) 'the only living Marianne Moore in captivity.' . . . The poems from this period were . . . not very interesting by-product[s] of her photogenic eccentricity: she does her baseball poems, her poems for Christmas and Valentine's Day; she has seen various things on TV and gives her poetic two cents. She is never, in these poems, grave enough for her subjects; even baseball she underestimates, turning athletes of remarkable prowess and beauty into adorable buffoons. . . The late poems are an example of genius in soft-focus" (Chiasson, "What Color Is Jerboa Fur?").

4. Since I began writing on Moore's later work in 1994, the field has expanded. John Emil Vincent's perceptive analyses of the refusal of closure in three late Moore poems (*Queer Lyrics* [2002]) offer direct encounters with what is on the page rather than with what is rumored to be there. Charles Berger explores the engagement of Moore's late work with that of her friend Wallace Stevens around legacy ("Moore after Stevens" [2007]). Benjamin Kahan's theorization of Moore's celibacy (her "hypereroticized abstinence" [520]) with particular attention to *Tell Me, Tell Me* ("'The Viper's Traffic-Knot'" [2008]) has advanced Moore studies, as has other work that recognizes the erotic energies of the late poetry—by Elizabeth Wilson ("El Greco's Daughter" [2005]); Cristanne Miller ("'By-Play'" [2008]); and Elien Arckens ("'In This Told-Backward Biography'" [2016]).

Eco-critical readings by David W. Gilcrest ("Rhetorical Redemption, Environmental Poetics, and the Case of the Camperdown Elm" [2001]), Kirby Olson ("Marianne Moore's 'The Camperdown Elm' and the Revival of Brooklyn's Prospect Park" [2011]), Sharla Hutchison ("The Eco-Poetics of Marianne Moore's 'The Sycamore'" [2011]), and others, of late poems like "The Camperdown Elm" and "Sycamore," locate Moore as an eco-activist, whose later work expands on environmental concerns present in earlier work and on related ethical concerns raised by linguistic co-optation through description. Zhaoming Qian ("Mai-Mai Sze, the Tao, and Moore's Late Poetry" [2013]) has revealed as influential Moore's reading of Sze's 1956 book *The Tao of Painting* and their subsequent correspondence. Other important interventions around Moore's late work include those by Catherine Gunther Kodat (*Don't Act, Just Dance* [2014]) on Moore's political response to the Cold War; Benjamin Johnson ("Marianne Moore's 'Abraham Lincoln and the Art of the Word'" [2015]) on Moore's post-1951 echoing of Lincoln's civic piety; Emily Setina ("Marianne Moore's Postwar Fables and the Politics of Indirection" [2016]) on Moore's translations of La Fontaine's *Fables*; Aurore Clavier ("'The First Grace of Style'" [2017]) on Moore's late work on dance; Zachary Finch ("'Passion for the Particular'" [2017]) on "Tell Me, Tell Me." My own essays about Moore's later poetry written over the past twenty-plus years are evolved and absorbed herein. This volume makes the first book-length argument for Moore's work of the period as a whole. That several critics have identified the later poems they examine as ars poetica supports the view that Moore wrote self-consciously about her own methods in this phase.

5. *Holding On*, 146ff. Nonetheless, Moore occasionally borrowed Mary's words (a form of collaboration), to either endorse or dispute them, and sometimes discussed poems with her.

6. July 30 in subsequent publications.

7. This version of the note appeared in *Partisan Review* (Fall 1956): 506. Throughout this book, I cite full poems where possible and relevant, but readers are encouraged to have a copy of Moore's poems to hand for reference. The 2017 *New Collected Poems* (*NCP*) and the 1967/1981 *Complete Poems* (*CP*) are good sources for the later work. Because Moore's notes function as part of her poetry, I will cite the notes linked to the lines quoted. Where textual differences among versions warrant, I cite poems' original magazine publications, versions from other collections, or drafts, all noted.

8. Chasar, *Everyday Reading*, 1–26.

9. Joan Shelley Rubin's *Songs of Ourselves* charts the shifting, crowded territory of U.S. poetry between 1880 and 1959 and demonstrates the absence of firm brow divisions in reading practices. She characterizes the poetry scene as *multivocal*—full of diverse types of poems, widely read by a population skilled at memorization, seeking intellectual and emotional stimulus. Readers of the period (as now) might enjoy both modernist poetry and old favorites. From early days, Moore's work reflected this complexity, actively challenging high/low divisions by including a wide range of materials and tones, often in one poem.

10. Ngai, *Our Aesthetic Categories*.

11. Braudy, *The Frenzy of Renown*; Marshall, *Celebrity and Power*.

12. Braudy, *The Frenzy of Renown*, 371–89.

13. Marshall, *Celebrity and Power*, 241, 244.

14. Bryant, *Women's Poetry and Popular Culture*, 2.

15. Glass, *Literary Celebrity in the Modern United States, 1880–1980*.

16. See, for example, Huyssen, *After the Great Divide*.

17. O'Hara, "Statement for *The New American Poetry*."

18. "Axis of the Hairfine Moon."

19. Henderson, "'In the Public Garden,'" 15. Henderson pinpoints Moore's late-phase performance focus, frames it in relation to her early work's different engagement with performers and playwright-celebrities (Shaw and Molière), and analyzes in depth her two late occasional poems as well as aspects of her performance techniques.

20. Filreis, "The End of the End of Poetic Ideology, 1960," 509–10.

21. Rukeyser, "The Rhythm Is the Person," 18.

22. Hughes, quoted in Gilroy, "Marianne Moore Wins Gold Medal."

23. Lowell to Bishop, November 22, 1964, in *Words in Air*, ed. Hamilton, 560.

24. Bishop, "Efforts of Affection," 139, 140.

25. Once attention is turned to this work, it will take time for many of the poems' dynamics recognizable by Moore's contemporaries to be even observed, let alone evaluated, by twenty-first-century readers and critics.

Chapter One

First epigraph *Note: RML*, VII:11:02 (1942–196-?): "August 9, 1937." This notebook is a repurposed 1937 date book; the printed dates have no relation to the date of Moore's entries. Second epigraph *Note: RML*, VII:04:05 (1961–70): 48.

1. Moore's unpublished memoir, cited in Dever, "'If She Were Here Tonight, She'd Be Right at Home.'" Elizabeth Bishop described Moore as resembling "a feminine, luminescent, delicate re-incarnation of Paul Revere" (Bishop to Moore, July 16, 1954, cited in *Holding On*, 421), but Moore referenced Washington twice when she recounted describing her desired hat to her milliner, in the article cited above and in a 1965 interview where she reported having told the milliner "I want a sort of George Washington Federal Troops hat, with tails in back" (Foley, "Genius at Work").

2. The clasp featured the 1921 Morgan Silver Dollar, with Lady Liberty in profile, and the words "E Pluribus Unum."

3. Moore's impersonation of Washington, in light of her 1932 poem "The Hero" (see the Introduction), invokes Washington's full story—including his slave ownership. The transvestite element of Moore's costume and its history as suffrage headgear (see note 7 in this chapter) raise questions about women's limited rights in American history, and Moore's advanced years add age dynamics to the identity/status questions. The silver-dollar clasp reminds us that Washington operates as guarantor of our currency (see Gregory, "Stamps, Money, Pop Culture and Marianne Moore").

4. Roffman, "'Mysteries Expound Mysteries,'" 193.

5. *Holding On*, 342.

6. Moore to John Warner Moore, February 28, 1950, *RML*, VI:39:23.

7. Mary Chapman notes that Moore wore a tricorne at a suffrage protest in the 1910s, when it was suffrage "parade headgear" of choice (*Making Noise, Making News*, 127), another historical echo in Moore's 1950s performance.

8. See discussion of Moore's active persona formation in *Holding On*, 342ff.

9. Tom Fool went ten for ten, including the 1953 Triple Crown of New York Handicap races (the Metropolitan, Suburban, and Brooklyn Handicaps).

10. Though Moore enjoyed being featured, she disliked the reductively sexist terms (as a "charmingly quixotic intellectual flirt") in which Winthrop Sargeant portrayed her, per her friend Chester Page (cited in *Holding On*, 359).

11. Moore met Ali in person in 1967 via George Plimpton, and they cowrote a poem (he wrote most) about Ali's upcoming fight with Ernie Terrell (Plimpton, *Shadow Box*, 124–29). Moore wrote the 1963 liner notes at the invitation of Miles Kreuger, a Columbia Records employee who had previously staffed Long John Nebel's all-night radio call-in show. Per Kreuger, Moore was a night owl and phoned in regularly (phone interview with author, June 10, 2018).

12. *Holding On*, 371. Since they taped over old shows, only two clips survive: great interviews with Robert Kennedy and Martin Luther King. Moore appeared on Wednesday, February 7, 1968. See Yoruba Richen's documentary *The Sit-In* (Peacock, 2020): https://www.peacocktv.com/the-sit-in-harry-belafonte. See also White, "Harry Belafonte and Marianne Moore on the Tonight Show," and Walsh, "49 Years Ago, Harry Belafonte Hosted the Tonight Show—and It Was Amazing."

13. While Moore's *Selected Poems* (1935) sold fewer than 2,000 copies total, sales began trending up with *Nevertheless* in 1944 (4,000-plus in three printings). The U.S.

edition of *Collected Poems* (1951) sold 6,600 copies the first year (its ten printings by 1961 sold more than 20,000), plus 3,500 U.K. copies. *Like a Bulwark* (1956) sold out its first printing of 2,500 copies in four months, followed by a second printing of 1,500; *O to Be a Dragon* (1959) went to four printings (8,800 copies) within one year; and *Tell Me, Tell Me* (1966) sold out two printings (totaling 10,500 copies) in nine months, followed by a third printing of 2,000. Moore's translation of *The Fables of La Fontaine* (1954) went to three printings in one year (8,000-plus copies), and 10,000 copies more were printed in the 1960s. Her *Marianne Moore Reader* (1961) had seven printings in eleven years, selling about 20,000 copies. Abbott, *Marianne Moore*, 13–18, 26–28, 34–41, 62–62, 69–71, 99–102, 42–53, 72–78.

14. Pound's status was complicated by his treasonous rants and his committal to St. Elizabeths psychiatric hospital.

15. See Jaffe, *Modernism and the Culture of Celebrity*. Moore enjoyed Eliot's *The Cocktail Party* several times on Broadway but disliked Celia's violent death ("[I] confess that it seems to me that one or the other might have been as strong as both, crucifixion and the ants"): January 21, 1950, *RML*, V:18:01. Eliot also explored fame, more privately—his stories for his godchildren on ways of creating fame and authority were published in 1939 as *Old Possum's Book of Practical Cats*, first set to music in 1954, and brought to the stage in 1981 as *Cats! The Musical*.

16. Moore's commentary was recorded at her 1965 reading at Harvard (*The Poet's Voice*).

17. Though David Anderson points to the relation of the tricorne to Moore's democratic interests, he focuses on her work of the 1920s and 1930s.

18. Kent, *Making Girls into Women*, 181, 187.

19. She seems rarely if ever to have cut her hair—so though the hair framing her face was white, her braid was brown.

20. The petite Moore preferred a men's size 42 shirt (*Holding On*, 308). Moore's friend Hildegarde Watson (artist and wife of *Dial* publisher James Sibley Watson) took great pleasure in dressing Moore for her performances, supplying elegant clothing and gardenia corsages. Cristanne Miller notes that "Moore adopted a style of dress that rides the line between masculinity and femininity" (*Cultures of Modernism*, 103–5).

21. Moore's interest in cross-dressing surfaces in a passage inscribed in a late-phase poetry notebook: the phrase "'Foremost of the Peach Orchard'" (in quotations) is followed by the citation "NYT Aug 9 1961" and a comment: "Alas, a communist!" (*RML*, VII:04:05 [1961–70]: 13). The first phrase comes from the obituary for Chinese female impersonator Mei Lan-Fang (women were forbidden the Chinese stage). His career spanned 1905–61, but, the obituary recounts, "he did not join the Communist Party until 1959." The article's subtitle reads "Top Chinese Star Was Noted as Female Impersonator": Moore's interests in things Chinese and in cross-dressing as well as Mei's status as a "top star" could all have drawn her to his story. She likely saw him on his 1930 world tour (*Times* reviewer Brooks Atkinson praised the "exquisite loveliness in pantomime and costume [that makes you] feel yourself vaguely in contact . . . with the strange ripeness of centuries"). In a 1952 letter to Ezra and Dorothy Pound, Moore recalls him and his performance as "a masterpiece of whom I would be ignorant had it not been for Gilbert Seldes [the *Dial*'s drama critic], who warned me not to miss him" (*SelLet*, 503).

22. Ball, on the other hand, though she had also refrained from having children early on, willingly acceded to that pressure when at thirty-nine she had her first child in June 1951, and her second practically on camera, as part of the sit-com's plot. The arrival of Little Ricky was celebrated on the cover of the first issue of *TV Guide*, making explicit television's investment in the battle over how to combine the historically unpaid female labor of reproducing the human race with the historically male world of paid work.

23. See Winthrop Sargeant's profile of Moore, "Profiles: Humility, Concentration, and Gusto," 64.

24. *Holding On*, 342.

25. See Appendix, 200.

26. Ngai, *Our Aesthetic Categories*, 183.

27. As she noted while reading "In Lieu of the Lyre": "I tend to bathos. I like bathos" (*The Poet's Voice*).

28. John Slatin recognizes the ways 1950s anti-feminism limited Moore's options, in "'Something Inescapably Typical.'"

29. The original zanies were sixteenth-century clowns who imitated the lead actors in the Italian commedia dell'arte, often jumping between roles erratically.

30. Ngai, *Our Aesthetic Categories*, 8.

31. Mak, "On Falling Fastidiously," 875. Mak explores Moore's 1920s interest in Chaplin's self-abnegating celebrity presentation as a "melding of person and persona," which helped shape her later persona.

32. Moore to Mary Craig Shoemaker, February 29, 1950, *RML*, V:60:03; Moore to John Warner Moore, October 1953 (labeled November), *RML*, VI:39:63.

33. *RML*, VII:11:02 (1942–196-?): "August 11."

34. Margaret Holley understands "Apparition of Splendor" to continue Moore's long line of war poems (from the World War I poem "The Fish" [1917] through 1948's military-minded "Like a Bulwark") (*PMM*, 140–41). "Apparition" can be read as a pacifist argument against continuation of the Korean War if the porcupine is read as a model American (and Mainer) because it resists oppression without actually firing its quills.

35. See, for instance, Howard, "Marianne Moore and the Monkey Business of Modernism," 3.

36. Vincent, *Queer Lyrics*, 89–119.

37. Ibid., 93–94.

38. "My tunic is closer than my cloak."

39. *PMM*, 18.

40. Rieke, "'Plunder' or 'Accessibility to Experience,'" 155. As Rieke elucidates, Moore felt increasingly ambivalent about the use of furs and other animal products in clothing.

41. Her notes suggest it was begun in January 1952 or December 1951. *RML*, VII:11:02 (1942–196-?): "August 9–15."

42. Moore's uses of quotation always involved puns on the meanings of those diacritical marks—which can mark borrowed words, dialogue, words used as words, titles, mottos, and irony.

43. Ermines only look spotted when dead, when the black fur of their tail-ends dot the royal vestments into which they are gathered.

44. Actually it's her *off-rhyme* scheme, in which the first, third, and fourth lines of most stanzas end with similar syllables or phonemes. This insistently variant pattern (stanza 6 departs entirely) supports the poem's assertion that "nothing's certain."

45. Vincent, *Queer Lyrics*, 95.

46. In her notes for this poem, Moore remarks of the Crow (with "his black never somber irridescent coat") that it is "Pleasant to be that sort of blackamoor / Conspicuously anonymous." *RML*, VII:11:02 (1942–196-?): "August 10."

47. H. D. to Moore, September 7, 1915, cited, with photo, in Willis, "Marianne Moore on May Day, 1906."

48. This ermine invokes several earlier references (the mountain goat in "An Octopus" has an "ermine body," a "wood-weasel" is an ermine in winter, and "New York" is "starred with tepees of ermine"). Levy borrows the phrase "special chastity" from Blackmur (Levy, *Criminal Ingenuity*, 65).

49. Having made the case for these characters serving in part as figures for Moore, I must also mention that beside notes about the Crow for this poem Moore writes "He/it doesn't describe me." *RML*, VII:11:02 (1942–196-?): "August 11." This notebook includes more than one such address to readers-to-come, often rather arch (turning the notebooks into a performance space as well); such protesting—whether ironic or sincere—easily suggests its opposite.

50. This kind of doubled meaning echoes in the invocations of several multihued objects: the settee made of "ebony violet" palisandre (rosewood), the black/purple violets, and the blue-black crow.

51. Moore, *Sister Arts*.

52. Costello, *Marianne Moore*, 192; Loiseaux, "Women Looking," 122–23.

53. Glavey, *The Wall-Flower Avant Garde*, 20–21.

54. Ibid., 4.

55. Ibid., 6.

56. Cited in ibid., 4.

57. Hall, *Marianne Moore*, 147.

58. Though her (younger) friend Elizabeth Bishop had had a first-refusal contract with the *New Yorker* since 1940, before 1953 Moore had never had a poem accepted there (a point of some bemused lamentation).

59. "For February 14th" was rejected because it "remained something of a cipher" and "Tell Me, Tell Me" was initially rejected as too "puzzling" but then taken with some edits. Howard Moss to Moore, January 27, 1959; Katharine White to Moore, September 18, 1959, both in *RML*, V:45:02.

60. See Hammill, "*The New Yorker*, the Middle Brow and the Periodical Marketplace in 1925," 18.

61. The proportion of comic poems in the magazine decreased steadily over the 1950s, and while Moore's first two accepted poems were comic, those after were not, though some involved humor.

62. Bishop, *Elizabeth Bishop & the* New Yorker, 40. Bishop published more than fifty poems there.

63. On the middlebrow debate, see Perrin, "On Blustering." Over the late 1950s and 1960s, many "serious" younger poets began appearing in the magazine, including Anne Sexton, W. S. Merwin, John Updike, W. H. Auden, etc. Moore was one of the few

poets of her generation and stature to appear, combining status as both sainted relic and active poet working in a new style.

64. Among them, he requested a change of title from the original "Caduceus," which was the name of Hermes' similar staff, with two snakes, not the symbol of medicine.

65. Moore, "An Interview with Donald Hall," 263.

66. Anderson, "Marianne Moore's 'Fertile Procedure,'" 90.

67. Actually, the article cited appeared in no. 180; this poem appeared in no. 186.

68. See discussions in Sielke, *Fashioning the Female Subject*, 83–84, and Miller, *Cultures of Modernism*, 89–111.

69. From her early, posthumously published poem "Emeralds" (*PMM*, 35).

70. "If I Were Sixteen Today," *CPr*, 503.

71. Hubbard, "Mannerist Moore," 122, 115.

72. Documented in the Metropolitan Museum of Art's 2019 show *Camp: Notes on Fashion*.

73. Moore's sound-alike friend Marion Morehouse was a photographer, E. E. Cummings's wife, and the first celebrity model (see *New York Times*, May 19, 1969, 47).

74. See Leavell, *Marianne Moore and the Visual Arts*, and Loiseaux, "Women Looking."

75. Note in Moore's appointment book for September 13, 1954, *RML*.

76. Moore to Allene Talmey, *Vogue*, 1950, *RML*, V:68:13.

77. The note in *NCP* (326) treats this material at greater length.

78. Brewer, *Dictionary*, 2410. In copying this passage into her notebook, Moore omitted the direct references to love making (italicized), suggesting the importance of the erotic here all the more, by the contrary logic of repression. In the early drafts, Moore cites Brewer on rosemary's symbolic associations to the linked set of erotic love, remembrance, and fidelity, and additional sources tying it to Christian legend. The phrase "Hath a dumb language" is repurposed from Sir Thomas More, on rosemary as a symbol of friendship.

79. Beauty is also presented as a source of status and wealth (*Vogue*'s implicit narrative includes the exchange of sex for money through "marrying well," often the backstory to affording the goods offered).

80. *RML*, I:04:10, "Rosemary" notes. "The Rosemary of Europe is unlike ours. It is an evergreen erect shrub, four to eight feet high . . . growing in sunny places, on rocks and old walls in countries around the Mediterranean Sea. . . While dedicated to the Virgin, it is really Rosemarious or Rosmarinus—Rose of the Sea; our Rosemary is really Sea Lavender . . . Elizabeth Todd Nash: *One Hundred and One Legends of Flowers*."

81. "The Past Is the Present," like "A Face" and "Poetry," appears in several versions that effectively put the initial text in motion over time, by introducing changes that enact what the poem claims. The initial version (active from *Observations* through the *Collected Poems*) rhymes, in direct contrast to the poem's claim that rhyme is outmoded—but the *Complete Poems* version cuts the rhymes, to offer an opposite structural argument, and thus reinforces (with less obvious, but still active, irony) the argument that form matters little.

82. When Moore works through drafts, the cut bits still resonate, buried in the poem's emotional frame.

83. Similar plays on Moore's names seem active in "Blue Bug" (see Chapter 2) and in "Sun" (see Chapter 5).

84. Tiffany, "Cheap Signaling."

85. Following Clement Greenberg, I use the term "kitsch" broadly here, as does Tiffany—to include familiar, received ideas that require little or no reflection to process. Per Greenberg, kitsch "has many different levels. . . A magazine like the *New Yorker*, which is fundamentally high-class kitsch for the luxury trade, converts and waters down a great deal of avant-garde material for its own uses" ("Avant Garde and Kitsch," 11).

86. Tiffany, "Cheap Signaling."

87. See discussion of Moore's relation to Plath and her husband, Ted Hughes, in Chapter 4.

Chapter Two

1. Along with social engagements, Moore's appointment books (*RML*) include notes on writing projects, correspondence, church music, errands, and housekeeping—cheek by jowl. The following items (from 1952) hint at the range and density of activity: "Fixing girdle on sewing machine/ Museum Mod Art 6:30/ Redon drawings -/ Monroe [Wheeler]. K. Burke. J. Flanner" (February 26); "Pulitzer Prize/ $500 [in red pencil]" (May 5); "Added 2 stanzas to poem/ Title: "Then the Ermine" (July 2); "MS of Allen Ginsberg/ mailed it . . . Empty Mirror" (July 4); "Ticket for Washington . . . Ezra & Mrs. Pound" (July 15); "Cat Morgan fr. TSE" (July 17); "Glenway's party for S and G Sitwell" (October 2); "Louise about protesting Franco/ Spain in Unesco/ Typing talk for Yale/ Oranges & pears & celery for Isabel Anderson" (November 24).

2. *Life*'s September 1953 photo-story emphasized her celebrity over her name: "Life Goes on a Zoo Tour with a Famous Poet," *Life* 35 (September 21, 1953): 202–4, 207.

3. Phillips, "The Students of Marianne Moore."

4. Wheeler and Gavaler, "Impostors and Chameleons," 72–77.

5. *PMM*, 195–97.

6. Wheeler and Gavaler, "Impostors and Chameleons," 68.

7. Cantwell, "The Poet, the Bums and the Legendary Red Men," 78, 82.

8. Moore and Mary Warner Moore to John Warner Moore, January 15, 1914, *RML*, VI:20:02, cited in *Holding On*, 118.

9. Wheeler and Gavaler, "Impostors and Chameleons," 65. Moore's failure to join the petition, in spite of her recognition of mistreatment, may have been due to fear of losing her salary (see Phillips, "The Students of Marianne Moore," and Wheeler and Gavaler, "Impostors and Chameleons").

10. Pound, *Selected Letters*, 143.

11. Sitwell, "Review of Poems," *CRMM*, 34; North, *The Dialect of Modernism*, 3–36.

12. Among them: "England" (1920), "New York" (1921), "The Jerboa" (1932), "Style" (1956), "Enough: Jamestown, 1607–1957" (1957), "Leonardo da Vinci's" (1959), "Combat Cultural" (1959), "Arthur Mitchell" (1962), "Blue Bug" (1962), and her baseball poems (1956 and 1961).

13. This version appeared first in *What Are Years* (1941), and thereafter. See *NCP* for the 1935 initial version, which asserts that colonizers, including the "dwarf-fancying Egyptian, the American, / the Dutch" and the "noble / Roman" "were not all intel- / lect and delicacy" and that the colonized, including "black savage[s]" and those "subject to the / deer-fur Crown," are "not all brawn / and animality" (134–35).

14. Kadlec finds her uses of quotational collage (tracing her poems' diverse ancestries), hybridized compound words, and "kinky semantic chains" of metonymically linked words to be means of refreshing the linguistic pool of words and ideas through a type of semantic crossbreeding ("Marianne Moore, Immigration and Eugenics," 30).

15. The original version had "Theirs is a race that 'understands'" (*NCP*, 119).

16. Miller, "Marianne Moore's Black Maternal Hero," 801. In the same year, racial tension surfaced also in a letter Moore sent to Rue Shaw, the president of the Arts Club of Chicago, telling Shaw that she need not invite Moore's fellow Pulitzer Prize winner Gwendolyn Brooks to a reception after Moore's reading there if it made Shaw uncomfortable (October 15, 1953). Moore begins by citing invitees suggested by *Poetry* editor Nicholas Joost, and then comments: "include the above named.—omitting Gwendolyn Brooks, alas, if the Club is not in the habit of welcoming Negroes. I am *very* pro-Negro but don't want to take you by surprise" (Newberry Library, Arts Club Papers, Series 3, Box 4, Folder 145). The letter is discussed in a post by Julianne Neely ("Kill Your Heroes") that characterizes Moore as racist based on this letter and a confused account of "The Hero" (see the Introduction for my analysis of the poem). The dynamic with Shaw seems more nuanced: in a time of fiercely enforced public segregation, Moore, who had served with Brooks on the National Book Award jury in 1951 (they gave it to Wallace Stevens for *Auroras of Autumn*), seems concerned for her hostess's and perhaps also for Brooks's discomfort. Such concern about a guest was expressed when Moore called ahead to a restaurant to check on its openness to serving blacks before inviting Leontyne Price to dinner there (Moore to Hildegarde Watson, February 17, 1956, Bryn Mawr). The question of comfort in public places was avoided with James Baldwin, whom Moore had to dinner at home, and with the members of her integrated church, where everyone was welcome. Brooks's poem "Lovers of the Poor" (1960) directly critiques white women who take classes at the "nice Art Institute" and want to be seen as charitable but won't directly engage with poor black people. The Arts Club is a separate group. Whatever Shaw's views, Moore's appointment book notes do not indicate that Brooks attended.

17. Moore's grandfather, pastor of Gettysburg's Presbyterian church in 1863, watched the battle from his roof, while her grandmother and her mother (then a one-year-old) retreated to the basement. After her grandmother's death three months later of a battleground fever, Reverend Warner sent his daughter to live with his parents. He lectured nationally about his experience, even addressing the House of Representatives, with Lincoln in attendance. This joint national and family catastrophe made Gettysburg key to the family narrative. Mary Warner Moore took her children to picnic there annually throughout their lives, and Marianne and her mother are buried there, beside her grandparents. Johnson ("Marianne Moore's 'Abraham Lincoln and the Art of the Word'") explores Moore's late life interest in Lincoln; this history lay the foundation for that interest and may have contributed to Moore's affinity for Washington, another emblematic American president.

18. *Holding On*, 370.

19. Gilroy, "Marianne Moore Wins Gold Medal"; Kahan, "'The Viper's Traffic-Knot,'" 529. Leavell reads this as an "uneasy joke" (*Holding On*, 370). Kahan reads this as Hughes's extrapolation from Moore's self-reference as a "Moor" in "Sun." Both poets were Missouri natives, friends, and part of the same circles.

20. Previously, Moore had been sports-associated via a prank recounted in *Troubadour*, the 1925 memoir by *Others* editor Alfred Kreymborg. He took Moore to a baseball game, in order to "give myself the pleasure at least once of hearing her stumped about something." But Moore commented knowledgably on the game and demonstrated familiarity with pitcher Christy Mathewson's book (244–45). Kreymborg massages the story, but, Leavell notes, Moore clearly astonished him (*Holding On*, 150). The high/low joke belonged effectively to both.

In 1963, Moore extended this joke when George Plimpton took her to a World Series game (with purposes like Kreymborg's). She claimed that the game first "caught her fancy" in 1949 (watching Roy Campanella calm down a pitcher with a "pat to [his] rump" ["The World Series with Marianne Moore," 53]). In his piece about their trip, Plimpton assumed the role of guide to the world of sport, but the Kreymborg story suggests Moore manufactured that role for him.

21. Tom Fool was doing well in June, when the poem appeared, but had not yet earned the Triple Crown.

22. The note documents Moore's slight rephrasing.

23. Cowles requested a poem, but Moore anticipated that *Flair* might reject "Letter Perfect" and even encouraged the editor to do so: "Dear Mr. Offergeld: If you do not like this, or Mrs. Cowles is doubtful of it, have no hesitation about returning it. Attempting it was a pleasure, and, remember, I was going to do it anyhow. Let no thought of obligation burden you, Mr. Offergeld. I enclose a return envelope" (*RML*, V:20:20). Laurence Stapleton reports that *Flair* initially asked Moore for an airplane-shaped piece: "[Moore] replied that she could not do that, but might be able to produce one in the shape of a rivet!" (*Marianne Moore*, 189).

24. Per James Schuyler, Moore "decided *Flair* was disgusting and bought it back" (letter to Kenneth Koch, January 1957, Koch Papers).

25. *SelLet*, 107.

26. In "The Woman in the Tricorn Hat," David Ross Anderson helpfully explicates "Is Your Town Nineveh?" as a reflection on the parallel operations of nature, divine order, and the politics of the twentieth-century American republic, all three of which depend on diversity, he argues (of species, of experience, and of citizens).

27. See discussions of similarly humble performance dynamics in Trousdale, "'Humor Saves Steps'"; Johnson, "Marianne Moore's 'Abraham Lincoln and the Art of the Word'"; and Mak, "On Falling Fastidiously." See also Herd, "'So He Who Strongly Feels, Behaves'" on the ways in which an ethics of precise description inform Moore's poetics of humility.

28. Moore confirmed her anti-McCarthyism in a letter to Bryher (September 28, 1954, Bryher Papers), noting that "The Committee recommends censure of Joseph McCarthy—this steadies me."

29. Mason, "'Another armored animal,'" 320.

30. "Ain't Misbehaving" (1929), score by Fats Waller, lyrics by Andy Razaf. Rerecorded by Waller in 1943 for *Stormy Weather*.

31. One classicist calls "Hometown" the first "potentially ascertainable epinicion"—a Greek victory ode performed upon the return of a champion—since Leopardi (Swanson, *Pindar's Odes*, 216). See discussion of "Blue Bug," below.

32. The *New York Herald Tribune*'s front-page commentary ("To the Dodgers") continues this, comparing Moore to Homer and Virgil, and calling the World Series struggle *epic*.

33. Moore apparently saw the song performed in a Burton Holmes Travelogue titled *The Charm of the South.*

34. The epigraph version is an unusual variant that itself breaks the tetrameter pattern—adding further rhythmic complexity here.

35. Conklin, "Dodgers' Music Score?"

36. "From 1938 to 1957 [this band] of unlikely musicians serenaded Dodger fans at Ebbets Field in Brooklyn, . . . [from] seats 1–8, row 1, section 8. Sometimes they sauntered up and down the aisles . . . [or] climbed on top of the Dodger dugout. . . [They] would razz a visiting-team strikeout victim back to his bench with ["The Worms Crawl In"]. As the player would sit down on his bench, the Sym-Phoney would accentuate the touchdown of his derriere with a blasting beat of the bass drum" (Frommer, *The Sports Junkie's Book of Trivia, Terms, and Lingo*, 21).

37. Conklin ("Dodgers' Music Score"), who describes the Sym-Phoney as "the ZANIEST," also provided a few phrases and two key structural ideas: building a contrapuntal poem and mixing high- and lowbrow elements together for that poem. He makes a point of interweaving slangy quotes from the Sym-Phoney band leader with highbrow musical analysis; calling *Three Blind Mice* a "canon in contrapuntal form," and offering an elite-sounding discussion of the folk origins of street melodies.

38. Moore to Hildegarde Watson, August 14, 1956, in Moran, "Selected Letters," 652.

39. Moore was unhappy with the initial version sent to *Hudson Review*, writing to Hildegarde that she was working "like a wild cat in a waste-basket" and that "I am full of self-contradictions and crudities. One is supposed to press on so fast as not to notice them. The whole thing may seem too infantile to print. I can't imagine submitting it to Sibley and Scofield!!" (August 14, 1956, in Moran, "Selected Letters," 652–53). But with more work, it improved: "received back my Dodger piece as 'not my best.'—So I set to work and ding-bing if it isn't my best now, it is not that I have spared labor. I have sent it to *the N[ew] Yorker*. Shall get it back (but as routine perhaps, rather than that it is too bad)! (Am hard to crush)" (September 10, 1956, in Moran, "Selected Letters," 662).

40. Howard Moss to Moore, September 12, 1956, *RML*, V:45:01.

41. "Hometown Piece" drafts folder, *RML*, I:02:23.

42. See also "Bird-Witted" (1936) and "Virginia Britannia" (1935).

43. Moore wears a cape but not the tricorne in the *Herald Tribune* photo above the poem, but she was well known for wearing both.

44. Asked on TV in 1952 why the Yankees did not have any black players, Jackie Robinson replied, "I think the Yankee management is prejudiced" (Scott, *Jackie Robinson*, 117).

45. Moore attended the second game with George Plimpton and Robert Lowell. In his account Plimpton expressed surprise that she wasn't excited when the Dodgers dominated ("The World Series with Marianne Moore," 57).

46. Though this poem has received little critical attention, Leavell mentions it as Moore's most ambitious self-portrait since "The Paper Nautilus," reading the shy pony as an analogy for Moore's own "half-reluctant" celebrity (*Holding On*, 378–79). Setina treats it in "Marianne Moore, Photography, and the Self-in-Flux," 276, also noting its two-way dynamic.

47. Holland, "Don't Pull Up for Doc," 72.

48. Moore was of course not alone in questioning the shifting cultural context she found herself navigating. The Frankfurt School (Horkheimer and Adorno, "Culture Industry") and Guy Debord in his *Society of the Spectacle* read the ubiquitous circulation of film and celebrity images to passive audiences as capitalist indoctrination and control.

49. *Holding On*, 378–79.

50. Moore's poetry notebook reveals that John Simon's review of a MoMA show including painter Odilon Redon was the source of the phrase (*RML*, VII:04:05 [1961–70]: 21): "The more one examines Redon's works, the more one realizes that one is being examined by them—that, like Big Brother, *they* are continually watching *us*. The thing that looks out at us from almost every work of Redon's is The Eye; melancholy, tragic, sinister, grotesque or merry, it is the very essence of 'eyeness.' It may reach out to us fondly, or fiercely stab us. If it is not nakedly an eye, then it is a face full of the eye or eyes, the whole countenance *reduced to a container for the eye* [my emphasis]" ("The Torments of Imagination," 26).

51. Indicated in Moore's poetry notebook (*RML*, VII:04:05 [1961–70]: 22): "I can imagine / or can I? / What I have not seen / in A Midsummer Night's Dream / or one of my own / Dr Williams Blue Bug / Arthur Mitchel [*sic*]." In the ballet itself Mitchell's costume consisted of strategically placed leaves and an evanescent capelet (see embedded video in Libbey, "Arthur Mitchell").

52. In so doing, it echoes a very similar literal image in Moore's "To the Peacock of France" (1917), which closes with a long final line, enacting the text:

"in whose chief interest and for whose spontaneous delight, your broad tail was unfurled."

53. Moore to Albert Gelpi, May 26, 1964, *RML*, V:21:40, cited in Willis, "Letter to Albert Gelpi," 11.

54. See Clavier, "'The First Grace of Style.'"

55. Garafola, "Lincoln Kirstein, Modern Dance, and the Left," 25.

56. "I am a political activist through dance," Mitchell said at the opening of his archive in 2016. "I believe that dance, and the arts more broadly, can be used as a catalyst for social change—this is why I started the Dance Theatre of Harlem" (press release for the exhibit *Arthur Mitchell: Harlem's Ballet Trailblazer*, Columbia University Rare Book & Manuscript Library).

57. See *Ten Thousand Miles along the Yellow River*, unidentified artist, China, Qing Dynasty, Metropolitan Museum of Art Online, https://www.metmuseum.org/toah/works-of-art/2006.272a,b/.

58. For example, the murals in the Tomb of Crown Prince Zhanghuai, Shaanxi History Museum.

59. Nicholson, *Aristocracy and Athletics in Archaic and Classical Greece*, 9. Pherenikos was also celebrated in Bacchylides' Ode 5. Not celebrated was the professional jockey who rode him to victory—since he challenged the patron's claim to inherent clan-based athletic superiority. Pindar reflects on this complexity in poems like "Olympian 1."

60. Though most Moore critics have ignored the parallel, a Pindar scholar hears echoes of his work in Moore's. "Marianne Moore's 'The Hero,' 'Virginia Britannia,' and 'Saint Nicholas' may not have been conceived as Pindaric odes, but in their music, structure, metric, and mythic content they are closer to Pindar than anything produced by Ronsard or Cowley" (Swanson, *Pindar's Odes*, 216). Amazingly, Swanson,

who doesn't mention "Blue Bug" or "Tom Fool," calls Moore's Pindarics both the most successful in centuries and unintentional! Stapleton also recognizes "Tom Fool" as Pindaric (*Marianne Moore*, 190).

61. The word *verse* also means "turn" (Lat. *vertere*).

62. See *Holding On*, 89–90, on Moore's enthusiasm for Greek language and poetry in college.

63. *πελῶ*, in Liddell and Scott, *Greek-English Lexicon*, 618.

64. Emerson marks such shapes as elemental to all human vision and knowledge in his essay "Circles," in "The eye is the first circle" (403).

65. *Pulu* may be a loan word from the Greek βαλλῶν.

66. The show *Redon, Moreau and Bresdin* ran at MoMA from December 6, 1961, to February 25, 1962 (see earlier note 50 on Simon). Moore also saw the lithograph at MoMA's 1952 show *Redon: Drawings and Lithographs*, which she attended with Monroe Wheeler, MoMA's director of exhibitions, per her appointment book. (Its presence there is documented in Lieberman, *Redon*, 6.) See Levy, *Criminal Ingenuity*, on Moore's surrealist links (xxiv–xxv). In naming his image thus, Redon invokes Poe's general edginess, and his "The Balloon Hoax" (1844).

67. Though many of Redon's paintings include eyes, Moore's reference to an eye revolving points to this image in particular (the other images reproduced are of people gazing at their viewers), as does her mention of a pastime that is work. Simon's essay ends with a quotation from Novalis that would have sounded familiar to Moore: "If we accept Novalis's definition of genius as 'the ability to deal with imaginary objects as with real ones, and to treat them as such, too' . . . then, surely, Redon was a genius in the purest possible sense" ("The Torments of Imagination," 27). Moore uses similar terminology to describe her work in "Poetry."

68. Costello, *Marianne Moore*.

69. Loiseaux, "Women Looking," 127.

70. NBC broadcast, March 23, 1962, NBC Archives, Smithsonian Museum. The tape reveals that Li Siau Than is the name of both an individual and his troupe. The troupe includes his (apparently German) wife and their son, Gerhart. Though Ameche explains that the stunt was Li père's in his youth, it is Gerhart (the son, presumably born in Germany in the early to mid-1940s) who performs the stand on *International Showtime*, with his parents assisting.

71. See Miller, *Marianne Moore*, 129–66.

72. Lincoln Kirstein to Moore, October 17, 1961, *RML*, XIVb:01:01.

73. Moore to Kirstein, October 31, 1961, *RML*, XIVb:01:01.

74. Quite a few villains in literary history are characterized as "Moors" and Moore cites several in her oeuvre; her reference to herself on several occasions as a "Moor" indicates that she was drawn to the pun and to exploration of racial and outsider dynamics.

75. Qian, *Modernist Response to Chinese Art*; Stamy, *Marianne Moore and China*.

76. *SelLet*, 313.

77. Stamy, *Marianne Moore and China*, 5.

78. Cited in Monroe, "Symposium on Marianne Moore," 210.

79. Vincent, *Queer Lyrics*, 95–96.

80. For more on their friendship, see McCabe, "'Let's Be Alone Together.'"

81. Monroe, "Symposium on Marianne Moore," 209.

82. Marshall, *Celebrity and Power*, 241, 244.

83. Family Correspondence, January 20, 1909, *RML*, VI:15a:2.

Chapter Three

1. This poem first appeared (1915) under another title, and took this title and form in *Observations* (1924). Moore here cites her Bible teacher, Rev. Kellogg, citing A. R. Gordon.

2. Spahr, *Everybody's Autonomy*.

3. Spahr notes that Stein (whose work Moore referred to in 1936 as "a triumph" [*CPr*, 341]) reached a wide audience through language that both repeats the immigrant's experience of immersion in multivalent English and redefines the individual (*Everybody's Autonomy*, 31, 45).

4. Linda Leavell, email to author, June 3, 2017.

5. Kirstein's brochure stressed the performance's Masonic roots. Included with Kirstein to Moore, January 7, 1956, *RML*, V:34:12.

6. For Price's backstory, see Tolliver, *Of Vagabonds and Fellow Travelers*.

7. Moore loved Price's Pamina: "Yes, I was seeing The Magic Flute when you were, and charmed by the delectable harmonies. . . . As for Pamina, I don't know how a voice could tiptoe about among the clouds as hers did; and her festooning draperies were so very stately. And I liked the fetters clattering and piling up in that barbaric scene." (Moore to Watson, January 20, 1956, in Moran, "Selected Letters," 609).

8. Dudziak, *Cold War Civil Rights*.

9. Moore to Watson, February 17, 1956, Hildegarde Watson Papers, Bryn Mawr Library.

10. Auden and Kallman, *The Magic Flute*, 66.

11. Wentletraps were Chinese imports.

12. Moore's notes include an illustration of a wentletrap shell.

13. The stanzas have an odd number of lines (per Masonic preference) and share the syllabic pattern 4/8/6/6/7/5/4/6/6/6/8.

14. Rockefeller Center's buildings connect through underground passages—the spiral stair is in 10 Rock, below the current *Today Show* studio, giving access to the skating rink.

15. Mackey, "The Legend of the Winding Stairs," 328.

16. See also Sainz, "A Masonic Poem on a Masonic Opera."

17. Koch, "New Books."

18. "Axis of the Hairfine Moon."

19. A letter from Moore to Louise Crane (February 26, 1955, *RML*, V:13:04) discusses the performance and the ticket.

20. *RML*, I:04:26.

21. Talmey to Moore, May 27, 1955, *RML*, V:68:13.

22. Moore refers to *Iberica* in draft notes for "Style" (*RML*, XII:11:02), and to Crane's Spanish connection in a note to "Tom Fool at Jamaica," where a drawing is sourced to "a fund-raising committee for Republican Spain . . . given to me by Miss Louise Crane" (*NCP*, 327).

23. Aurore Clavier also discusses Moore's poems as balancing acts and "written dance" ("The First Grace of Style,'" 215).

24. *PMM*, 152.

25. Etchebaster, a Basque Frenchman, reigned as "real tennis" champion in New York for twenty-six years.

26. Clavier, "'The First Grace of Style'"; see also *PMM*, 168–69.

27. Kodat, *Don't Act, Just Dance*, 1–14. See also Hallinan, "The 1958 Tour."

28. Among them, Walter Terry, who reviewed Moiseyev for the *New York Herald Tribune*, and others discussed by Frances Saunders in *The Cultural Cold War*.

29. Kodat, *Don't Act, Just Dance*, 5, 7.

30. See http://www.tv.com/shows/the-ed-sullivan-show/episodes/; seasons 10 and 11.

31. *New Yorker* editor Katharine White wrote to Moore: "I was particularly delighted with your poem on the Moiseyev dancers, in part because you did that one-man fight so brilliantly. I shall never forget how funny and charming it was, and now, to my great happiness, you have celebrated it for all time" (July 10, 1959, *RML*, V:45:02).

32. Moore documented her daily activities in her appointment books. She doesn't mention having seen the show in her letter to Hildegarde Watson about the lunch, nor does that year's appointment book mention it, though it does the other three occasions.

33. Moore was invited by Sol Hurok, the impresario who organized the tour.

34. Though it didn't feed people at the St. Regis, the 1950s TV world was actively engaged in a brow-crossing enterprise, with its opera broadcasts, variety shows, and foreign circuses, and with shows like *Sunrise Semester*—one of the first distance-learning TV shows, taught by NYU comparative literature professor Floyd Zulli. On the day that Moore lunched with Moiseyev at the St. Regis, her calendar indicates she was also reading Camus's *The Stranger* to keep up with Zulli's 6:30 a.m. TV lectures.

35. Kodat notes that Americans would have recognized a parallel between the Nanai people of the Soviet Arctic and the Alaskan Inuit, since the Alaska Statehood Act was in the news (*Don't Act, Just Dance*, 4).

36. In the *New Yorker* and *CP* versions, these two lines are set in quotes, representing a claim which line 3 disputes. *NCP* reprints the *O to Be a Dragon* version.

37. The troupe was formed to blur lines of cultural hierarchy in order to bond diverse Soviet audiences, of varying ethnicities and brow preferences. Kodat cites Moiseyev's aims for the troupe: "to 'create national dances . . . reject everything extraneous . . . raise the skill of the performance of folk dances to the highest artistic level, and . . . improve ancient dances in such a way as to influence the creation of new national dances.' The company's mission was . . . to streamline and modernize (without making modernist) 'ancient,' ethnic dances so that they would embody . . . a Soviet vision of cultural unity-in-diversity . . . adding gymnastic and ballet values to what otherwise are quite simple steps" (Kodat, *Don't Act, Just Dance*, 3–4).

38. Typescript of "Combat Cultural" sent to the *New Yorker* with Moore's penciled edits. *RML*, I:01:31.

39. Kappel, "Notes on the Presbyterian Poetry of Marianne Moore," 50.

40. Leader, "'The teacher was speaking of unrhymed verse,'" 118.

41. Willis, "Contrarieties Equally True."

42. As John Ashbery put it, Moore's readers feel "excited and dismayed at the prospect of 'ending up the décor,' as the French say of a car that drives off the road" ("Straight Lines over Rough Terrain," *CRMM*, 224).

43. Absent evidence of a specific request, Moore seems to have evolved this poem as in line with the prior invitations to write Christmas poems (see Chapter 1). It was an immense success with the editors.

44. "Saint Nicholas" is Moore's first apostrophic poem since the early 1920s' "A Grave" (1921) and "To a Snail" (published 1924, written prior) (*PMM*, 51). Moore's first known poem, written at the age of eight, was "Dear St Nicklus; / This Christmas morn / you do adorn / Bring Warner a horn / And me a doll / That is all. / December 25th 1895" ("MM's First Poem").

45. Barbara Church.

46. Moss to Moore, September 30, 1958, *RML*, V:45:01. The arrangement paid 50 percent beyond the normal rate.

47. In between, Moore offered the *New Yorker* another Saint-linked poem, for Valentine's Day, eventually titled "For February 14th." That poem did not focus on its Saint, and they rejected it as too puzzling; see Chapter 4.

48. Their "looking alike" seems, via Moore's notes, to be based on another image of Jerome, in the Belles Heures de Jean de France, where he has a lion's-mane-like beard.

49. She also wrote a few less-evolved poems of this type that she did not publish.

50. Henderson, "'In the Public Garden,'" 107ff.; Johnson, "Marianne Moore's 'Abraham Lincoln and the Art of the Word,'" 72ff.

51. Perhaps the cupolas of Dunster Hall (Red), Eliot House (Blue), and Baker Hall (Gold), all at Harvard; Simmons College for women also has a blue cupola.

52. As with "Arthur Mitchell," and later "In Lieu of the Lyre," the poem's composition before the fact requires the poet to imagine some day-of effects. Here she substitutes her first Boston taxi ride for her taxi to this event. This "scriptural" driver echoes the scriptural start to other poems (like "Is Your Town Nineveh?" "Tom Fool," "Sojourn in the Whale," etc.) and sets up the scriptural echoes of Psalm 23 in the hymn she cites here. If as in the others the scriptural story echoed here is that of Jonah, the taxi (and driver) figure the Whale, giving us Moore as Jonah, belched up on the beach here, a survivor/immigrant.

53. *RML*, VII:04:10 (1935–55): 13, cited in Stapleton, *Marianne Moore*, 256.

54. Stapleton, *Marianne Moore*, 197.

55. Moore cites Watts's verse three: "Your sure provisions gracious God / attend me all my days; / oh, may your house be my abode, / and all my work be praise. / Here would I find a settled rest, / while others go and come; / no more a stranger, nor a guest, / but like a child at home." The poem enters both the chapel and Watts's text, literally. The steady 8/6/8/6 syllable count of the hymn lines (common meter) creates a counterpoint to the less steady syllabic pattern (variants on the initial stanza's 7/6/9/6/11) of most of the poem's stanzas (ten have five lines, but stanzas 10 and 11 have three and eight lines, respectively).

56. A third poem—"Melchior Vulpius / c. 1560–1615" (1958)—makes its contrapuntal concern explicit, describing Vulpius as "a contrapuntalist— / composer of chorales" (*NCP*, 217) and following that with direct quotations from Vulpius's hymn "God be praised in heaven above," which again Moore alters to create a counterpoint with her framing poem. Moore had heard the hymn performed at her church in June 1957 and took notes (*RML*, VII:11:02: pages marked November 13–16).

Johnson ("Marianne Moore's 'Abraham Lincoln and the Art of the Word,'" 71–72) also reads Moore's interest in counterpoint's harmonizing of disparate voices as a metaphor for creating community and recognizes "something akin to musical counterpoint" in the echoes of stanza 1 in stanza 3, harmonizing public and private concerns. The poem also creates a simultaneous *stylistic* counterpoint, of end-stopped praise lines with "modernist" enjambed structure. Moore continues her experimentation with form and popular access to art and reflection here ("We have to trust this art / this mastery which none / can understand"). See also Pat Willis's blog on this anthem ("Melchior Vulpius," 2012: https://moore123.com) and Rukeyser, "The Rhythm Is the Person."

57. The three lines in stanza 10 all end with the "*-al*" sound, as do lines 3, 4, and 8 of stanza 11. This poem features an odic shape like that of "Blue Bug," with an initial turn, a counterturn on a pivot, and a closing stand.

58. Her appointment book indicates that Moore had attended a birthday dinner for Holocaust documentarian Julien Bryan on May 23, 1958, at which he received a turquoise Iranian camel.

59. *CP*, 293.

60. The two relevant articles are: "A Refugee Bill Gains in Senate" and "Young Refugees Long for America," both *New York Times,* August 21, 1957, p. 13, 14, *RML*, VII:11:02 (1942–196-?): "November 18." Clippings laid in.

61. Herd, "'So He Who Strongly Feels, Behaves,'" 483–84.

62. A gradual is a medieval chant in celebration of the Eucharist. Moore viewed two books of graduals at the Morgan Library on June 4, 1958, while she was composing this poem (May 25 to June 10, 1958). (See 1958 Appointment Calendar (*RML*) and June 16, 1958, letter to Hildegarde Watson [Moran, "Selected Letters," 777ff.].)

63. She had visited to read at least once in the interim.

64. Moore notes receiving the invitation on April 26, for a reading on May 11; she sent the poem to Davis for review on May 4 (1965 Appointment Calendar, *RML*).

65. Stuart Davis, phone interview with the author, June 6, 2017.

66. Unlike "Public Garden," "In Lieu" has no stable stanza form or rhyme scheme—though rhymes do occur. The first stanza starts off with an internal rhyme on "debarred" and "Harvard." As the poem progresses, rhymes appear sporadically in tension with the many conversational lines, which are not syllabically measured but patterned with indentations.

67. Author's transcription of recording of Moore's *Advocate* reading, May 11, 1965 (*The Poet's Voice*).

68. "To Brooklyn Bridge," l. 29.

69. In both poems Trachtenberg is mentioned in the notes and Crane is invoked through allusions.

70. Moore's notes don't mention Dr. Fang being there but do mention Dr. Levin (1965 Appointment Calendar, May 11).

71. This Macaronic poem—playing on brow levels within English vocabulary ("cogitating" vs. "thinking") and across languages—was originally titled "Occasionem Cognosce" (the motto of the Lowell family, meaning "recognize opportunity") when first published as a broadsheet in 1963; and it has also been collected as "I've Been Thinking."

72. In his email of July 10, 2019, Davis was 90 percent sure that Moore wore the tricorne at the 1965 reading.

73. The speaker's third-person self-references initially operate in tension with her first-person presence ("one debarred," "Brooklyn's [or Mexico's] *ineditos*," "one whose 'French aspect' was invented," and "a too outspoken outraged refugee from clichés"). But she reappears in first person (another veil-and-reveal dynamic) in stanza 3, still

almost incognito in Latin ("gratia sum" ["I am grateful"]), and then in a declarative English "I am." In stanza 4 she returns as the third-person "guest," and then is further repressed along with the implied "I offer" in the final phrase: "These reflections, Mr. Davis, / in lieu of the lyre." Moore underscores this tension in the note (recycled from "Tom Fool"), emphasizing (via Fang) that she "broke Mme. de Boufflers's injunction" to not talk about oneself.

74. In the *Harvard Advocate* version, Moore misstated Roebling's name as William.

75. Stuart Davis, email correspondence with the author, July 10, 2019.

76. Ngai, *Our Aesthetic Categories*, 1.

77. Ibid., 172.

Chapter Four

Epigraph: *RML*, VII:11:02 (1942–196?): "August 11."

1. See Sargeant, "Profiles: Humility, Concentration, and Gusto," 38; and Kramer, "Freezing the Blood and Making One Laugh," *CRMM*, 230.

2. Kahan, "'The Viper's Traffic-Knot,'" 523.

3. Eliot, "Tradition and the Individual Talent," 40, 41.

4. Erkkila, *The Wicked Sisters*, 102.

5. Pound, "Marianne Moore and Mina Loy," *CRMM*, 22.

6. Animals also played a key role in Moore's emotional shorthand. In many poems the bodies of armored animals protect them from the dangerous world by ingeniously evolved means. While they represent themselves, they also signal a canniness and moral status linked to humans and inherited from fables, and all stand in for Moore in some respects.

7. Per Leavell, "Marriage" responded to Scofield Thayer's proposal ("'Frightening Disinterestedness'").

8. "Dear Miss Moore: I am thoroughly shocked at my casualness in returning my your! shell-books, and hope that you will forgive me; also, that you will accept what is left of this Paper Nautilus as a form of 'interest'—I ordered it from the Mr. Webb of the shell books, and he wrote back that he would pack it just as carefully and successfully as he used to pack birds eggs, 45 years ago; but I am afraid he has lost the knack! . . . PS: Toby, the Siamese kitten, has just knocked the box containing the shell onto the ground, delighted with its lightness. I don't dare open it to see what's left!" (Louise Crane to Moore, February 20, 1937, *RML*, V:05:01).

"Dear Miss Crane, It is well I did not know when I received the mysterious box, that a nautilus was inside, or my hand might have shaken so as to injure it. A nautilus has always seemed to me something supernatural. The more I look at it the less I can *credit it*, this large yet weightless thing, with a glaze like ivory on the entrance and even on the sides. How curious the sudden change of direction in the corrugations, and the transparent oyster white dullness of the paper. The wings are so symmetrical I should not know any part had been broken if you had not said so." (Moore to Louise Crane, February 27, 1937, *SelLet*, 381).

As a poet and skilled observer Moore added value to her epistolary exchanges—the pun in her name (more!) marks this pattern of supplement. As her celebrity grew, her circle also shared a glamor benefit. She occasionally repaid a gift like Crane's paper nautilus with a poem (the germ of "The Paper Nautilus" glows in the phrases of her letter), and she daily returned gifts of affection and material goods with detailed and imaginative descriptions that bespoke her engagement with her correspondent. As Elizabeth Bishop noted, "to send you a post-card is to get back something worth a thousand of them" (Bishop to Moore, June 2, 1938 [*One Art*, 74]). Sabine Sielke describes this as "women establish[ing] their own economy of exchange, seemingly apart from the cultural commerce in which women serve as gifts and communication between men" (*Fashioning the Female Subject*, 122). See also Siofra McSherry's discussion of Moore's embeddedness within a community of patronage and gifts in the 1920s, "To fulfill a private obligation.'"

9. Moore bears witness to the complexity of civilian war experience in "In Distrust of Merits." See Galvin, *News of War*, 2017.

10. In this precursor to (the weirder) "Then the Ermine:" Moore introduces a creature that could be either Hildegarde or herself "emerg[ing] daintily," who is described in terms of the distinctive markings of a protean range of animals, including weasels, skunks (once classified as weasels), chipmunks, goats, ermines, otters, and pole-cats.

11. The poem portrays her as a member of the same weasel family to which Moore and her brother had long assigned themselves. The poem celebrates Hildegarde's attentive provision to Moore of distinctive clothing (often duplicating Hildegarde's own). See, for example, Moore's letter of December 13, 1941, in Moran, "Selected Letters," 373–74.

12. The book was *Man Eaters of Kumaon*, by Jim Corbett (which argues that tigers don't normally eat humans). Moore sent the poem to Crane, noting: "Since I'm thanking you Louise, you don't have to thank me for the peculiar poem. (I can't think of a worse favor than enclosing a friend a poem.)" (*RML*, V:13:02). The self-deprecating comment seconds the poem's point that poets who fuss dazzle less than the "unobtrusiveness" of affectionate care.

13. "Efforts of Affection" (1948) combines an invocation of Jubal and Jabal—descendants of Adam and Eve (part of a complex history of romantic and filial affections, Gen. 4:19–21)—with a citation from Bottom ("hay, sweet hay, which hath no fellow"), an example of the unpredictability of love, which we're told further down "can make one / bestial or make a beast a man," but which, the poem concludes, is most noteworthy for the ongoing "efforts of affection [that] / attain integration too tough for infraction." "By Disposition of Angels" (1948) recognizes the departed shining down from above:

> Steadier than steady, star dazzling me, live and elate,
> No need to say, how like some we have known; too like her,
> Too like him, and a-quiver forever. (*NCP*, 184)

But while "Disposition" hints at love amid the stars, "Armor's Undermining Modesty" (1950) claims to reject both:

> No wonder we hate poetry,
> and stars and harps and the new moon. If tributes cannot
> be implicit,
>
> give me diatribes and the fragrance of iodine,
> the cork oak acorn grown in Spain;
> the pale-ale-eyed impersonal look
> which the sales-placard gives the bock beer buck. (*NCP*, 188)

This witty poem (echoing the sardonic "I too dislike it" of "Poetry") manages to conclude with a sentimental "imperishable wish" for a service ethic like that of the grail knights who did "not let self bar / their usefulness to others who were / different."

14. Poetry Notebook, *RML*, VII:11:02 (1942–196-?): "August 9."

15. Though Moore omits overt sexual reference from her work, her friends described her as a very embodied person. In 1935, writing about Moore's *Selected Poems*, T. S. Eliot and Wallace Stevens both attributed an erotic energy to her work: "[Moore] is not a writer. She is a woman who has profound needs," offered Stevens ("A Poet That Matters," *CRMM*, 117). Eliot defended Moore's unusual choices of poetic material, which might be perceived to detour around both passion and the traditional definitions of what's important, arguing that "we all have to choose whatever subject matter allows us the most powerful and most secret release; and that is a personal affair. The result is often something that the majority will call frigid; for to feel things in one's own way, however intensely, is likely to look like frigidity to those who can only feel in accepted ways" (introduction to *The Selected Poems of Marianne Moore*, *CRMM*, 107).

16. "What of chastity? It confers a particular strength" ("If I Were Sixteen Today" [1958], *CPr*, 503). In a 1921 letter to Bryher, defending her life choices, Moore noted, "What you say is true; the physical is important as well as the spiritual and I don't doubt that a thousand derangements are the result of our misunderstanding of the physical. . . [B]ut, as Freud says, our capacity for transferring energy from one field to another is almost infinite and the adjustments of one need to another, involve so many things that it is no easy matter to be absolute as to what course of action we are compelled to adopt for our all round best good" (*SelLet*, 153).

17. Sedgwick, *Tendencies*, 8.

18. While Valentine's Day invokes a saint, Chaucer's *Parliament of Fowles* created Valentine's connection to romantic love by citing his name day in early spring as the day on which birds met to choose their mates for the year, suggesting the courtly tradition of mutual choice, rather than arranged marriage.

19. Moss to Moore, January 27, 1959: "Dear Miss Moore: In spite of our best efforts, I'm sorry to have to say that OVERTURE remained something of a cipher. And so I must return it to you, with our regret." *RML*, V:45:02.

20. Moore described her process to Moss shortly thereafter (February 8, 1959): "(I improved a line or two of the valentine that baffled you and the *Herald Tribune* seems pleased with it—to my relief. I don't quite bear out my advice to beginners, 'pay no attention to acceptances and rejections. Write what you yourself like and be loyal to it!')" As with her *Vogue* editor, Moore makes explicit to Moss her openness to reshaping works to fit editors' needs. *RML*, V:45:02.

21. White to Moore, January 6, 1960, *RML*, V:45:02. Emphases added.

22. Alternatively, the "you" in line 5 might be understood as an address to readers, or, as Elizabeth Wilson suggests (see below), to Moore herself.

23. Miller, *Marianne Moore*, 201.

24. The line may also come from another Harris poem, yet to be identified.

25. Her boldness is represented as a Vine in the poem, suggesting that she was either tipsy or otherwise uncontrollably forward. One could read the Vine as merely a fast-growing plant that pushes open doors, but the epigraph (included in the copy

Harris sent Moore in 1958 but not in the published version) suggests alcohol: "'when ye come to the lees, it is foolish to spare.' Hesiod." *RML*, V:24:32.

26. It balances the claim to value in drink with a number of "beg pardons" that suggest that Harris may be addressing it directly to Moore: "Before the insistent vine / Often a door will jar; / But my excessive green // Once heedlessly un-thou'd / A fair and blest savante / And I beg her pardon now. // No harm was ever meant / Except for a wicked wish / To travel in her train." *The Risk of the Vine*, xv.

27. That request (and her reworking of Harris's poem) may remind some of her history with Hart Crane's "The Wine Menagerie," another poem about alcohol's effects. In 1926, as *Dial* editor, Moore suggested sweeping revisions to that poem, which Crane accepted in order to get it published but complained about later. Though the incident has echoed through modernist studies as an example of intrusive editing, John Emil Vincent interprets Moore's cuts and changes as representative of a clash of poetic visions rather than editorial censure (*Queer Lyrics*, 59–88). Originally, Crane's poem like Harris's viewed wine as an expander of vision and loosener of inhibitions, but Moore cut that out, reducing the poem to half its length and renaming it "Again." Crane's original ending refers to two biblical stories (the decapitations of Holofernes [beheaded while drunk] and John the Baptist [beheaded because Herod promised while drunk]); Moore's invocation of Noah toward the end of "For February 14th" parallels Crane's similar structure. His poem closed with a couplet delivered as a whispered commentary: "'— And fold your exile on your back again; / Petrushka's valentine pivots on its pin.'" The speaker leaves the bar alone again, invoking the romantic misery suffered by the puppet Petrushka over the Ballerina, in Stravinsky's 1911 ballet. In her 1920s anti-sentimental phase Moore cut those lines from the version of Crane's poem published in the *Dial*, but she may be viewed as repairing her breach with Crane in her own late-life venture back into the realm of the heart. Both "The Wine Menagerie" and "For February 14th" speak of alternative romance plots. Seven years later Moore again affirmed her continued engagement with Crane's work in "Granite and Steel" (see Chapter 5).

28. This supports Wilson's view of Moore's questions to "you" in line 5 as addressed not to Valentine but to herself, as part of a retrospective reconsideration of her own life choices around romance that ends with her endorsement of her choice of a life devoted to writing, but in the process reminds readers of the trade-offs involved.

29. The painting was exhibited in London in the 1830s with that title. "English and Continental Treasures on Loan to Glasgow," *Illustrated London News*, December 19, 1959, 907 (partial page clipping in "Saint Valentine" drafts folder, *RML*, I:04:12). The article included two images each by Moore's two favorite painters, El Greco and Blake, including a Blake illustration of Chaucer's *Canterbury Tales*.

30. In offering as a gift a vignette of this (falsely named) Vera, Moore's ekphrasis assigns to the poem a physical body (El Greco's portrait) that now exists both within and outside the poem.

31. Hubbard, "Mannerist Moore."

32. The syllable "me" repeats eight times in stanza 1.

33. Vincent, *Queer Lyrics*, 103.

34. The editorial took Moore's last line as its title: "Yes, Yes, Yes, *Yes*."

35. The question mark in the title was retained in Moore's 1967 version of the *Complete Poems* but removed by the editors of the 1981 edition. Since it seems important to the poem's response dynamic, I cite the earlier version here.

36. The *NCP* version of the body of "Love in America?" (263) differs slightly but importantly, as discussed, but I cite the *NCP* notes.

37. "Love in America" drafts folder, *RML*, I:02:59.

38. Holley reads this line as a quotation of Molly Bloom at the end of *Ulysses* (*PMM*, 190), and Vincent takes it as an orgasmic shout that doubles as the poem's climax, a direct reminder of the presence of sexuality in America (*Queer Lyrics*, 102–7).

39. *SelLet*, 312.

40. Gregory, "Confessing the Body."

41. Moore to Ginsberg, July 4, 1952, cited in Hyde, *On the Poetry of Allen Ginsberg*, 13–14.

42. Moore to Plath, July 13–14, 1958, Mortimer Rare Book Room, Smith College Library, cited in Pollak, *Our Emily Dickinsons*, 164.

43. Moore to Henry Allen Moe of the Guggenheim Foundation, November 1961 (*RML*): "I think her very gifted but feel cold toward this 'project.' And way of presenting it. You are not subsidized for having a baby especially in view of a world population explosion." Cited in Pollak, *Our Emily Dickinsons*, 167.

44. Plath's "The Tour" (1962) angrily addresses a maiden aunt unable to deal with sexuality, fertility, or strong emotion. The speaker cites the words "bitter" and "averse"—terms that were part of Moore's characterization of Plath's *The Colossus* in a letter to Plath's editor Judith Jones (also 1962), which Jones then shared with Plath (Pollak, *Our Emily Dickinsons*, 169–70): "I am bitter? I'm averse? / Here's your specs, dear, here's your purse. // Toddle on home to tea now in your flat hat" (Plath, *Collected Poems*, 238).

45. As exemplified by his inclusion in *The Waste Land* of quotations from his arguments with his first wife, Vivienne Haigh-Wood, and the discourse of their housemaid Ellen Kellond, both without acknowledgment. Eliot, *The Waste Land*, 127n5; Gregory, *Quotation and Modern American Poetry*, 67, 203; see also Miller, *T. S. Eliot*, 4.

46. Steuben Correspondence, *RML*, V:63:18.

47. Glass design by Lloyd Atkins, engraving design by Frank Eliscu (Steuben Glass, *Poetry in Crystal*, 44–45).

48. Moore enclosed an image of a "pegasus giraffe by [Bruno] Munari" with her July 28, 1933, letter to Benét (*SelLet*, 312). Reference to a "paddock full of leopards and giraffes" appears in "Marriage" (1923), which seems to invoke her friend Bryher, who also used fond animal names for her friends (Bryher sometimes called H. D. *giraffe*) and whose marriage of convenience to Robert McAlmon (of which Moore disapproved) was part of the poem's subtext.

49. Moore to Eliot, July 15, 1962: "I have revised my giraffe—don't like the digression of informality in original." *RML*, V:18:05.

50. Carrington ("Metaphysical") also understands the poem to explore the relation and relative virtues of confessional and modernist work. She argues that the poem, while ambivalent, implies a preference for the impersonal, even while Moore manages "deviously" to be personal in addressing her friend Eliot.

51. Author's correspondence with Perry Morley. Thanks to her and to Susanna Morley Smithson and Janet Sidaway for sharing details on the background to the "giraffe house" name and on Eliot's and the Morley family's name play.

52. Moore mixes up Susanna (who was away at school) with Peregrine here. *Camelopardalis reticulata* is a Latin species name within the genus *Giraffa*. Moore here

quotes Morley's letter to her, which mentioned his "remarkable visitor in the shape of T. S. Eliot." See Frank V. Morley to Moore, June 7, 1946, and Moore to Morley, June 9, 1946, *RML*, V:4:20.

53. In September she had offered to pay Eliot for his proposed editing of her *Collected Poems*, referring to herself as a *gosling* (an innocent in money matters) (Moore to Eliot, September 5, 1946). He declined, noting that the editing was both his job and unfinished, and asking, "Does that not cook your gosling?" (Eliot to Moore, October 5, 1946). *RML*, V:17:26.

54. Eliot to Moore, November 21, 1946, and Moore to Eliot, December 1, 1946, *RML*, V:17:26. Like Moore and her family, Eliot and his friends inhabited a universe of animal names and stories. There Eliot was Elephant, "because he never forgets" (Susanna Morley Smithson, email correspondence to author). Simultaneously he was Br'er Possum (to Ezra Pound's Br'er Rabbit, via Uncle Remus), a teller of animal tales to the Morley children; those tales became *Old Possum's Book of Practical Cats*.

55. Leavell, "'Frightening Disinterestedness,'" 65, 69.

56. Next to an extended borrowing set in quotes, Pound pencils "? . . . Marianne" (*Waste Land*, 6). Though editor Valerie Eliot added a note denying that this could refer to Marianne Moore, there is no more likely candidate.

57. "Eliot . . . is a faithful friend of the objects he portrays; altogether unlike the sentimentalist who really stabs them treacherously in the back while pretending affection." ("A Note on T. S. Eliot's Book" [1918], in *CPr*, 35.)

58. *Letters of T. S. Eliot: Volume 1: 1898–1922*, 47. Moore was not entirely obliging to Eliot, however—she rejected his submission to the *Dial* of his first wife Vivienne's story "The Paralyzed Woman," finding that "it has not for us, that finality which you feel it to have" (Moore's undated reply to Eliot [1925], *RML*, V:17:24).

59. After Mary Warner Moore's death Eliot wrote to Moore sending his "affectionate sympathy" (Eliot to Moore, July 16, 1947, *RML*, V:18:01). Vivienne Eliot also died in 1947. Though Eliot and his wife had long lived apart (they separated in 1933, and she was committed to an asylum by her brother in 1938), he seemed strongly affected by her death. Moore and Eliot each may have felt open to new connection after the drawn-out end of a relationship. Indeed, Moore instructed the stonemason carving her mother's and her shared gravestone to leave a space under her name, in case "a line [were] ever to be inserted there, designating marriage" (Moore to George Meals, November 6, 1947, *SelLet*, 467).

60. Eliot to Moore, May 8, 1956, *RML*, V:18:04, cited in *Holding On*, 356.

61. Eliot/Moore correspondence, 1957, *RML*, V:18:04.

62. Berry worked for Moore from 1946 until Moore's death in 1972 and they had a strong rapport (*Holding On*, 328–30ff.). Berry described Moore in an interview as having been quite affected by the news that Eliot had married: "I think Marianne Moore really loved T. S. Eliot, I really do. And they seemed to enjoy each other so much, being together. But when she got the message he'd married, that was a little more than I think that she could take. She felt quite bad about it for quite a while, quite a while." *Voices and Visions: Marianne Moore*. Video.

63. See, for instance, letters between Moore and Eliot of October 23 and 31, 1934, *RML*, V:17:25.

64. It's also relevant that Moore had famously spoken up for "literalists" ("of the imagination") before, also as part of an argument with a modernist authority—specifically

Yeats, whom Moore debates on the value of "literalists" like Blake, in her endnotes to "Poetry." This debate continues that pattern.

65. Berryman discusses his anti-Eliot motivations in his National Book Award acceptance speech, cited in Haffenden, *The Life of John Berryman*, 352. Carrington ("Marianne Moore's Metaphysical Giraffe") also makes this clear connection, reads it as part of the transition toward the popular in Moore's later work, and notes Moore's sympathy for the confessionals, though with different emphasis.

66. All drafts are from the "To a Giraffe" drafts folder, *RML*, I:04:44.

67. Interview quoted in Costello, *Marianne Moore*, 15.

68. She'd cited the same scene in "Efforts of Affection" (1948), another love poem.

69. The consolations of metaphor are profound, Moore tells us, citing Ennis Rees's introduction to the *Odyssey*. Moore's "quotation" condenses two of Rees's paragraphs: "If [Homer's] fables were not essentially and obviously metaphorical—saying life is a battle, life is a journey—one is at liberty to doubt if they would have lasted so well. . . . After all, the myth of death and rebirth, the journey from sin to redemption—in short, the return, is surely one of the most central and universal images in the human soul" (Rees, introduction to *The Odyssey of Homer*, ix–x). Moore cites Rees's "metaphorical" in her draft but changes it to "metaphysical" in the final version.

70. In another version, "*giraffeable*."

71. Eliot was no more "succulent" than Moore. His gender, combined with his money and fame, made the difference.

72. Moore to Eliot, July 15, 1962, *RML*, V:18:05.

73. Cited in Miller, *T. S. Eliot*, 4.

74. See Willis, "Contrarieties Equally True."

75. This concern with permission echoes "The Octopus" (1924).

76. See discussion earlier in this chapter. *RML*, VII:11:02 (1942–196?): "August 9."

77. Kramer, "Freezing the Blood and Making One Laugh," *CRMM*, 233, 230, 233, 231.

Chapter Five

Epigraph: *Becoming*, 177; first published, thus, in 1916. The *Observations* variant of this poem (*NCP*, 11), titled "Fear Is Hope," differs markedly from the 1916 version, which is much closer to the version in *TMTM*, reprinted in *CP*, 234.

1. Several of these have been discussed in previous chapters.

2. One year after *Tell Me, Tell Me*, Moore published her famously incomplete *Complete Poems* (1967), which included four new poems in a section called "Hitherto Uncollected." Her last published poems were included in a posthumous 1981 version of the *Complete Poems*, edited by Patricia Willis and Clive Driver.

3. Moore did not explicitly support a major cause in her poems, yet her late work firmly advocates for animal rights, refugees, and parks, and against ageism—along with her less direct but long-term advocacy for race and gender equity and for expanded dialogue.

4. See Kahan's discussion in "'The Viper's Traffic-Knot,'" 524ff.

5. As Elien Arckens notes, though Moore might question procreative sexuality, she also "of course . . . would wish that her queer archival poetry continue to be read and, hence, survive its writer" ("'In This Told-Backward Biography,'" 125).

6. See Finch, "'Passion for the Particular.'"

7. Written in 1911, "Sun" (aka "Sun!") was published in 1916, 1923, and then, greatly altered, in 1924 in *Observations*, under the title "Fear Is Hope." It then disappeared from Moore's canon until 1957, when it returned in nearly its 1916 version.

8. The principal differences between the 1966 version and the 1916 version (see *Becoming*, 177) lie in the difference of person in line 3 ("us" vs. "you"—the "us" likely introduced by Moore's 1916 editor [ibid., 178]), the shift in the poem's shape over time, and the changes in the phrasings in lines 8/9 and 11/12.

9. *Becoming*, 177.

10. Stanzas 3 and 4 include the sun imagery:

We passed the School, where Children strove
At Recess—in the Ring—
We passed the Fields of Gazing Grain—
We passed the Setting Sun—

Or rather—He passed Us—
The Dews drew quivering and chill—
For only Gossamer, my Gown—
My Tippet—only Tulle— (*The Pocket Emily Dickinson*, 112)

Like Dickinson's, Moore's poem includes a male figure in or on a vehicle (the prince in the caravan), who is outraced by the sun but headed toward Immortality. Dickinson's speaker is a woman invited into the carriage with this figure, called Death, while Moore's speaker is not in the vehicle and is plural, represented as two aspects of one individual—called Fear and Hope. But an allegorical figure of Deth is present here too, via the epigraph. In both poems the Sun figures Time and is linked to Death. In Moore's poem the speakers have no gender assigned, and the Sun's lack of gender is stressed: "You are not male nor female."

"Prevalent at One Time," a late poem unpublished in Moore's lifetime, may also be taken to refer to 479. This short poem about riding alone in a semicircular black gig (a type of carriage) without fears about one's health (the closing line is "I'm no hypochondriac") suggests a lack of anxiety about death and arguably an embrace of immortality. That poem's action repeats the jumping forward and backward in time operative in several other poems examined in this chapter, and its parallels to the much earlier poem "Sun" also collapse time. What was "prevalent at one time" remains of interest here.

11. Pollak, *Our Emily Dickinsons*, 137.

12. Moore seems to refer to a similar sense of poetry as a source of immortality in "Old Tiger" (1932; see below).

13. Moore had also reintroduced work from much earlier in her career in *O to Be a Dragon* (1959), republishing there "I May I Might I Must" (1909), "To a Chameleon" (1916), and "A Jellyfish" (1909).

14. The backward format echoes an early poem in which Moore manipulates time by running it backward: "To-morrow will be / Yesterday unless you say the / Days of the week back- // Ward." (This poem, against holding grudges, which Moore published only in 1917, shares the title "The Past Is the Present" with a separate poem.) The format echoes also a suggestion in filmmaker Jean Cocteau's "Preface to the Past" (cited

in "Carnegie Hall: Rescued"), a philosophical preparation for *his* own death. He notes that at the end one's life risks looking ridiculous unless we "run the film backwards," the alienated perspective giving it new grandeur.

15. Moore "quotes" and alters several other of Crane's phrases: "O catenary curve" imitates Crane's diction and his use of the word "curve" pointedly, but she imports the word "catenary" from Alan Trachtenberg's book about the construction of the Brooklyn Bridge; "O path amid the stars / crossed by the seagull's wing!" and "O radiance that doth inherit me!" reorganize several of Crane's lines including "O Thou whose radiance doth inherit me," "immaculate sigh of stars / Beading thy path," and "the seagull's wings shall dip and pivot him." "O steel! O stone!" redoes Crane's "O, Steel and stone!" (The phrase "o path amid the stars" also echoes a phrase cited by Trachtenberg ["this path among the stars"], from a 1913 melodrama by Dorothy Landers Beall also called "The Bridge" [*PMM*, 173], but the cadence and the key words come from Crane.)

16. See Chapter 4, note 27.

17. Lionel Trilling argues that "Marianne Moore, much more than Carl Sandburg, is [Whitman's] true descendent" (cited in Redding, "'One must make a distinction, however,'" 326). Nonetheless, Bishop's "Efforts of Affection" cites Moore responding to a question about Whitman (perhaps ironically): "E*liz*abeth, don't speak to me about that man!" (143).

18. Written before Brooklyn was consolidated into New York City.

19. *Emma Lazarus: Selected Poems and Other Writings*, 233.

20. "In the Public Garden," "In Lieu of the Lyre," "Rescue with Yul Brynner," and "Tell Me, Tell Me."

21. Moore refers to this crisis in "Rescue with Yul Brynner." See Bentz, "Cracking the Door."

22. Following that she gives two "clarifications" of her own work—a synopsis of the plot of the fantasy narrative "My Crow Pluto" that appears in this volume and a rejection of a reading of her 1924 poem "Marriage," holding that it "in no sense suggest[s] a philosophy of marriage." Since this take would be to many readers patently false, the example undermines the essay's claim to want to explain her own work or to reassure us of her trustworthiness in that regard. She puts attentive readers on guard.

23. *RML*, VII:04:05 (Poetry Notebook 1961–70): page 45, image 50.

24. Ellis's Introduction cites Landor's full *Imaginary Conversations*, in which Diogenes says to Plato, "I meddle not at present with infinity or eternity; when I can comprehend them I will talk about them" (xxiii).

25. Moore organized the placement of poems in his *Selected Poems* of 1951.

26. This becomes yet another Christmas gift poem at the close.

27. *NCP* reprints a typo (Timothy) from the first publication, but Moore corrected the name of the painter invoked, Thomas Cole, in the *Complete Poems*.

28. The poem in the *New Yorker* on September 23, 1967, was preceded on August 5, 1967, by the *New York Times* op-ed citing the attractions of Brooklyn, including its trees: "Brooklyn has trees—a group of massive English elms in Fort Greene Park, and sycamores arching over South Portland Avenue; but its crowning curio is the Camperdown Elm in Prospect Park not far from the boathouse, planted in 1872. It has eighteen cavities, is in need of cleaning and bracing under its heavy horizontal limbs.

Funds could make it serve as an outdoor classroom, demonstrating techniques of tree care. Will it be here in 1972? (Camperdown Fund, 171 Congress Street, Brooklyn, Mrs. Graff)" (Moore, "Topics")

See Gilcrest ("Rhetorical Redemption, Environmental Poetics, and the Case of the Camperdown Elm") and Olson ("Marianne Moore's 'The Camperdown Elm' and the Revival of Brooklyn's Prospect Park") for more on the poem's eco-activism and its context.

29. Specifically invoked through the compound adjective "tree-loving," Bryant's apple-tree poem also tells the story of a tree: beginning when the speaker plants it ("Come, let us plant the apple tree"), looking forward to its life laden with fruit, birds, and children, on past the speaker's imagined death while the tree lives on, up to the tree's decline and near demise. At that point children will ask who planted it, and the poet and his poem will be recalled.

> "Who planted this old apple-tree?"
> The children of that distant day
> Thus to some aged man shall say;
> And, gazing on its mossy stem,
> The gray-haired man shall answer them:
> "A poet of the land was he,
> Born in the rude but good old times;
> 'T is said he made some quaint old rhymes
> On planting the apple-tree." (Bryant, *Poetical Works*, 224)

This poem has long been recited ritually on Arbor Day, as parks-minded citizens "Cleave the tough greensward with the spade." Bryant's injunction to plant trees was fulfilled enormously when 500,000 were installed in the new Central Park. Both poets break the poetic fourth wall by assigning their speaker/poets an action external to the poem: where Bryant plants trees, Moore conserves them.

30. Durand's painting also gestures toward apple trees (in the untrammeled, "Edenic" American landscape), through its explicit revision of Cole's earlier painting *Expulsion from the Garden of Eden*.

31. William Cullen Bryant, "A New Public Park," *New York Evening Post*, July 3, 1844, in Branch, *Reading the Roots*, 337–38.

32. Nevius and Nevius, *Inside the Apple*, 85–87. Bryant loved the beauties of wilderness and had been impressed with European parks. Though *he* could escape the city for recreation in nature, his editorial emphasized the need of local green space for city dwellers of lesser means.

33. Willis, "Camperdown Elm," 95.

34. In "Mercifully," Moore seems to consider all people a variety of tree, when she notes that one of the few things that can disgust her is "a person without a tap root."

35. Earth, that nourish'd thee, shall claim
> Thy growth, to be resolved to earth again,
> And, lost each human trace, surrendering up
> Thine individual being, shalt thou go
> To mix forever with the elements,
> To be a brother to the insensible rock,
> And to the sluggish clod, which the rude swain

Turns with his share, and treads upon. The oak
Shall send his roots abroad, and pierce thy mould." ("Thanatopsis," ll. 22–30)

36. Hazlitt, "On Sitting for One's Picture," 36.

37. The poem's "end" refuses closure, calling for further action by readers.

38. Bryant mourns the brilliant Cole's passing and sketches his life and legacy. Per Bryant, Cole's greatest teachers were the trees around him in his Ohio youth. The eulogy was delivered before the National Academy of Design, founded by Cole and painter/inventor Samuel Morse.

39. Durand's painting also blurs the line between poetry and visual art in several ways—by including a poet, by taking its name from a poem, and by including some text—in the form of Cole's and Bryant's names, carved in the elm's trunk.

40. Moore's friendly reputation was reinforced by her protégée Elizabeth Bishop's "Invitation to Miss Marianne Moore" (1948), which represented her as a kind of good witch, whom the speaker entreats: "From Brooklyn, over the Brooklyn Bridge, on this fine morning, / please come flying." The poem invokes Moore's favorite haunt—the Bryant Park library where she often met friends and fans under Durand's *Kindred Spirits* (Willis, "Camperdown Elm"). She is one "For whom the grim museums will behave / like courteous male bower-birds, / for whom the agreeable lions lie in wait / on the steps of the Public Library, / eager to rise and follow through the doors / up into the reading rooms" (*The Complete Poems, 1927–1979*, 83). Even stone animals flock to Moore's side, sensing her benevolence. Bishop too feels the strong attraction but marbles her portrait of Moore's compassion with reminders of a contrasting "slight censorious frown," suggesting an additional ability to be critical.

41. All three include trees—as does "Mercifully."

42. Jonson, *Timber.*

43. Gilbert, "'These Things,'" 34.

44. Jonson, *Timber.* In the preceding paragraph Jonson *Notes*: "Truth lies open to all. . . I thank [the ancients] that have taught me, and will ever; but yet dare not think the scope of their labour and inquiry was to envy their posterity what they also could add and find out. / If I err, pardon me" (*Timber*).

45. Vincent, *Queer Lyrics*, 117–18.

46. The *New Yorker* version reproduced in *NCP* introduces an extra, repetitive line not in Moore's drafts, as line 7 ("a cat's-eye yellow crack in the shutter"). Moore removed it in *CP.*

47. The "Retreat" in the title describes this literal ascent, working as a verbal noun, activating the military meaning of the word alongside the sense in which it may also refer to the house.

48. The *CP* version closes with "can't make the owner's loss less hard" (241).

49. Willis, "Contrarieties Equally True." Moore's initial draft invoked Blake's poem explicitly, in a stanza later deleted, which closed:

He was the prey of a two-fold delusion—
that his war was holy
and that a tiger was a deity
since even in a poem

a "tiger burning bright"
had made him faint.

Willis, "Tippoo's Tiger," 5.

50. Likewise "Old Tiger" (written in 1918 and published once, in 1932) may be understood to address Blake. That poem suggests a similar sense of poetry as a source of immortality: "you know that it is not necessary to live in order to be alive." "Voracities and Verities" (1947) can also be read through a Blakean lens, as can Moore's unpublished late poem "Prevalent at One Time," with its "tiger-skin rug."

51. Jarrell, "The Humble Animal," *CRMM*, 134.

52. Willis, "Archiving Moore," 256.

Epilogue

1. Warhol and Johnson were friends; Johnson met Moore on several occasions and tried to correspond with her, but she did not take up his invitations. Whether or not Warhol and Moore ever met, both attended Capote's Black and White Ball.

2. Warhol and Liston: https://www.youtube.com/watch?v=75wlL1K4RNI; Moore and Spillane: https://moorearchive.org/contextandhistory. Where Warhol is paired with boxer Sonny Liston, and Dali with pitcher Whitey Ford, Moore sits beside crime novelist Mickey Spillane, who confesses to Moore that "What I really wanted to be all my life was a poet." As Kahan notes, this juxtaposition is amusing not just for the high/low difference but because Spillane's violent, highly eroticized books contrast directly with Moore's renown as a celibate spinster. In the ad their stereotyped roles are reversed, as Moore smilingly drinks champagne while sporting her trademark tricorne and a stylish suit, and Spillane drinks milk and wishes he were a poet.

Though Kahan sees Moore's celibacy as precluding lesbian sexual relationships along with heterosexual ones, the voiceover at least opens that possibility in letting us know that both Moore and Spillane "like our food. They like our girls. They like our style." Warhol's appearance in his ad, as a gay man with a high voice, similarly plays against the heterosexual innuendo embedded in the Braniff brand (with its flight attendants' Gucci outfits and "air strips") to suggest alternative sexualities.

3. The personal lives of these two immigrants to New York from the Pennsylvania interior had intriguing parallels. Both were lifelong bachelors, with nonstandard sexual histories; both lived for decades as adults in New York sharing beds with their mothers as well as devoted religious practices. Upon their deaths, both left large estates (Warhol's far exceeding Moore's), having both lived frugally for decades in the midst of wealth. Both are understood to have moved through distinct phases in their careers, including a latter phase that some see as involving a sellout of highbrow values. The two are buried 175 miles apart, in Gettysburg and Pittsburgh, in their family plots. Warhol's grave has a twenty-four-hour camera feed.

4. "*Correspondance*" is spelled with a closing "dAnce," a triple pun on the concept of a "correspondence school," the French spelling of the English word *correspondence*, meaning *connection* (and more specifically, the title of a poem by Baudelaire), and dancing.

5. *Not Nothing: Selected Writings by Ray Johnson*, 38.

6. See Roffman, "'Mysteries Expound Mysteries.'"

7. See McRae, "'Another Armored Animal.'"

Appendix

1. Though she never met John Milton Moore, who lived most of his life in an asylum and died in 1925, Marianne noted a feeling of connection to him in an interview with Rex Reed in 1966: "My father was an engineer, so I inherited a love of bridges. Especially the Brooklyn Bridge. Its catenary curve takes my fancy" (Reed, "Marianne Moore," 127).

2. Mary Warner Moore initially moved the family to relatives in Ben Avon, PA—then two years later to Carlisle.

3. Leavell ("'Frightening Disinterestedness'") posits that Moore refused a marriage proposal from Scofield Thayer not because she wasn't interested in men but because his offer sprang from a philanthropic rather than romantic motive. Leavell surmises that Thayer, Moore's sexually ambiguous and wealthy fan, sought to ensure Moore's financial stability. But his several laudatory *Dial* essays "flaring" Moore after her Dial award also exhibit a sparky, even amatory tone.

4. Burke, in *Voices and Visions: Marianne Moore*. Video, 38:20.

5. *Holding On*, xviii.

6. Moore's syllabic meter counts syllables rather than beats, without end stops; it sounds like prose when read aloud.

7. DuPlessis, "No Moore of the Same," 6.

8. Moore's "Roses Only" critiques gender hierarchies. Like Mina Loy in "Parturition" (1914), Moore transforms a familiar female role to mean dangerously, lacerating from within the carpe diem tradition of Herrick's "Gather ye rosebuds" poem. Though it's addressed to a "you," the keen wit of "Roses Only" marks its rose as emblematic of Moore and her choice to remove herself from the standard love market. The poem rejects looks, emotions, and status-as-love-object as prime criteria of women's value, wittily enacting a simultaneous rejection of the poetry of sentiment often associated, negatively, with female poets. But the poem does not reject the realm of the body or sexuality—since both are emphasized by the poem's own strong physical presence on the page, the controlled undulation of the lines, and the playful language that teasingly conceals almost as much as it shows.

9. "Thorns" can also be pronounced heavily as a near rhyme with "us."

10. Now e-books allow readers to stretch lines to the width of their screens.

11. In the *Others* anthology version (1917) "thorns" was not in end-line position and the rhyme on "make us"/"minus" held. Moore made the pointed change in the *Observations* version, reworking both lines to maintain the syllable scheme (see *Becoming*, 83, 229). The 1935 *Selected Poems* version returned to the *Others* text, and Moore omitted the magnificent "Roses Only" from collections thereafter.

12. As with "Roses Only," the significant shapes of some other Moore poems have remained hidden by the exigencies of book publishing, while still others have been more visible and occasionally remarked by critics. Moore seems to have been content knowing these evidences of witty skill were there, largely unseen. See chapters for more examples.

13. The shapes suggest a desire to physically bring the world outside into her poems, and to represent that inside/outside tension.

14. Leavell (*Marianne Moore and the Visual Arts*, 57–63) discusses Moore's early visual design as a version of cubism—whereas those painters explored defamiliarizing

relations among visual illusion, media, images, and words, Moore foregrounded her linguistic medium in space.

15. Willis, "Contrarieties Equally True." Moore's "Poetry" borrows from and corrects Yeats's characterization of Blake as a "too literal realist of the imagination." Moore holds that true poets must be, like Blake, "literalists of the imagination." In following him, her note suggests, they too will express those "figures seen by the mind's eye, [which] when exalted by inspiration, were 'eternal existences,' symbols of divine essences" (*NCP*, 297). Though she was devotedly religious throughout her life, Moore's vision was not exclusively Christian; her sense of access to underlying spiritual forces involved questioning human cultural hierarchies, including religious hierarchies, of all kinds. As Leavell describes, "rather than lamenting the loss of traditional values in an increasingly diverse world Moore witnesses truth in the diversity itself. . . Moore shared with the visual artists she knew . . . a moral resistance not only to conventions in art but to conventional, hierarchical standards of any kind; and ultimately the belief that such standards obstruct one's ability to see the 'spiritual forces'" (*Holding On*, 136). This visionary element drives the poems' invitation to readers to see things otherwise.

16. And in the process, as Aaron Jaffe (*Modernism and the Culture of Celebrity*) has outlined, he increased his own, through an economics of scarcity, in which modernists' fame was inversely proportional to their few, innovative works, augmented by the special literary PR of authoritative introductions and reviews.

17. "Miss Moore is, I believe, one of those few who have done the language some service in my lifetime. . . [She] has no immediate poetic derivations. . . [Her] use of rhyme is in itself a definite innovation in metric. . . Of the light rhyme Miss Moore is the greatest living master. . . [Her] poems form part of the small body of durable poetry written in our time," etc. (introduction to *The Selected Poems of Marianne Moore*, *CRMM*, 106, 108, 109).

18. Redding, "'One must make a distinction, however.'" Redding's chief examples are "Poetry" (1919–25) and "The Labours of Hercules" (1921), in which "Moore attempts to define the proper relation between the egalitarian tendencies of democracy and the cultural distinction sought by art . . . [arguing] that the pleasures of difficult art need not be sacrificed in the name of bringing about a more egalitarian society" (308). "On the contrary, these poems imply that" democratic politics should protect a "respect for aesthetic complexity, personal individuality and social difference" (308). Redding points also to the formative role of her suffrage work on Moore's early poetry (299–301), and Chapman (*Making Noise, Making News*) notes Moore's early sporting of a tricorne hat as a suffrage symbol (127).

19. Redding, "'One must make a distinction, however,'" 311. Redding invokes Moore's essay "Henry James as a Characteristic American" as demonstrating her identification with "James's contradictory desire to be both an American and an artist" (305).

20. Ibid., 318.

21. Ashbery, *Selected Prose*, 112; cited in Roffman, "'Mysteries Expound Mysteries,'" 186.

22. See Miller, "Distrusting." Of the sixteen poems Moore published during World War II, eleven clearly respond to the war in some way. She had previously written

poems about World War I, including "The Fish" (1918), "Reinforcements" (1918), and "Isaiah, Jeremiah, Ezekiel, Daniel" (1915).

23. *PMM*, 116.

24. *SelLet*, 410–11.

25. Moore wrote to Elizabeth Bishop in 1942, "I too resist obliqueness just now, of any kind in anyone" (January 31, 1942, cited in Kalstone, *Becoming a Poet*, 90).

26. Miller respects the poem's efforts but sees it as finally a failure because it seems to conclude that eternal beauty makes sense of suffering. Rachel Galvin (*News of War*, 252–72) reads it instead as a self-reflexive handling of the complexities of civilian witness and the rhetorical limitations of war poetry. Expanding on that, when the poem is viewed performatively, any failure to resolve advances its larger success at portraying struggle: it enacts the world's difficulty, including the difficulty of concluding. Its title undercuts not just military merit but Moore's own claims to merit here—or to any success in a world where so much is lost. Because of the poem's failure to convince even its poet ("I would not believe it"), the concluding couplet affirms its fit with the radical optimism Moore describes in "The Hero": "hope not being hope / until all ground for hope has / vanished."

27. Moore published eight poems in the very prowar *Nation* between 1943 and 1952. She left when poetry editor Margaret Marshall was dismissed and the book review section was cut to a single page, in a moment of financial difficulty for the magazine (Guttenplan, *The Nation*, 140).

28. Jarrell, "Poetry in War and Peace," *CRMM*, 141.

29. See Setina, "Marianne Moore's 'Light Is Speech.'"

30. Nonetheless, the two maintained a friendly correspondence afterward. A 1953 letter indicates that Jarrell understands that Moore had moved on: "Your regarding my criticism of you as a trouble of mine that you can feel sympathetic toward, and not simply as a necessary trial, is a joy to me" (November 2, 1953, *RML*, V:30:33).

31. This kind of dialogue also occurs among other poems across versions, though critics have not recognized it much. The increased availability of variora aids comparative analysis.

32. Unpublished poems could be gathered in an appendix.

33. I differ with Hugh Kenner, who holds that Moore's notes "are not like the notes to *The Waste Land*, part of our education, we are not meant to look up the sources" (*A Homemade World*, 102). While the sources aren't necessary for engaging, they may add valuable context.

Bibliography

ARCHIVAL SOURCES

Bryher. Papers. General Collection, Beinecke Rare Book and Manuscript Library, Yale University, New Haven, CT.

Koch, Kenneth. Papers. New York Public Library, New York, NY.

Mitchell, Arthur. Papers. Columbia University Rare Book and Manuscript Library, New York, NY.

Moore, Marianne. Papers. Rosenbach Museum and Library, of the Free Library of Philadelphia, Philadelphia, PA.

NBC Archives. Smithsonian Museum, Washington, DC.

Shaw, Rue. Papers. Newberry Library, Chicago, IL.

Watson, Hildegarde. Papers. Bryn Mawr College Library, Bryn Mawr, PA.

SECONDARY SOURCES

Abbott, Craig S. *Marianne Moore: A Descriptive Bibliography.* Pittsburgh: University of Pittsburgh Press, 1977.

Aldington, Richard. "Review of *Observations.*" *The Criterion* 3, no. 11 (July 1925): 588–92. Reprinted in *CRMM*, 74–75.

Anderson, David Ross. "Marianne Moore's 'Fertile Procedure': Fusing Scientific Method and Organic Form through Syllabic Technique." *Paideuma* 33, no. 2–3 (Fall–Winter 2004): 83–108.

———. "The Woman in the Tricorn Hat: Political Theory and Biological Portraiture in Marianne Moore's Poetry." *Journal of Modern Literature* 22, no. 1 (Fall 1998): 31–45.

Arckens, Elien. "'In This Told-Backward Biography': Marianne Moore against

Survival in Her Queer Archival Poetry." *Women's Studies Quarterly* 44, no. 1 & 2 (Spring/Summer 2016): 111–27.

Ashbery, John. "Straight Lines over Rough Terrain." *New York Times Book Review*, November 26, 1967, 1, 42. Reprinted in *CRMM*, 222–26.

Auden, W. H., and Chester Kallman, trans. *The Magic Flute: The New English Translation of the Libretto of Mozart's Famous Opera*. New York: Random House, 1956.

"Axis of the Hairfine Moon." *Times Literary Supplement*, November 22, 1957, 704.

Bentz, Adam T. "Cracking the Door: 'Mr. Immigration' and the Hungarian Refugee Crisis." *Pennsylvania Legacies* 47, no. 2 (Fall 2016): 20–25.

Berger, Charles. "Moore after Stevens: Beyond the Last Thought." *Wallace Stevens Journal* 31, no. 2 (Fall 2007): 131–47.

"Best Living Poet." *Newsweek* 38 (December 24, 1951): 69–71. Reprinted in *CRMM*, 150–53.

Bishop, Elizabeth. *The Complete Poems, 1927–1979*. New York: Farrar, Straus and Giroux, 1983.

———. "Efforts of Affection: A Memoir of Marianne Moore." In *The Collected Prose*, ed. Robert Giroux, 121–56. New York: Farrar, Straus and Giroux, 1984.

———. *Elizabeth Bishop and the* New Yorker: *The Complete Correspondence*. Edited by Joelle Biele. New York: Farrar, Straus and Giroux, 2011.

———. *One Art: Letters*. Selected and edited by Robert Giroux. New York: Farrar, Straus and Giroux, 1994.

Branch, Michael, ed., *Reading the Roots: American Nature Writing before Walden*. Athens: University of Georgia Press, 2004.

Braudy, Leo. *The Frenzy of Renown: Fame and Its History*. New York: Random House, 1986.

Brewer, E. Cobham. *Dictionary of Phrase and Fable*. New York: Harper Brothers, 1894.

Bryant, Marsha. *Women's Poetry and Popular Culture*. New York: Palgrave/Macmillan, 2011.

Bryant, William Cullen. *The Poetical Works of William Cullen Bryant*. New York: D. Appleton, 1916.

Cantwell, Robert. "The Poet, the Bums and the Legendary Red Men." *Sports Illustrated*, February 25, 1960, 74–84.

Carrington, Ruth. "Marianne Moore's Metaphysical Giraffe." In *Marianne Moore: Woman and Poet*, edited by Patricia C. Willis, 145–54. Orono, ME: National Poetry Foundation, 1990.

Carson, Luke. "Republicanism and Leisure in Marianne Moore's Depression." *Modern Language Quarterly* 63, no. 3 (September 2002): 315–42.

Chapman, Mary. *Making Noise, Making News: Suffrage Print Culture and U.S. Modernism*. New York: Oxford University Press, 2014.

Chasar, Mike. *Everyday Reading: Poetry and Popular Culture in America*. New York: Columbia University Press, 2012.

Chiasson, Dan. "What Color Is Jerboa Fur?" *The Believer* (December 2003/January 2004).

Clavier, Aurore. "'The First Grace of Style': Marianne Moore and the Writing of Dancing." In *TFCMM*, 203–19.

Conklin, William R. "Dodgers' Music Score? Off-Pitch Sym-Phoney Band Is Base." *New York Times*, August 12, 1956, S3.

Costello, Bonnie. *Marianne Moore: Imaginary Possessions*. Cambridge, MA: Harvard University Press, 1981.

Crane, Hart. *The Bridge*. 1930. In *The Complete Poems and Selected Letters and Prose*, edited by Brom Weber, 45–117. New York: Doubleday Anchor, 1966.

Debord, Guy. *Society of the Spectacle*. 1967. Detroit: Black and Red, 1983

Dever, Joseph X. "'If She Were Here Tonight, She'd Be Right at Home.'" *Philadelphia Evening Bulletin*, November 17, 1972, 8B.

Dickinson, Emily. *The Pocket Emily Dickinson*. Edited by Brenda Hillman. Boston: Shambhala, 2009.

Dudziak, Mary. *Cold War Civil Rights: Race and the Image of American Democracy*. 2000. Rev. ed. Princeton: Princeton University Press, 2011.

DuPlessis, Rachel Blau. "No Moore of the Same: The Feminist Poetics of Marianne Moore." *William Carlos Williams Review* 14, no. 1 (Spring 1988): 6–32.

Eliot, T. S. Introduction to *The Selected Poems of Marianne Moore*, vii–xiv. New York: Macmillan, 1935. Reprinted in *CRMM*, 105–9.

———. *The Letters of T. S. Eliot: Volume 1: 1898–1922*. Edited by Valerie Eliot and Hugh Haughton. New Haven, CT: Yale University Press, 2011.

———. "Tradition and the Individual Talent." 1919. In *Selected Prose of T. S. Eliot*, edited by Frank Kermode, 37–44. New York: Harcourt, 1975.

———. *The Waste Land: A Facsimile and Transcript of the Original Drafts Including the Annotations of Ezra Pound*. Edited by Valerie Eliot. New York: HBJ, 1974.

Emerson, Ralph Waldo. "Circles." 1841. In *Essays and Lectures*, 403–14. New York: Library of America, 1983.

Erkkila, Betsy. *The Wicked Sisters: Women Poets, Literary History, and Discord*. New York: Oxford University Press, 1992.

Filreis, Al. "The End of the End of Poetic Ideology, 1960." In *The Oxford Handbook of Modern and Contemporary American Poetry*, 507–29. New York: Oxford University Press, 2012.

Finch, Zachary. "'Passion for the Particular': Marianne Moore, Henry James, Beatrix Potter and the Refuge of Close Reading." In *TFCMM*, 221–35.

Foley, Eileen. "Genius at Work: I Write Because I Can't Help It." *Philadelphia Evening Bulletin*, October 26, 1965.

Freire, Paulo. *The Pedagogy of the Oppressed*. New York: Continuum, 2007.

Frommer, Harvey. *The Sports Junkie's Book of Trivia, Terms, and Lingo*. Lanham, MD: Taylor Trade Publishing, 2005.

Galvin, Rachel. *News of War: Civilian Poetry 1936–1945*. New York: Oxford University Press, 2017.

Garafola, Lynn. "Lincoln Kirstein, Modern Dance, and the Left: The Genesis of an American Ballet." *Dance Research* 3, no. 1 (Summer 2005): 18–35.

Gilbert, Roger. "'These Things': Moore's Habits of Adduction." In *TFCMM*, 33–48.

Gilcrest, David W. "Rhetorical Redemption, Environmental Poetics, and the Case of the Camperdown Elm." *ISLE: Interdisciplinary Studies in Literature and Environment* 8, no. 2 (Summer 2001): 169–80.

Gilroy, Harry. "Marianne Moore Wins Gold Medal." *New York Times*, April 14, 1967, 36.

Glass, Loren. *Literary Celebrity in the Modern United States, 1880–1980*. New York: New York University Press, 2004.

Glavey, Brian. *The Wall-Flower Avant Garde: Modernism, Sexuality and Queer Ekphrasis*. New York: Oxford University Press, 2016.

Green, Fiona. "Marianne Moore and the Hidden Persuaders." In *Writing for* The New Yorker*: Critical Essays on an American Periodical*, edited by Fiona Green, 58–78. Edinburgh: Edinburgh University Press, 2015.

Greenberg, Clement. "Avant Garde and Kitsch." 1939. In *Art and Culture: Critical Essays*, 3–21. Boston: Beacon Press, 1961.

Gregory, Elizabeth. "Confessing the Body: Sexton, Plath, Lowell, Ginsberg and Berryman." In *Modern Confessional Writing: New Critical Essays*, edited by Jo Gill, 33–49. New York: Routledge, 2005.

———, ed. *The Critical Response to Marianne Moore*. Westport, CT: Praeger, 2003.

———. *Quotation and Modern American Poetry: "'Imaginary Gardens with Real Toads.'"* Houston: Rice University Press, 1995.

———. "Stamps, Money, Pop Culture and Marianne Moore." *Discourse* 17, no. 1 (Fall 1994): 123–39. Excerpted in *CRMM*, 234–46.

Gregory, Elizabeth, and Stacy Carson Hubbard, eds. *Twenty-First Century Marianne Moore: Essays from a Critical Renaissance*. New York: Palgrave, 2017.

Gullette, Margaret. *Declining to Decline: Cultural Combat and the Politics of the Midlife*. Charlottesville: University of Virginia Press, 1997.

Guttenplan, D. D. *The Nation: A Biography*. New York: The Nation Company, 2015.

Haffenden, John. *The Life of John Berryman*. London: Routledge & Kegan Paul Books, 1982.

Hall, Donald. *Marianne Moore: The Cage and the Animal*. New York: Pegasus, 1970.

Hallinan, Victoria. "The 1958 Tour of the Moiseyev Dance Company: A Window into American Perception." *Journal of History and Cultures* 1 (2012): 51–64.

Hamilton, Saskia, ed. *Words in Air: The Complete Correspondence between Elizabeth Bishop and Robert Lowell.* New York: Farrar, Straus and Giroux, 2010.

Hammill, Faye. "*The New Yorker*, the Middle Brow and the Periodical Marketplace in 1925." In *Writing for* The New Yorker: *Critical Essays on an American Periodical*, edited by Fiona Green, 17–35. Edinburgh: Edinburgh University Press, 2015.

Harter, Odile. "Marianne Moore's Depression Collectives." *American Literature* 85, no. 2 (June 2013): 333–61.

Hazlitt, William. "On Sitting for One's Picture." 1823. In *Table Talk: Opinions on Books, Men and Things*, 1:25–36. New York: Wiley & Putnam, 1845.

Henderson, Bruce. "'In the Public Garden': Marianne Moore Performing and Performing Marianne Moore." PhD diss., Northwestern University, 1983.

Herd, David. "'So He Who Strongly Feels, Behaves': Marianne Moore's Ethical Detail." *Twentieth-Century Literature* 63, no. 4 (December 2017): 475–98.

Holland, Gerald. "Don't Pull Up for Doc." *Sports Illustrated*, November 13, 1961, 70–78.

Holley, Margaret. *The Poetry of Marianne Moore: A Study in Voice and Value.* Cambridge: Cambridge University Press, 1987.

Horkheimer, Max, and Theodor W. Adorno. "The Culture Industry: Enlightenment as Mass Deception." 1944. In *The Dialectic of Enlightenment*, 120–67. New York: Continuum, 1994.

Howard, Richard. "Marianne Moore and the Monkey Business of Modernism." In *Marianne Moore: The Art of a Modernist*, edited by Joseph Parisi, 1–12. Ann Arbor, MI: UMI Research Press, 1990.

Hubbard, Stacy Carson. "Mannerist Moore: Poetry, Painting, Photography." In *Critics and Poets on Marianne Moore: "A Right Good Salvo of Barks,"* edited by Linda Leavell, Cristanne Miller, and Robin Schulze, 113–36. Lewisburg, PA: Bucknell University Press, 2005.

Hutchison, Sharla. "The Eco-Poetics of Marianne Moore's 'The Sycamore.'" *ISLE: Interdisciplinary Studies in Literature and Environment* 18, no. 4 (Autumn 2011): 763–78.

Huyssen, Andreas. *After the Great Divide: Modernism, Mass Culture, Postmodernism.* Bloomington: Indiana University Press, 1987.

Hyde, Lewis. *On the Poetry of Allen Ginsberg.* Ann Arbor: University of Michigan Press, 1984.

Jaffe, Aaron. *Modernism and the Culture of Celebrity.* Cambridge: Cambridge University Press, 2005.

Jarrell, Randall. "The Humble Animal." *Kenyon Review* 4, no. 3 (Autumn 1942): 408–11. Reprinted in *CRMM*, 133–36.

———. "Poetry in War and Peace." *Partisan Review* 12 (Winter 1945): 120–22. Reprinted in *CRMM*, 139–41.

Johnson, Benjamin. "Marianne Moore's 'Abraham Lincoln and the Art of the Word': Poetry, Celebrity and Civil Religion." *Texas Studies in Literature and Language* 57, no. 1 (Spring 2015): 53–79.

Johnson, Ray. "Is Marianne Moore Marianne Moore?" In *Not Nothing: Selected Writings by Ray Johnson*, edited by Elizabeth Zuba, 38–40. Los Angeles: Siglio, 2014.

Jonson, Ben. *Timber: Discoveries Made upon Men and Matter.* 1640. Online.

Kadlec, David. "Marianne Moore, Immigration and Eugenics." *Modernism/modernity* 1, no. 2 (April 1994): 21–49.

Kahan, Benjamin. "'The Viper's Traffic-Knot': Celibacy and Queerness in the 'Late' Marianne Moore." *GLQ* 14, no. 4 (2008): 509–35. Collected in *Celibacies: American Modernism and Sexual Life*, 56–80. Durham, NC: Duke University Press, 2013.

Kalstone, David. *Becoming a Poet: Elizabeth Bishop with Marianne Moore and Robert Lowell.* Ann Arbor: University of Michigan Press, 2001.

Kappel, Andrew. "Notes on the Presbyterian Poetry of Marianne Moore." In *Marianne Moore: Woman and Poet*, edited by Patricia C. Willis, 39–50. Orono, ME: National Poetry Foundation, 1990.

Kenner, Hugh. *A Homemade World: The American Modernist Writers.* New York: Knopf, 1975.

Kent, Kathryn. *Making Girls into Women: American Women's Writing and the Rise of Lesbian Identity.* Durham, NC: Duke University Press, 2003.

Koch, Kenneth. "New Books." *Poetry* 90 (April 1957): 47–50. Reprinted in *CRMM*, 195–97.

Kodat, Catherine Gunther. *Don't Act, Just Dance: The Metapolitics of Cold War Culture.* New Brunswick, NJ: Rutgers University Press, 2014.

Kramer, Hilton. "Freezing the Blood and Making One Laugh." *New York Times Book Review*, March 15, 1981, 7, 22–23. Reprinted in *CRMM*, 230–34.

Kreymborg, Alfred. *Troubadour.* New York: Boni and Liveright, 1925.

Landor, W. S. *Imaginary Conversations and Poems: A Selection.* London: J. Dent, 1950.

Lazarus, Emma. *Emma Lazarus: Selected Poems and Other Writings.* Edited by Gregory Eiselstein. Peterborough, Ontario: Broadview Press, 2002.

Leader, Jennifer. "'The teacher was speaking of unrhymed verse': Marianne Moore, E. H. Kellogg, and the Poetry of Modernist Hermeneutics." In *TFCMM*, 113–28.

Leavell, Linda. "'Frightening Disinterestedness': The Personal Circumstances of Marianne Moore's 'Marriage.'" *Journal of Modern Literature* 31, no. 1 (Fall 2007): 64–79.

———. *Holding On Upside Down: The Life and Work of Marianne Moore.* New York: Farrar, Straus and Giroux, 2013.

———. *Marianne Moore and the Visual Arts: Prismatic Color.* Baton Rouge: Louisiana State University Press, 1995.

Levy, Ellen. *Criminal Ingenuity: Moore, Cornell, Ashbery, and the Struggle between the Arts*. New York: Oxford University Press, 2011.

Libbey, Peter. "Arthur Mitchell: What to Watch and Read." *New York Times*, September 19, 2018.

Liddell, H. G., and R. Scott. *Greek-English Lexicon*. Oxford: Oxford University Press, 1975.

Lieberman, William S. *Redon: Drawings and Lithographs; Picasso: His Graphic Art*. New York: MoMA, 1952.

"Life Goes on a Zoo Tour with a Famous Poet." *Life Magazine* 35 (September 21, 1953): 202–4, 207.

Loiseaux, Elizabeth Bergmann. "Women Looking: The Feminist Ekphrasis of Marianne Moore and Adrienne Rich." In *In the Frame: Women's Ekphrastic Poetry from Marianne Moore to Susan Wheeler*, 121–44. Newark: University of Delaware Press, 2009.

Mackey, Albert G. "The Legend of the Winding Stairs." In *The Symbolism of Freemasonry*, 328–47. N.p., 1882.

Mak, Clifford. "On Falling Fastidiously: Marianne Moore's Slapstick Animals." *ELH* 83, no. 3 (Fall 2016): 873–98.

"Marion Morehouse Cummings, Poet's Widow, Top Model, Dies." *New York Times*, May 19, 1969, 47.

Marshall, P. David. *Celebrity and Power: Fame in Contemporary Culture*. Minneapolis: University of Minnesota Press, 1997.

Mason, Dancy. "'Another armored animal': Modernist Prosthesis and Marianne Moore's Posthumanist Animiles." *Feminist Modernist Studies* 1, no. 3 (2018): 318–35.

McCabe, Susan. "'Let's Be Alone Together': Bryher's and Marianne Moore's Aesthetic-Erotic Collaboration." *Modernism/modernity* 17, no. 3 (September 2010): 607–37.

McRae, Calista. "'Another Armored Animal': Robert Lowell's Allusions to Marianne Moore." *Arizona Quarterly* 72, no. 2 (Summer 2016): 1–28.

McSherry, Siofra. "'To fulfill a private obligation': Marianne Moore, Her Patrons, and the Social Economy of the Gift." *NANO: New American Notes Online* (July 2017).

Miller, Cristanne. "'By-Play': The Radical Rhythms of Marianne Moore." *Foreign Literature Studies/Wai Guo Wen Xue Yan Jiu* 30, no. 6 (December 2008): 20–32.

———. *Cultures of Modernism: Marianne Moore, Mina Loy and Else Lasker-Schüler*. Ann Arbor: University of Michigan Press, 2007.

———. "Distrusting: Marianne Moore on Feeling and War in the 1940s." *American Literature* 80, no. 2 (June 2008): 353–79.

———. *Marianne Moore: Questions of Authority*. Cambridge, MA: Harvard University Press, 1995.

———. "Marianne Moore's Black Maternal Hero: A Study in Categorization." *American Literary History* 1, no. 4 (1989): 786–815.

Miller, James E. *T. S. Eliot: The Making of an American Poet*. College Park: Pennsylvania State University Press, 2005.

Monroe, Harriet. "Symposium on Marianne Moore." *Poetry* 19 (January 1922): 208–26. Reprinted in *CRMM*, 35–40.

Moore, Lisa L. *Sister Arts: The Erotics of Lesbian Landscapes*. Minneapolis: University of Minnesota Press, 2011.

Moore, Marianne. *Becoming Marianne Moore: The Early Poems, 1907–1924*. Edited by Robin G. Schulze. Berkeley: University of California Press, 2002.

———. *The Complete Poems of Marianne Moore*. Rev. ed. New York: Macmillan/Viking, 1981.

———. *The Complete Prose of Marianne Moore*. Edited by Patricia C. Willis. New York: Viking, 1986.

———. "Henry James as a Characteristic American." In *CPr*, 316–22.

———. "An Interview with Donald Hall." In *A Marianne Moore Reader*, 253–73. New York: Viking, 1961.

———. "Love in America?" *Saturday Evening Post* 239 (December 31, 1966): 78.

———. *New Collected Poems of Marianne Moore*. Edited by Heather Cass White. New York: Farrar, Straus and Giroux, 2017.

———. *Observations*. 1924. Rev. ed. 1925. Edited by Linda Leavell. New York: Farrar, Straus and Giroux, 2016.

———. *The Poet's Voice; Poets Reading Aloud and Commenting upon Their Works: Marianne Moore*. Cambridge, MA: Harvard University Press, 1978. Audiotape.

———. *The Selected Letters of Marianne Moore*. Edited by Bonnie Costello, Celeste Goodridge, and Cristanne Miller. New York: Alfred A. Knopf, 1997.

———. *Selected Poems*. Edited by T. S. Eliot. New York: Macmillan, 1935.

———. *Tell Me, Tell Me: Granite, Steel, and Other Topics*. New York: Viking, 1966.

Moore, Marianne C. "Topics: Crossing Brooklyn Bridge at Twilight." *New York Times*, August 5, 1967, 17.

Moran, Eileen. "Selected Letters of Marianne Moore to Hildegarde Watson." PhD diss., Bryn Mawr College, 1985.

Neely, Julianne. "Kill Your Heroes: Examining Marianne Moore's Fraught Racial, Misogynistic, Capitalist Politics." *Vida Online*, April 27, 2018.

Nevius, Michelle, and James Nevius. *Inside the Apple: A Streetwise History of New York City*. New York: Free Press, 2009.

Ngai, Sianne. *Our Aesthetic Categories: Zany, Cute, Interesting*. Cambridge, MA: Harvard University Press, 2012.

Nicholson, Nigel James. *Aristocracy and Athletics in Archaic and Classical Greece*. Cambridge: Cambridge University Press, 2005.

North, Michael. *The Dialect of Modernism: Race, Language and Twentieth-Century Literature*. New York: Oxford University Press, 1994.

O'Hara, Frank. "Statement for *The New American Poetry*." In *Standing Still and Walking in New York*, 112. Bolinas, CA: Grey Fox Press, 1975.

Olson, Kirby. "Marianne Moore's 'The Camperdown Elm' and the Revival of Brooklyn's Prospect Park." *Journal of Ecocriticism* 2, no. 3 (July 2011): 16–27.

Page, Chester. *Memoirs of a Charmed Life in New York*. Bloomington, IN: iUniverse, 2007.

Perrin, Tom. "On Blustering: Dwight Macdonald, Modernism and *The New Yorker*." In *Writing for* The New Yorker: *Critical Essays on an American Periodical*, edited by Fiona Green, 228–48. Edinburgh: Edinburgh University Press, 2015.

Phillips, Siobhan. "The Students of Marianne Moore: Reading the Ugly History of the Carlisle Indian Industrial School, Where the Poet Taught." *Poetry Foundation* (March 14, 2017).

Plath, Sylvia. *The Collected Poems*. Edited by Ted Hughes. New York: Harper Perennial, 2008.

Plimpton, George. *Shadow Box: An Amateur in the Ring*. New York: Putnam, 1977.

———. "The World Series with Marianne Moore: Letter from an October Afternoon." *Harper's Magazine* (October 1964): 50–58.

Pollak, Vivian. *Our Emily Dickinsons: American Women Poets and the Intimacies of Difference*. Philadelphia: University of Pennsylvania Press, 2016.

Pound, Ezra. "Marianne Moore and Mina Loy." *Little Review* 4 (March 1918): 56–58. Reprinted in *CRMM*, 22–23.

———. *The Selected Letters of Ezra Pound, 1907–1941*. Edited by D. D. Paige. New York: New Directions, 1971.

Qian, Zhaoming. "Mai-Mai Sze, the Tao, and Moore's Late Poetry." *Paideuma* 40 (2013): 349–68.

———. *The Modernist Response to Chinese Art: Pound, Moore, Stevens*. Charlottesville: University of Virginia Press, 2003.

Redding, Patrick. "'One must make a distinction, however': Marianne Moore and Democratic Taste." *Twentieth Century Literature* (Summer 2012): 296–332.

Reed, Rex. "Marianne Moore." In *Do You Sleep in the Nude?*, 124–28. New York: NAL, 1968.

Rees, Ennis. Introduction to *The Odyssey of Homer*, translated by Rees. New York: Random House, 1960.

Rieke, Alison. "'Plunder' or 'Accessibility to Experience': Consumer Culture and Marianne Moore's Modernist Self-Fashioning." *Journal of Modern Literature* 27, nos. 1–2 (Fall 2003): 149–70.

Roffman, Karin. "'Mysteries Expound Mysteries': Marianne Moore's Influence on John Ashbery." In *TFCMM*, 185–99.

Rubin, Joan Shelley. *Songs of Ourselves: The Uses of Poetry in America*. Cambridge, MA: Harvard University Press, 2007.

Rukeyser, Muriel. "The Rhythm Is the Person." *Saturday Review* 42 (September 1959): 17–18.

Sainz, Inmaculada Sanz. "A Masonic Poem on a Masonic Opera." *Reden: Revista espanola de estudios norteamericanos*, no. 15–16 (1998): 93–109.

Sargeant, Winthrop. "Profiles: Humility, Concentration, and Gusto." *New Yorker*, February 16, 1957, 38–77 passim.

Saunders, Frances Stonor. *The Cultural Cold War: The CIA and the World of Arts and Letters*. New York: New Press, 2001.

Scott, Richard. *Jackie Robinson*. Los Angeles: All America, 1990.

Sedgwick, Eve Kosofsky. *Tendencies*. Durham, NC: Duke University Press, 1993.

Setina, Emily. "Marianne Moore, Photography, and the Self-in-Flux." *English Language Notes* 44, no. 2 (Fall–Winter 2006): 275–82.

———. "Marianne Moore's Postwar Fables and the Politics of Indirection." *PMLA* 131, no. 5 (October 2016): 1256–73.

———. "Marianne Moore's 'Light Is Speech,' *Decision* Magazine, and the Wartime Work of Intellectual Exchange." In *TFCMM*, 167–83.

Sielke, Sabine. *Fashioning the Female Subject: The Intertextual Networking of Dickinson, Moore, and Rich*. Ann Arbor: University of Michigan Press, 1997.

Simon, John. "The Torments of Imagination." *Arts Magazine* (February 1962): 20–27.

Sitwell, Edith. "Review of *Poems*." *The Sackbut* 2 (December 1921): 38. Reprinted in *CRMM*, 34–35.

Slatin, John. "'Something Inescapably Typical': Questions about Gender in the Late Work of William Carlos Williams and Marianne Moore." *William Carlos Williams Review* 14, no. 1, Special Issue: Marianne Moore (Spring 1988): 86–103.

Spahr, Juliana. *Everybody's Autonomy: Connective Reading and Collective Identity*. Tuscaloosa: University of Alabama Press, 2001.

Stamy, Cynthia. *Marianne Moore and China: Orientalism and the Writing of America*. New York: Oxford University Press, 1999.

Stapleton, Laurence. *Marianne Moore: The Poet's Advance*. Princeton: Princeton University Press, 1978.

Steuben Glass. *Poetry in Crystal: Interpretations in crystal of thirty-one new poems by contemporary American poets*. New York: Spiral Press, 1963.

Stevens, Wallace. "A Poet That Matters." *Life and Letters Today* 13 (December 1935): 61–65. Reprinted in *CRMM*, 113–18.

Swanson, Roy Arthur. *Pindar's Odes*. Indianapolis: Bobbs-Merrill, 1974.

Terry, Walter. "Dance: Russian Blaze; America on Fire Too." *New York Herald Tribune*, April 20, 1958, section 4: 6.

Tiffany, Daniel. "Cheap Signaling: Class Conflict and Diction in Avant-Garde Poetry." *Boston Review*, July 15, 2014.

———. *My Silver Planet: A Secret History of Poetry and Kitsch*. Baltimore: Johns Hopkins University Press, 2013.

"To the Dodgers." *New York Herald Tribune* 116, no. 40,334 (October 8, 1956): 1.

Tolliver, Cedric. *Of Vagabonds and Fellow Travelers: African Diaspora Literary Culture and the Cultural Cold War*. Ann Arbor: University of Michigan Press, 2019.

Trousdale, Rachel. "'Humor Saves Steps': Laughter and Humanity in Marianne Moore." *Journal of Modern Literature* 35, no. 3 (2013): 136–37.

Vincent, John Emil. *Queer Lyrics: Difficulty and Closure in American Poetry*. New York: Palgrave, 2002.

Voices and Visions: Marianne Moore. New York: Annenberg Media, NY Center for Visual History, 1986. Video.

Walsh, Joan. "49 Years Ago, Harry Belafonte Hosted the Tonight Show—and It Was Amazing." *The Nation*, March 6, 2017.

Wheeler, Lesley, and Chris Gavaler. "Impostors and Chameleons: Marianne Moore and the Carlisle Indian School." *Paideuma* 33, no. 2–3 (2004): 53–82.

White, Andrew. "Harry Belafonte and Marianne Moore on the Tonight Show." *RML* blog, April 3, 2020. https://rosenbach.org/blog/harry-belafonte-and-marianne-moore/.

Willis, Patricia C. "Archiving Moore." In *TFCMM*, 255–60.

———. "Camperdown Elm." In *Marianne Moore: Vision into Verse*, 95–97. Philadelphia: Rosenbach Museum and Library, 1987.

———. "Contrarieties Equally True: Marianne Moore and William Blake." In *TFCMM*, 89–111.

———. "Letter to Albert Gelpi." *Marianne Moore Newsletter* 3, no. 1 (Spring 1979): 10–11.

———. "Marianne Moore on May Day, 1906." *Marianne Moore Newsletter* 5, no. 1 (Spring 1981): 21.

———. *Marianne Moore: Poetry*. Blog. www.moore123.com.

———. "MM's First Poem: 'Dear St. Nicklus.'" *Marianne Moore Newsletter* 5, no. 2 (Fall 1981): 23.

———. "Tippoo's Tiger." *Marianne Moore Newsletter* 2, no. 2 (Fall 1978): 2–7.

Wilson, Elizabeth. "El Greco's Daughter: Necessary Deflection in Marianne Moore's 'For February 14th' and 'Saint Valentine.'" In *Critics and Poets on Marianne Moore: "A Right Good Salvo of Barks*, edited by Linda Leavell, Cristanne Miller, and Robin Schulze, 192–207. Lewisburg, PA: Bucknell University Press, 2005.

Index

"MM" indicates Marianne Moore. Moore's poetry is listed under the main heading: Moore, Marianne, poetry by.

About the Author

Elizabeth Gregory, PhD, directs the WGSS Program and the Institute for Research on Women, Gender & Sexuality at the University of Houston, where she is a professor of English. Her research focuses both on American modernist poetry (*Quotation and Modern American Poetry: "'Imaginary Gardens with Real Toads'"* [1995], *The Critical Response to Marianne Moore* [2003], and with Stacy Carson Hubbard *Twenty-First Century Marianne Moore: Essays from a Critical Renaissance* [2017]) and on women's work and fertility (*Ready: Why Women Are Embracing the New Later Motherhood* [2012/2007]). Her transcription/edition of *Moore's 1961–1970 Poetry Notebook* was recently published as part of the Marianne Moore Digital Archive (moorearchive.org, 2021).